Origami Sea Life

Second Edition

Other books by John Montroll:

Origami Sculptures

Prehistoric Origami *Dinosaurs and Other Creatures*

Animal Origami for the Enthusiast

Origami for the Enthusiast

Origami
Sea Life

Second Edition

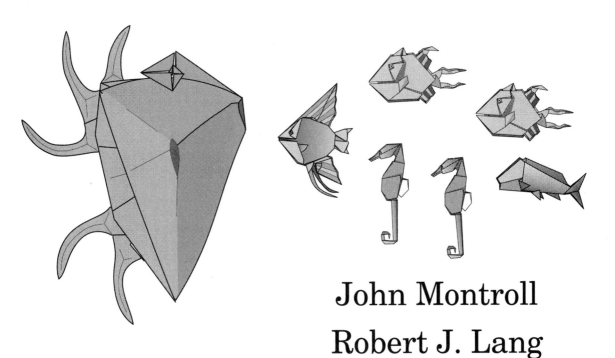

John Montroll
Robert J. Lang

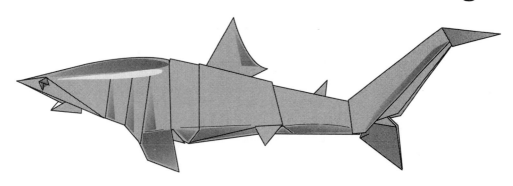

Dover Publications, Inc.
New York

To Shigeo, Tsuneo, Junko,
   Hiroshi, Koji, and Toshiyuki

To Peter and Diane

Copyright © 1990 by John Montroll and Robert J. Lang.
All rights reserved under Pan American and International Copyright Conventions.

Published in Canada by General Publishing Company, Ltd., 30 Lesmill Road, Don Mills, Toronto, Ontario.
Published in the United Kingdom by Constable and Company, Ltd., 3 The Lanchesters, 162–164 Fulham Palace Road, London W6 9ER.

This Dover edition, first published in 1991, is an unabridged and unaltered republication of the second edition of the work originally published in 1990 by Antroll Publishing Company, Vermont.

Manufactured in the United States of America
Dover Publications, Inc., 31 East 2nd Street, Mineola, N.Y. 11501

Library of Congress Cataloging-in-Publication Data

Montroll, John.
   Origami sea life / John Montroll, Robert J. Lang. — 2nd ed.
      p.   cm.
   ISBN 0-486-26765-2 (pbk.)
   1. Origami.   2. Fishes in art.   I. Lang, Robert J.   II. Title.
TT870.M572   1991
736'.982—dc20
                                                        91-2997
                                                        CIP

Introduction

The sea is nearly a world unto itself; it is vast, ecologically rich, complex, and yet, we are acquainted with only the tiniest fraction of its varied life. Its denizens include both the largest and smallest of creatures, creatures timid and aggressive, creatures mundane and outlandish. The sea was the cradle of life some four billion years ago; nearly every major phylum of life evolved in its waters, and many fanciful forms appeared over the eons. Its present inhabitants are the subject of this book.

The unique shapes of sea life, from the five-pointed starfish to the many-spined lionfish, are attractive subjects for origami. At the same time, they pose unusual challenges to the origami designer. We, the authors, were independently moved to develop designs for origami sea life in large part because of the challenge in providing the detail necessary to do the subjects proper justice. Although both of us have written origami books independently, we chose to pool our efforts in this, our first joint effort.

Ordinarily, such a collaboration would be fraught with stylistic incompatibilities. However, the modern advances in computer graphics have enabled us to create consistent, easy-to-follow directions for each model. The directions use the Randlett-Yoshizawa notation with our own enhancements for more advanced procedures, and the style of folding is that of the modern purist: every model is folded from one square sheet of paper with no cuts.

Although several people helped with the production of this book, we are especially indebted to two people. Our sincerest thanks go to Andy Montroll for his help and to Diane Lang for her help, patience, and understanding.

John Montroll and Robert J. Lang

April, 1990

Contents

✳ Simple

✳✳ Intermediate

✳✳✳ Complex

✳✳✳✳ Very Complex

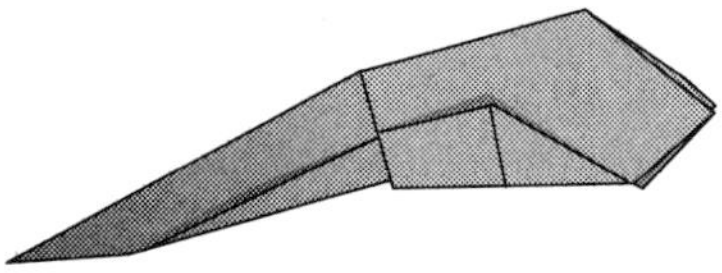

Tadpole
✳
Page 24

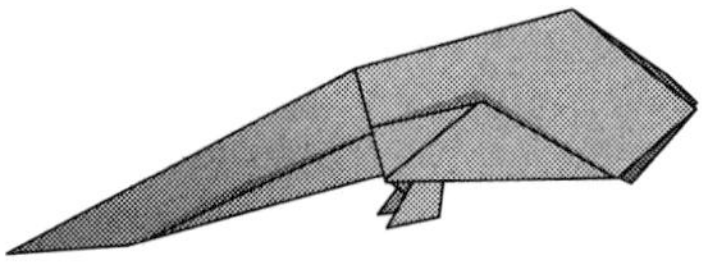

Tadpole with Hind Legs
✳
Page 26

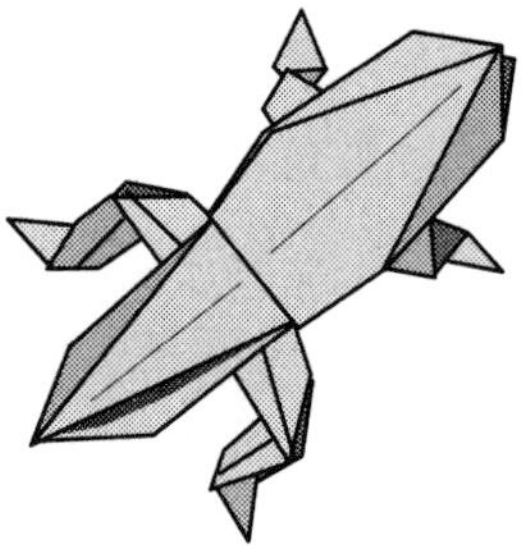

Froglet
✳✳
Page 28

Frog
✳✳
Page 34

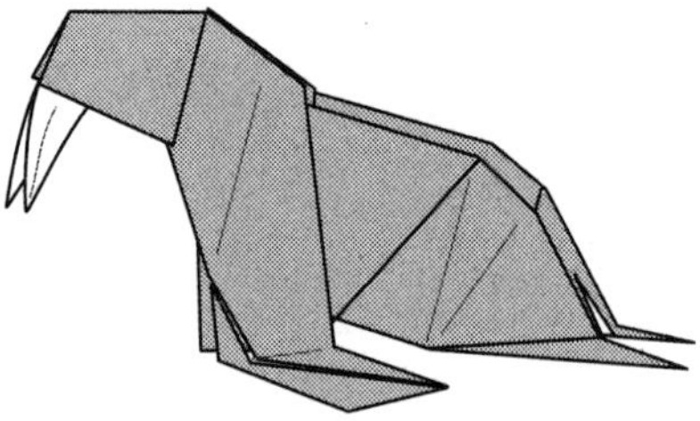

Walrus
✳✳
Page 38

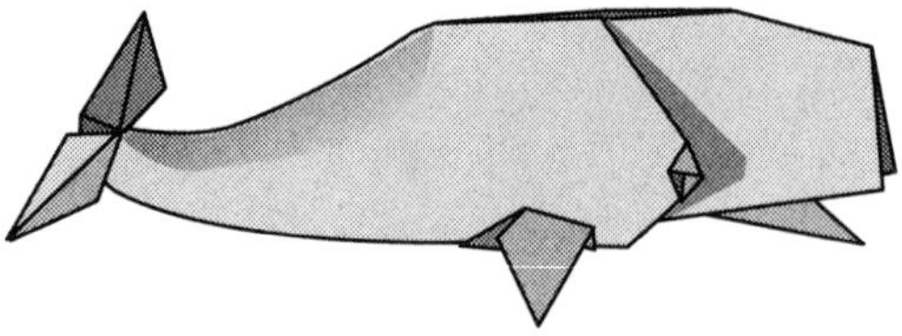

Sperm Whale
✳✳
Page 41

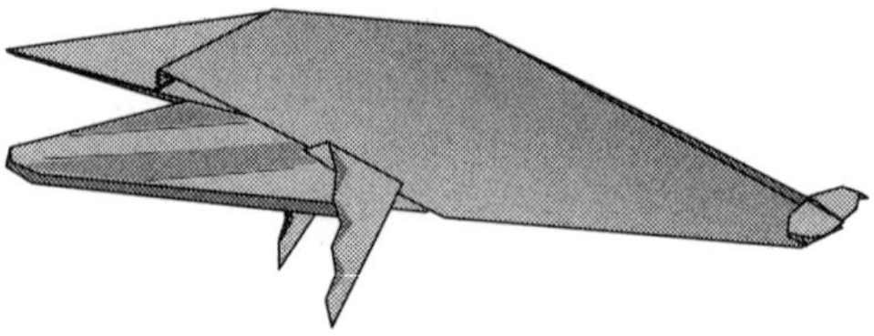

Humpback Whale
✳✳
Page 44

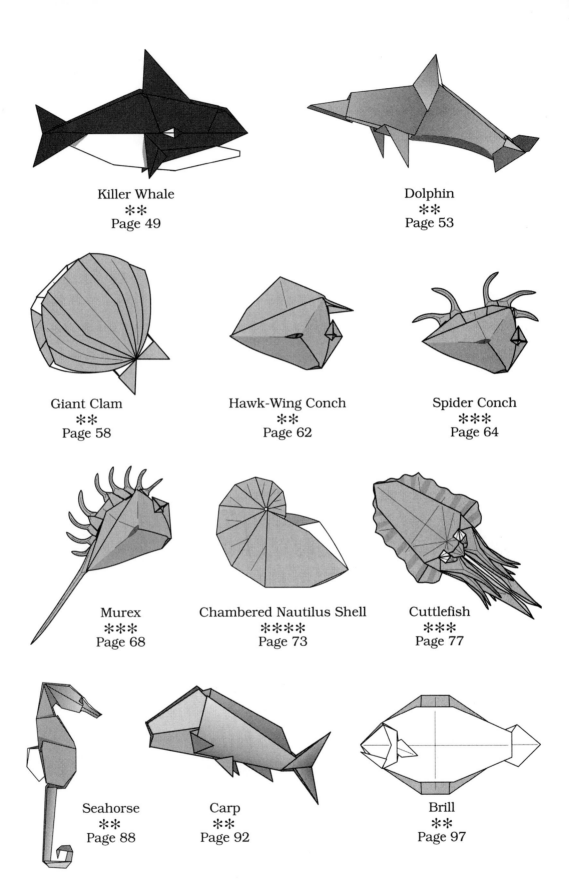

Contents 7

Ocean Sunfish
**
Page 103

Triggerfish
**
Page 108

Angelfish
***
Page 112

Goldfish
***
Page 118

Cichlid
***
Page 126

Sailfish
***
Page 133

Barracuda
***
Page 140

Blue Shark
***
Page 147

Angler Fish
***
Page 155

Blackdevil Angler
****
Page 161

Lionfish
✳✳✳✳
Page 174

Starfish
✳✳
Page 186

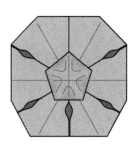

Sand Dollar
✳✳✳
Page 191

Atlantic Purple Sea Urchin
✳✳✳✳
Page 195

Bay Barnacle
✳
Page 202

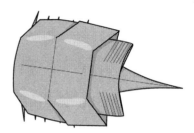

Horseshoe Crab
✳✳✳
Page 203

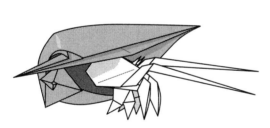

Hermit Crab
✳✳✳
Page 208

Blue Crab
✳✳✳✳
Page 215

Fiddler Crab
✳✳✳✳
Page 225

American Lobster
✳✳✳✳
Page 237

Contents 9

A History of Origami Sea Life

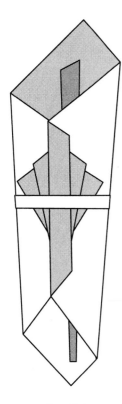

An example of the noshi, *a folded paper ornament signifying wishes for good luck. Traditional noshi enclosed a strip of dried abalone.*

Origami, the art of paper folding, was developed in Japan over a period of some fifteen centuries. Japan is a land with limited natural resources, and its people have always adapted what materials were at hand for their needs. Thus, paper, which could be made from the abundant trees, was used widely as a structural and decorative medium. In the national religion, Shinto, both abstract and representational figures are used as decorations and for ceremonial purposes. Quite early on, such figures were made from paper, and such figures were the original origami designs.

The natural world shaped Japanese culture in many ways. Those aspects of nature that were most familiar to everyday life figured the most heavily in ceremonial practices. The sea played a major role in the culture of Japan, an island nation; it provided much of the food in the daily diet, and a wide body of ceremony sprang up about the sea and its denizens, such as the *ika*, or squid, *ebi*, or shrimp, and *maguro*, or tuna. It was inevitable that sea life would become the subject of origami, and that those creatures that graced the Japanese table would also grace the world of origami.

As early as the twelfth century, sea life and origami were combined in the abstract *noshi-awabe*, a pleated paper ornament in which a strip of dried abalone (*awabe*) was placed. *Noshi* were attached to gifts to signify the hope of the giver that the recipient would enjoy good fortune. They are still used in Japan for this purpose, although the twentieth century has taken its toll on this tradition. One is now as likely to find the *noshi* design merely printed on the wrapping paper as separately folded and attached.

Representational origami sea life is also hundreds of years old. One of the earliest existing sets of origami instructions is contained in the classic work *Kan-no-mado* ("Window on Mid-Winter"), which includes directions for folding 48 popular traditional origami designs. Among various animals and human figures, the *Kan-no-mado* includes several sea creatures—a shrimp, a crab, an octopus, and a lobster. All four designs, interestingly enough, make heavy use of cuts in the paper.

An aside about cuts is in order here. Now that origami is a worldwide phenomenon with tens of thousands of devotees, it is widely assumed that the traditional rules for origami are "one square, no cuts." In fact, these strictures are of relatively recent origin. While many of the traditional origami designs are in fact folded from a single uncut square—the crane being the most famous—many are not. In fact, none of the sea creatures from the *Kan-no-mado* are without cuts. This is because origami sea life, more than almost any other genre, places unusual demands upon the designer, due to the large numbers of limbs, irregular shapes, and mismatched points. Only in the past few years have origami sea creatures appeared that were not highly stylized, indistinct, from multiple sheets, or cut.

Early sea life

It was not until the mid-twentieth century that one-piece, no-cut sea life began to appear in the origami literature; yet, because of the difficulty in producing realistic sea life, most remained highly stylized. Arthropods—crabs, lobsters, and shrimp—with a full complement of legs were unheard of, and fish were rarely identifiable as more than simply "fish." Yet, slowly, a body of origami sea life designs evolved.

Many of them were the product of the father of twentieth-century origami, the Japanese master Akira Yoshizawa. Yoshizawa began developing new designs in the 1930s and 1940s in relative obscurity. However, as his designs and photographs of finished works began to appear in Japanese books and magazines, his stature grew and his reputation spread to the Western world. His masterwork, *Origami Dokuhon*, was published in 1957, and, among more traditional sea creatures (a simple fish and frog), it contained a lobster, albeit legless, from an equilateral triangle.

Several other Japanese folders were active throughout the 1950s and 1960s as well, and added to the ranks of origami sea life. Typical of the period were Isao Honda's *The World of Origami*, published in 1965, which included a legless shrimp with cut antennae, a seal with cut rear flippers, a penguin, several generic fish, a goldfish with cut fins, the traditional frog, and a crab with cut legs; and Kunihiko Kasahara's *Creative Origami*, published in 1967, which contained a legless crawfish (from a right triangle), a goldfish, a shark, a blowfish (with cuts), a seahorse, a whale, and an octopus, crab, and squid, each with four legs apiece.

Four sea creatures from the Kan-no-mado, *ca. 1797. (Top to bottom): shrimp, crab, lobster, octopus.*

Meanwhile, in the West, origami was growing steadily in popularity, and Western folders were beginning to see their designs in print. Robert Harbin's *Secrets of Origami* (1963) contained traditional designs such as a frog, a cut octopus, and original Western creations including an angelfish, a whale, a seal, and a sea horse. James Minoru Sakoda's *Modern Origami* (1969) further expanded the Western repertoire with a seal, an angelfish, and a two-legged lobster.

Recent developments

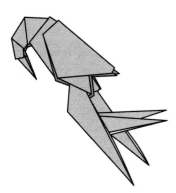

Kunihiko Kasahara's lobster, from Creative Origami.

Kunihiko Kasahara's *Viva Origami* (1983) was a breakthrough publication for Japanese origami, as it contained the first Japanese publication of highly complex models from squares—all designs of a young Japanese physicist, Jun Maekawa. Many of the designs were multipointed, including ten-fingered human figures and a frog whose feet had three and four toes each; however, the only crustacean, a crab, was disappointingly given only two legs. However, in his next book, *Top Origami* (1985), Kasahara included work from many different folders, including a host of shells of unprecedented realism from Kawasaki Toshikazu. Toshikazu was the first folder to develop a successful general method for achieving a spiral shell, which he accomplished by weaving four points around each other. *Top Origami* contained several shells from Toshikazu: an ivory shell, a turban shell, and a murex; the last, however, was heavily cut to produce its points.

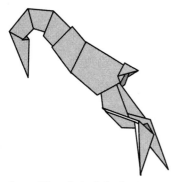

Isao Honda's lobster, from The World of Origami.

Meanwhile, Yoshizawa had produced his self-proclaimed second masterwork, *Origami Dokuhon II* (1984), which included instructions for the first time for his one-piece uncut crab, as well as a starfish from a Bird Base, a three-armed squid, a flying fish, a dolphin, a seahorse, and two other fish. Although the instructions for the crab were not published until 1984, photographs had been published in Japan many years earlier, making it possibly one of the earliest of the "realistic" designs. *Dokuhon II* also contained photographs (no instructions) of a sea turtle, scallops, a two-legged hermit crab, and an octopus.

In the West, several books containing complex models had appeared by this time, but the first to include a substantial aquarian offering was John Montroll's *Origami for the Enthusiast* (1979), which contained a fish, goldfish, seahorse, whale, and sunfish. It was the first publication of fish with the appropriate number and locations of fins. He followed it with *Animal Origami for the Enthusiast*

(1985), which (like *Top Origami*) contained a frog with the appropriate number of toes, as well as an angelfish, a crab, a seal, a walrus, and a lobster. The last was a major feat of origami design, achieving for the first time all eight legs, claws, antennae, and even eyestalks.

Most recently, Peter Engel's *Folding the Universe* (1989) has taken the subject matter of sea life to new heights; it contains an angelfish, a butterflyfish, a discusfish, a dollar bill crab, a crab from a square, and, for the first time, octopus and squid of unusual realism, including eyes, funnels, and the appropriate number of legs. *Folding the Universe* was an unusual origami book in that a significant fraction of the book was given over to material other than folding instructions. In it, Engel examined the very roots of origami, the process of folding design and how it related to creativity, engineering, and geometry. And in doing so, he touched on why the design of origami sea life is so difficult.

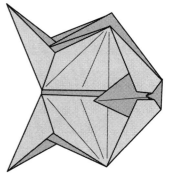

James Minoru Sakoda's angelfish, from Modern Origami.

Design

Of all the phyla of the animal kingdom, sea creatures pose some of the most difficult challenges to the origami designer. In large part, this is due to the natural environment in which they have evolved. Unlike their land-based brethren, sea creatures are continuously supported by water on all sides. This has resulted in creatures with large numbers of abnormally long legs at one extreme, and creatures without any appendages at all at the other. Neither extreme lends itself easily to origami design.

Ultimately, systematic origami design is based on symmetry. The square has certain symmetries; the subject has other symmetries. Most of the effort of the designer consists of altering the symmetry of the square to approximate that of the subject. The process of design is simple if the symmetry of the square already matches that of the subject—for example, if the subject has four limbs that may be made from the square's four corners. If the subject has many more limbs than four, additional points must be developed from the edge of the square and possibly even from the middle, which requires more complex and difficult folding.

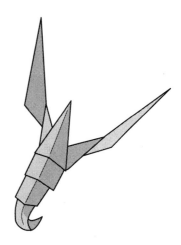

James Minoru Sakoda's lobster, from Modern Origami .

Fish offer a unique problem to the origami designer. The early part of the design of a subject consists of developing a geometric shape, called a "base," that has the same number, location, and size of points as the subject. Points are usually derived in pairs. Yet, the dorsal, ventral, anal, and caudal fins of a fish are singular. The designer is faced with the problem of either constructing a base with unmatched points or wastefully "throwing away" one of a pair of points by hiding it or tucking it away inside the model.

Mollusks, those creatures with shells, pose a different problem from fish. Most shells are symmetric, but it is the wrong kind of symmetry. Seashells often have a chiral symmetry (that is, they come in right- and left-handed versions), typified by a spiral structure. Such a shape does not have reflection symmetry—that is, the shell is not the same as its mirror image—but most origami bases do. Thus, design of a shell calls for wholly new design techniques to achieve the spiral. Things are further complicated when you add in extra spines, as many shells, particularly those of the family *Muricidae*, possess.

And then there is simply the problem of numbers. Supported by water, the limbs of sea creatures have evolved to enormous lengths compared to their diameters. Some creatures appear to be nothing more than collections of long, spindly legs, antennae, and eyestalks. To the origami designer, long legs are an anathema; they consume large amounts of paper and are extremely difficult to make with an aspect ratio (the ratio of length to width) of more than 5:1. Many sea creatures have all their limbs with aspect ratios of 100:1 or more. Add to that the fact that arthropods—crabs, lobsters, and shrimp—routinely have ten or more such appendages (echinoderms—sea urchins and sea stars—can have hundreds), and it becomes clear why the origami designers of old used cuts with such abandon.

In one way, however, arthropods are suited to origami. An inevitable by-product of folding shapes with many appendages is the presence of sharp lines at the joints between the appendages and the main body. In fact, origami models must necessarily have a sharp line or edge whenever a point changes size or direction, and the eye is inevitably drawn to these lines. This interaction between the observer and the paper affects the origami design in two ways. First, if several such lines are close to one another, the eye is drawn toward the group, which detracts attention from the rest of the model and gives the impression of clutter. Second, the eye tends to interpret the line as a joint in the subject, whether there is supposed to be one or not. Fortunately, underwater arthropods (and their terrestrial relatives as well) have joints wherever an appendage changes size or direction,

John Montroll's lobster, from Animal Origami for the Enthusiast.

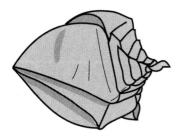

Toshikazu Kawasaki's ivory snail, from Top Origami.

just like an origami appendage. Thus, little effort is required to convert a point into a leg. With an arthropod, if the number and locations of legs can be achieved, the rest quickly follows.

The opposite extreme from the leggy, jointed arthropods are those creatures with too few legs; those of the amorphous body. These include sea slugs, sea cucumbers, coral, and sponges. Origami, even at its most realistic, is successful only as a cartoon, an abstraction. It must somehow include those features of the subject that are the most distinctive. The human eye is most readily drawn to outlines and geometric features—number and location of appendages, for example—and so those features are what origami designers have concentrated on. However, the amorphous subjects, such as coral or sponges, are recognized not by their outlines but by their textures, and origami textures have not been well developed. Similarly, other subjects that are difficult to achieve with origami are creatures that are light and feathery, such as sea lilies, and creatures with many limbs but no natural joints to use to hide fold lines, such as starfish and octopi.

Over the past few years, the challenges inherent in the design of realistic origami sea creatures attracted both of the authors to the genre. Independently, we developed techniques to form legs, antennae, claws, fins, flukes, legs, and spines; then, learning of the other's developments, we decided to pool our efforts. The result is this book. In *Origami Sea Life*, we have developed creatures of the water of all types: fish, seashells, crabs, lobsters, whales, amphibians, echinoderms, and mollusks. While many of the designs are simple enough for the novice folder, many of them are among the most complex ever published, and should prove challenging to even the most advanced folder.

One of the encouraging aspects of present-day origami is the speed at which the field is evolving. Ten years ago, many of the designs contained in this book would have been unthinkable. Ten years from now, who knows what might be possible?

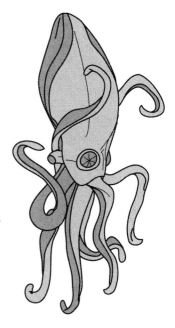

Peter Engel's octopus, from Folding the Universe.

Paper

The paper requirements of this book are minimal. In short, every model in this book can be folded from a standard ten-inch square of origami paper. This is widely available from artist's supply stores and stationery shops, by mail order from The Origami Center (see addresses), and from stores in the Japanese district of many major cities.

However, while origami paper may be the most convenient material to fold, it is not always the best. Conventional origami paper is somewhat springy, which makes subtle shaping difficult. The layers in models without locking folds tend to spread apart over time, making the models unsuitable for long-term display.

Foil-backed paper, such as Christmas wrapping paper, may also be used for the models in this book and offer greater longevity. Foil paper consists of a thin layer of foil bonded to a thicker layer of paper; the metal maintains its shape over time and furthermore allows the model to be shaped, which lets you add some three-dimensional character to the model. While Christmas wrapping paper is a good source (and obviously, the Christmas season is the best time to shop for it), many stationery stores and card shops carry some year round. Exceedingly thin gold and silver foil-backed paper is also available from many art stores, and is suitable for the most delicate models, including the crustacea in this book.

There are, however, also significant drawbacks to foil paper. Any model folded from foil-backed paper is quite fragile, and its appendages are easy to bend and distort. They may be bent back into place, but any creases made in foil-backed paper are usually indelible. And after several cycles of being bent and straightened, the paper weakens and will no longer hold its shape. Also, the color range is somewhat limited; the paper side is always white, while the foil side may be gold, silver, green, or red—but that's about all. Several patterned foil gift wraps are also available, but their patterns are usually garish rather than subtle and detract from the lines of the model.

Another paper that is especially suitable for folding small, intricate models is "tissue-foil," which is homemade. To make it, you spray a sheet of ordinary kitchen aluminum foil with an artist's spray adhesive, and carefully lay down a sheet of colored tissue paper over it; then repeat on the other side. The result is a three-layer laminate that has all the malleability of foil-backed paper, but the colors and surface texture of the two sheets of tissue.

One great advantage that tissue-foil has over foil-backed paper is that the metal layer is thicker in the former. The metal does not break after a sharp crease is made, unlike foil-backed paper, and thus it is less likely to crack or rip during a difficult fold. In fact, it is possible to completely unfold a tissue-foil model, smooth out the paper, and have it look as good as new! The disadvantage of this property is that precreasing is next to useless; creases cannot be easily reversed, and so this paper is much harder to work with.

Still, the results of tissue foil—especially with insects and other arthropods—can be impressive. The colored tissue paper is slightly translucent, and the reflection of the foil through the tissue gives the appearance of depth. Because the reflection adds a gray component to the color of the laminate, the color of the tissue will be altered. Earth tones—browns, grays, greens—do particularly well for animals and insects. You should be careful, however, about the tissue paper; most kinds use unstable color dyes that fade quickly. Earth tones tend to fade more gracefully than brighter colors.

For larger models, none of the foil-based papers are sturdy enough for long-term display. However, a folding technique called "wet-folding" can be used to make quite large, sturdy sculptures. In wet-folding, a heavy paper is dampened before folding, which makes it malleable enough to fold; when the paper dries, it becomes rigid and resistant to damage.

To fold a model "wet," you should use a large square of paper—50 centimeters square is a good size—and have handy a small dish of water and a dampened cloth. The paper should be fairly heavy; 28–40# ledger is a range of appropriate weights. Watercolor paper, available from art stores, is available in a variety of weights, colors, and textures in large sizes, and is probably the most accessible source of wet-folding paper. So-called "calligraphy parchment," (actually, not parchment at all), although only available in white and beige, is one of the best wet-folding papers you can find.

The paper should be dampened lightly and evenly with the cloth before folding. If you are cutting the square from a rectangle, dampen the paper before cutting the square, as the paper will expand slightly more in one direction than the other. Take care not to overdampen the paper. It should be leathery, not soggy. If the surface is shiny with water or creases become fuzzy with loose fibers, then it is too wet, and you should stop and let it dry a bit before continuing to fold.

Once the model is folded, it must be constrained to hold its shape until the paper has dried. Paper clips should be used sparingly, as they will leave a mark when the paper is dry. Depending on the surface of the paper, draftsman's tape can be used to hold the model in position until the paper is dry and can be stripped off afterward without leaving any marks.

One of the great benefits offered by wet-folding is the ability to make highly three-dimensional models by rounding and shaping the paper as you fold. (All of the models in the photographs were wet-folded.) As with any paper, wet-folding calls for its own set of folding techniques. Because the paper is so thick and stretches, depending on the dampness of the paper, it is difficult to fold precisely, and long, skinny points are difficult to make neatly. On the other hand, some procedures—notably closed sinks—are easier to perform with a wet-folding paper than with any other type, and the paper has enough give in it to let the folder cover up minor misalignments. Perhaps its greatest advantage, though, is its permanence. A wet-folded model can be easily transported and is resistant to minor dents; with only moderate care, a wet-folded origami model will keep its beauty for years.

Sea Life

The oceans and seas of the world contain some of the most wonderous and beautiful forms of life on this planet. Practically every large grouping or phylum of life is represented. This is hardly surprising since, as we can tell from fossil records, life began in the water.

The animals in the oceans have adapted to so many habitats so excellently that it can be said that if there is water, there is probably life, whether it be plant, animal, single-celled or multi-celled. They have adapted to feed on one another and escape from one another. Complex hunting and defense mechanisms abound even in the least complex species.

To give an idea of the variety of environments in the aquatic systems of our planet, here is a brief listing.

Coastal/Intertidal

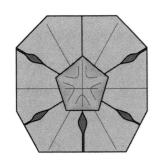

Found along shorelines, sand dollars live where they filter food out of the water.

The intertidal and coastal zones consist of the shoreline and waters immediately offshore. The intertidal zone is that region between high and low tides. The creatures who live there must cope with regular exposure to air and wave action and do so in many ways. Crabs, for example, can leave the water but must return periodically to remoisten their gills. Barnacles and oysters secure themselves securely to a rock or piling. The creatures of the intertidal zone are the most familiar to us, closely followed by those that live in the shallow waters immediately offshore.

Offshore/Open Ocean

The sailfish swims in the open oceans at speeds of up to 60 miles per hour.

The open ocean is the home of the large game fish and whales. There dwell the sailfish and tuna, the shark and orca. There are no hiding places in the open ocean so the inhabitants have evolved for speed. Many of the pelagic species are quite wide-ranging; some species of whales migrate halfway around the globe each year.

Deep Sea

Living in the deep sea, the angler fish uses its florescent lure to attract its prey.

Far below the depths to which light can penetrate live the deep-sea dwellers. Until recently, most of these species were little-known, and even now we are only beginning to learn about their lives through the use of specialized manned submersibles. Although no light can penetrate to such depths, many deep-sea creatures have specialized organs to create light, through a process known as bioluminescence.

Coral Reef

The coral reef may be the most productive environment in the world. Built from the exoskeletons of the coral, the reefs are found in shallow tropical waters where they shelter an amazing variety of life. The diversity and colors of the coral reef's inhabitants are unmatched by any other ecosystem.

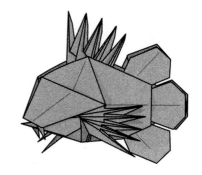

The colorful lionfish can be found along reefs.

Mangrove Swamp/ Salt Marsh

Mangroves and marsh grasses are found in estuaries, places where fresh water and salt water come together, for example, at the mouths of rivers. They are immensely important as nursery areas for many different species, as they provide calmer waters than the offshore zones and are rich in nutrients from decaying vegetable matter. Besides fish and crustacea, salt marshes are home to a variety of terrestrial animal life as well.

Fiddler crabs are one of the most numerous inhabitants of the mangrove swamps.

Freshwater Lakes and Rivers

Freshwater lakes and rivers are found in all climatic zones, from the temperate regions to the tropics. They are home to many important commercial species of fish and crustacea and offer low levels of dissolved salts and, in faster, colder streams and rivers, a high level of dissolved oxygen.

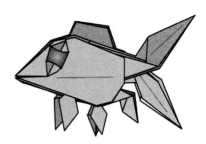

The freshwater goldfish is a popular aquarium pet.

Symbols

Lines

— — — — — — — — — —   Valley-fold, fold in front.

—··—··—··—··—··—   Mountain-fold, fold behind.

———————————   Crease line.

··   X-ray or guide line.

Arrows

 Fold in this direction.

 Fold behind.

 Unfold.

 Fold and unfold.

 Turn over.

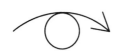 Sink, reverse fold, push here, or three-dimensional folding.

 Place your finger between these layers.

Frog Metamorphosis

The metamorphosis of a tadpole into a frog is a fascinating sequence of events which can be witnessed at almost any pond in the world. Frogs lay many jelly-like, nearly transparent eggs in the water. Tadpoles hatch from the eggs and breathe through gills. The young tadpole initially has no legs at all. Soon, however, the hind legs begin to form. Then the front legs appear. When the gills have changed to lungs the tadpole has become a young frog ready to go on land. Finally the tail disappears.

Adult frogs are tailless amphibians. With their powerful hind legs, they are very good at leaping. They breathe through their mouths and also through their moist skin. During the winter they hibernate at the bottom of ponds.

Tadpole

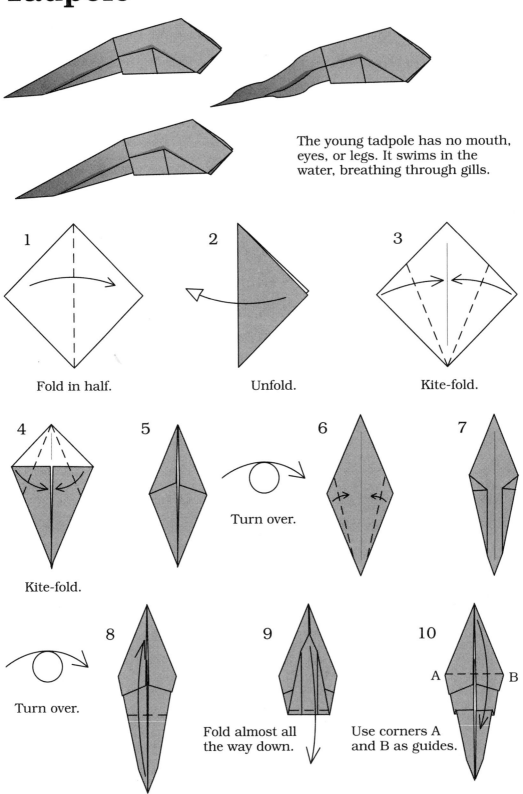

The young tadpole has no mouth, eyes, or legs. It swims in the water, breathing through gills.

1 Fold in half.

2 Unfold.

3 Kite-fold.

4 Kite-fold.

5

6 Turn over.

7

8 Turn over.

9 Fold almost all the way down.

10 Use corners A and B as guides.

A   B

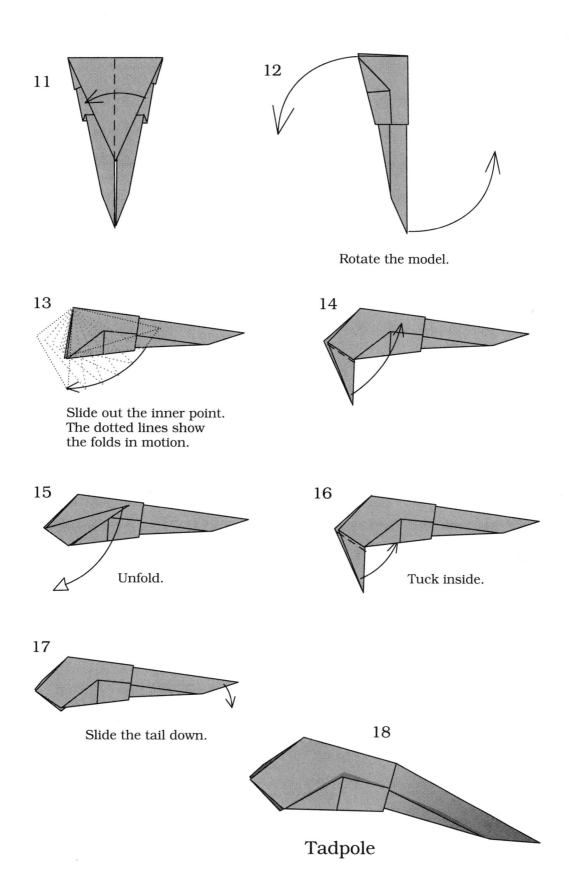

11

12

Rotate the model.

13

Slide out the inner point.
The dotted lines show
the folds in motion.

14

15

Unfold.

16

Tuck inside.

17

Slide the tail down.

18

Tadpole

Tadpole with Hind Legs

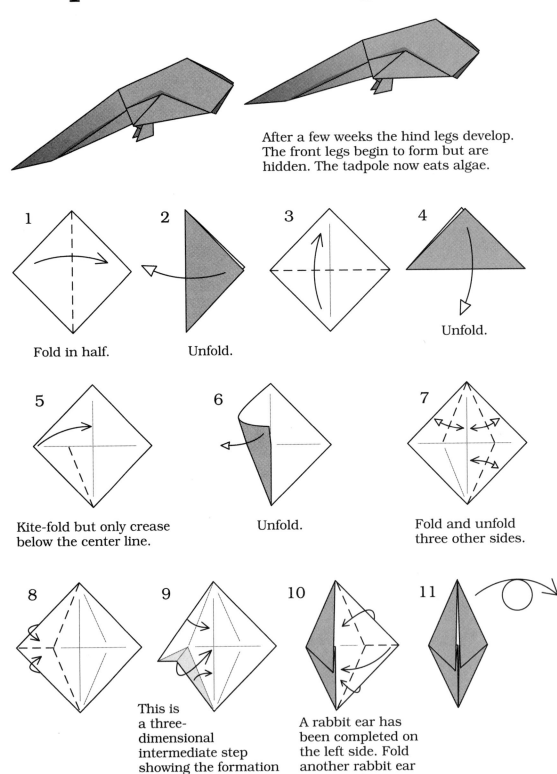

After a few weeks the hind legs develop. The front legs begin to form but are hidden. The tadpole now eats algae.

1
Fold in half.

2
Unfold.

3

4
Unfold.

5
Kite-fold but only crease below the center line.

6
Unfold.

7
Fold and unfold three other sides.

8

9
This is a three-dimensional intermediate step showing the formation of the rabbit ear.

10
A rabbit ear has been completed on the left side. Fold another rabbit ear on the right.

11

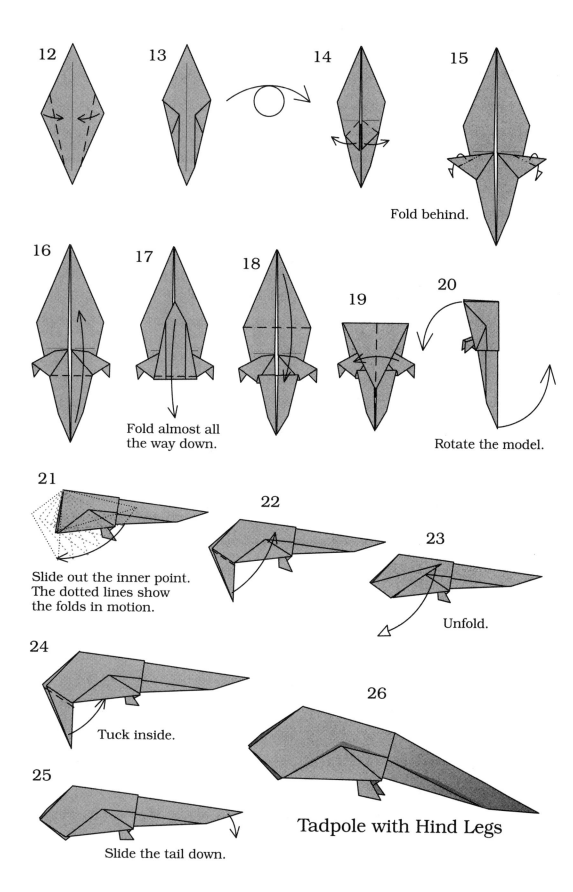

12

13

14

15

Fold behind.

16

17

Fold almost all
the way down.

18

19

20

Rotate the model.

21

Slide out the inner point.
The dotted lines show
the folds in motion.

22

23

Unfold.

24

Tuck inside.

25

Slide the tail down.

26

Tadpole with Hind Legs

Froglet

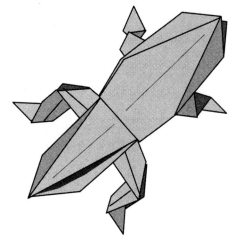

After a few months, the tadpole changes much more. The front legs appear. The gills disappear while the mouth becomes wider. The eyes become larger. It stops eating, digesting the materials in its tail. With a shrinking tail, the young frog is now ready to leave the water.

1

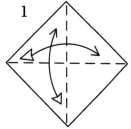

Fold and unfold.

2

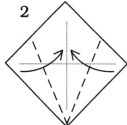

Kite-fold.

3

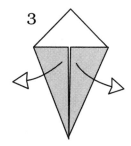

Unfold.

4

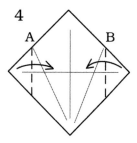

Use the points A and B as guides.

5

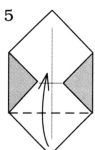

6

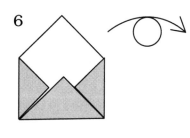

7

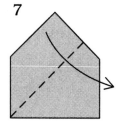

8

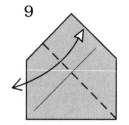

Unfold.

9

Fold and unfold.

10

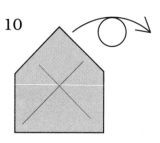

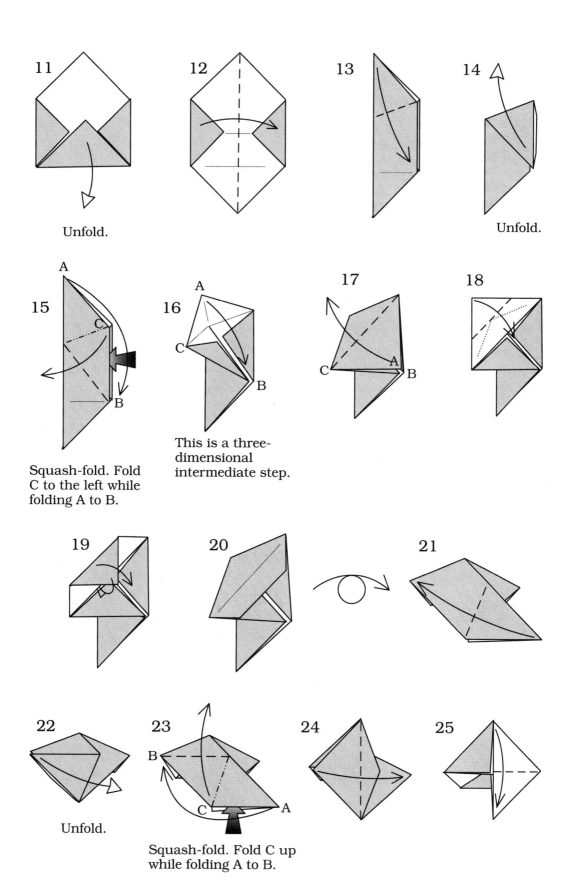

11

Unfold.

12

13

14

Unfold.

15 A

Squash-fold. Fold C to the left while folding A to B.

16 A

C

B

This is a three-dimensional intermediate step.

17

C A B

18

19

20

21

22

Unfold.

23 B

C A

Squash-fold. Fold C up while folding A to B.

24

25

26

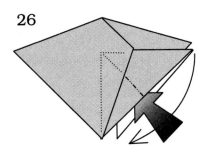

Reverse-fold.

27

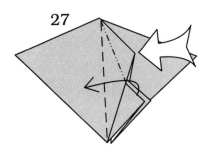

Spread-squash-fold.

28

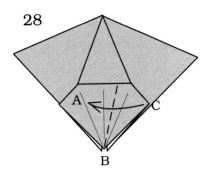

Fold line B–C to line A–B.

29

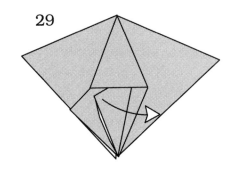

Unfold.

30

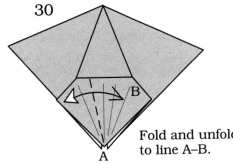

Fold and unfold to line A–B.

31

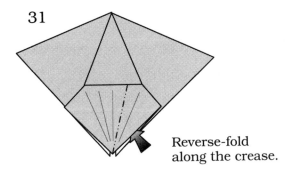

Reverse-fold along the crease.

32

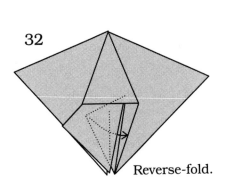

Reverse-fold.

33

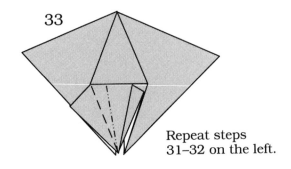

Repeat steps 31–32 on the left.

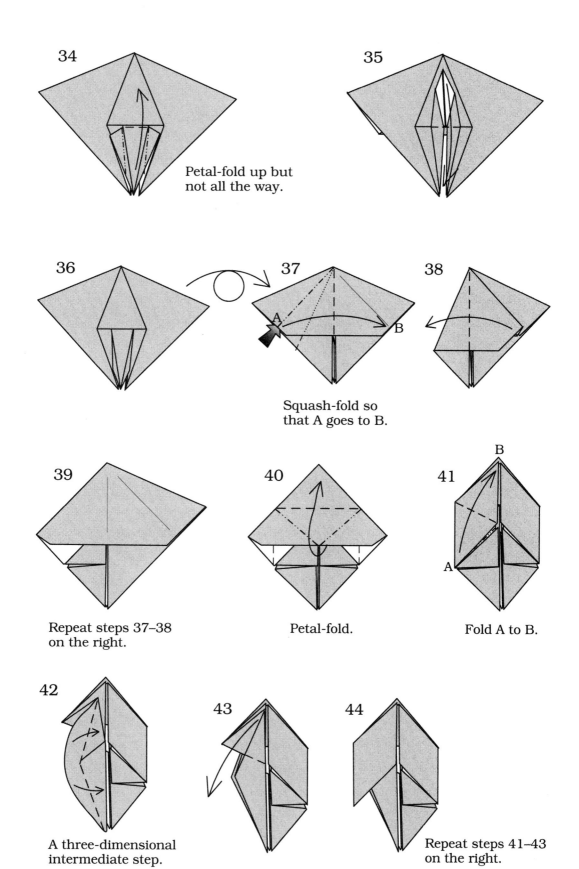

34 Petal-fold up but not all the way.

35

36

37 Squash-fold so that A goes to B.

38

39 Repeat steps 37–38 on the right.

40 Petal-fold.

41 Fold A to B.

42 A three-dimensional intermediate step.

43

44 Repeat steps 41–43 on the right.

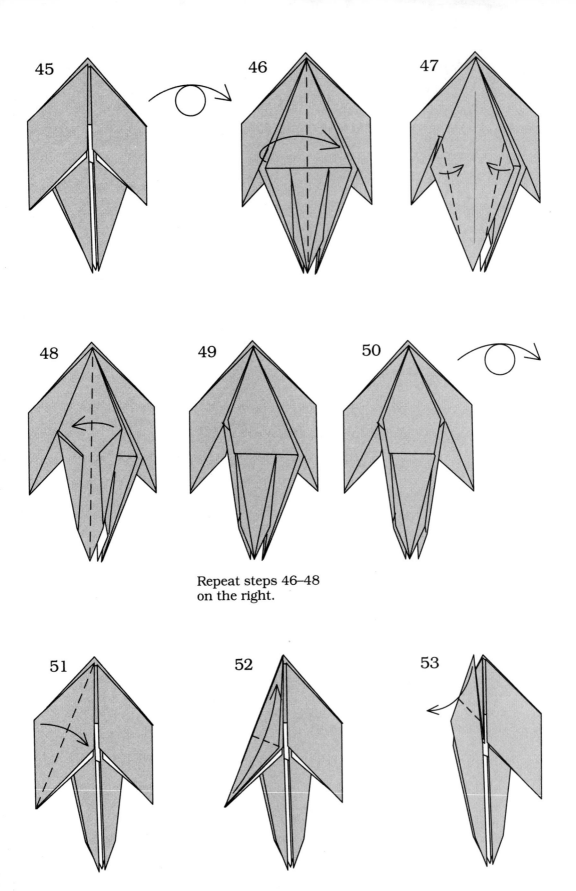

Repeat steps 46–48
on the right.

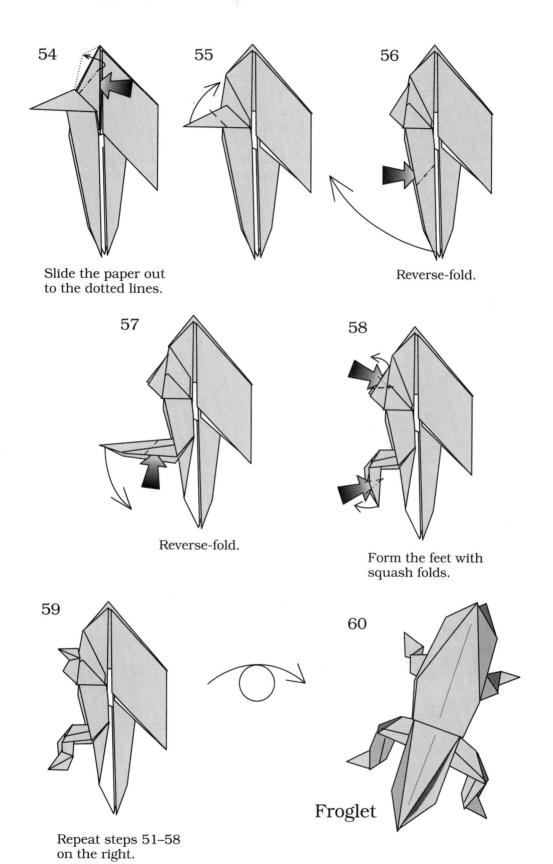

54

55

56

Slide the paper out
to the dotted lines.

Reverse-fold.

57

Reverse-fold.

58

Form the feet with
squash folds.

59

Repeat steps 51–58
on the right.

60

Froglet

Frog

Frogs (order *Anura*) are found throughout the world. They range in size from half an inch to almost a foot. They feed on insects and other small animals which they catch with their long sticky tongues.

1

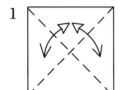

Fold and unfold.

2

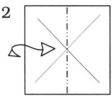

Fold behind and unfold.

3

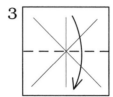

4

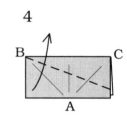

B   C

A

Fold up so that point A lies along line B–C.

5

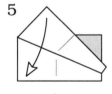

Unfold.

6

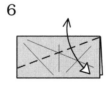

Fold and unfold.

7

8

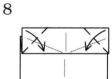

9

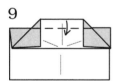

10

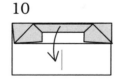

11

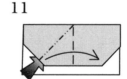

Squash-fold.

12

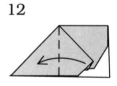

13

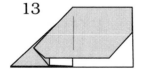

Repeat steps 11–12 on the right.

14

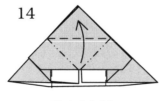

Petal-fold.

15

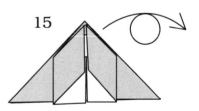

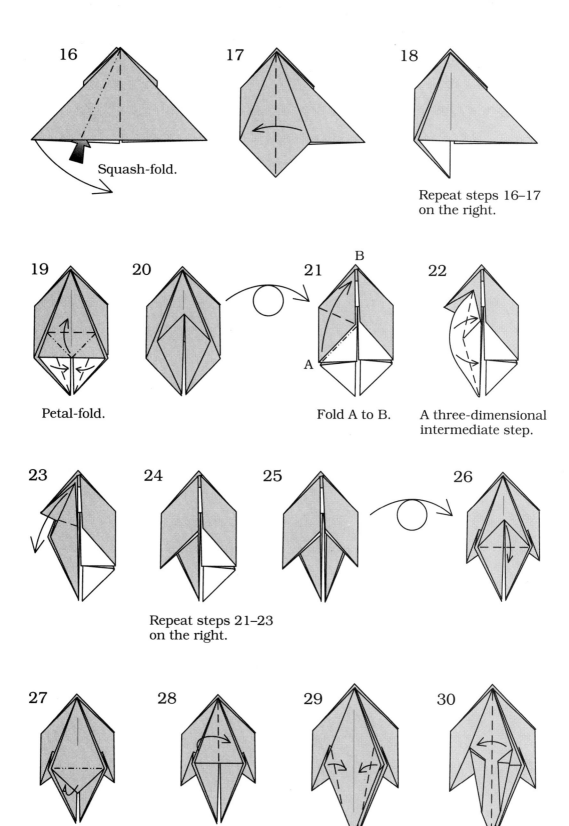

16 Squash-fold.

17

18 Repeat steps 16–17 on the right.

19 Petal-fold.

20

21 B A Fold A to B.

22 A three-dimensional intermediate step.

23

24 Repeat steps 21–23 on the right.

25

26

27 Fold inside.

28

29

30

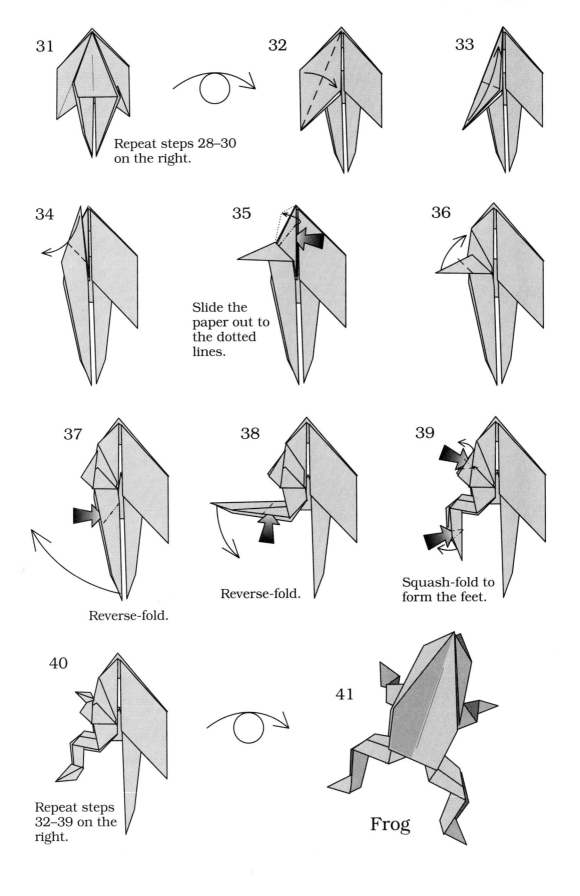

31

Repeat steps 28–30
on the right.

32

33

34

35

Slide the
paper out to
the dotted
lines.

36

37

Reverse-fold.

38

Reverse-fold.

39

Squash-fold to
form the feet.

40

Repeat steps
32–39 on the
right.

41

Frog

Sea Mammals

Among the many groups of animals that have returned from land existence to life in the sea, the whales have readapted the most successfully. These mammals feed on other sea life and are well adapted for swimming, with their streamlined shapes and powerful adaptations for swimming. Seals, walruses, and sea lions, while spending portions of their time out of the water are most at home under the surface, and whales, though they still breathe air, are entirely aquatic.

Whales may be most easily distinguished from fish by their tail fins; those of a whale are horizontal, while those of a fish are vertical. There are two groups of whales, the toothed whales, and the baleen whales. Toothed whales include dolphins, porpoises, killer whales, and sperm whales, and feed on squid and fish. The baleen whales, which include the blue whale, the largest of all living animals, feed on small crustacea called krill, which it strains through its baleen, large plates that hang from the upper jaw.

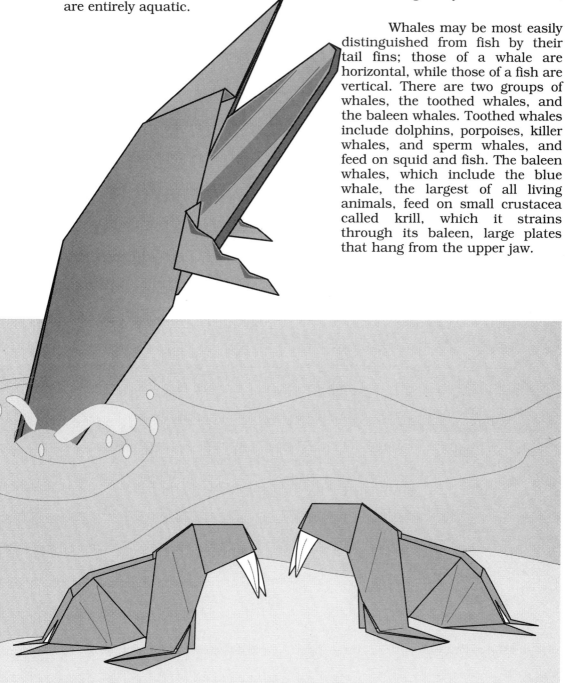

Walrus

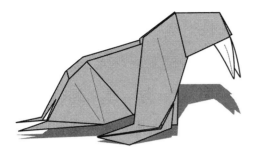

The Walrus (*Odobenus rosmarus*) is one of the most comical-looking animals in the world. With his oversize tusks and bushy moustache, the male walrus resembles an old sea captain. Although walruses seem very lethargic sprawled on northern beaches and ice floes, they are actually capable of great speed on land as well as in the water. They feed primarily on fish and shellfish and may grow up to 15 feet long.

1

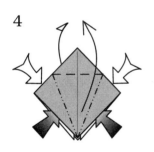

Crease the diagonals.
Turn the paper over.

2

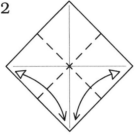

Fold and unfold.

3

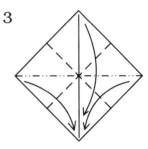

Make a Preliminary Fold.

4

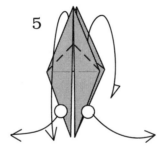

Petal-fold in front
and back to make a
Bird Base.

5

Hold each of the two bottom
flaps and pull them out to
the sides. Simultaneously,
swing the top flap down.

6

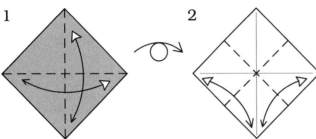

Flatten it out.

7

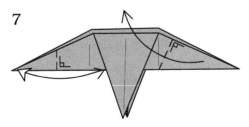

Fold and unfold on the left;
fold the right point up.

8

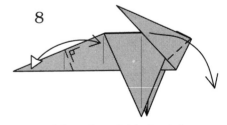

Fold and unfold the left point;
fold the right point down.

9

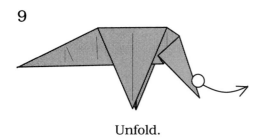

Unfold.

10

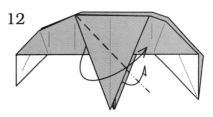

Crimp each side on
existing creases.

11

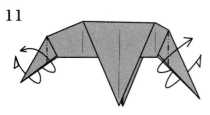

Pull out one layer
from each side.

12

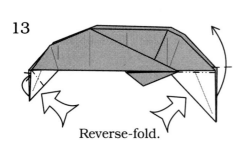

Fold the front and back points
as far to the right as possible.

13

Reverse-fold.

14

Reverse-fold.

15

Crimp the body.

16

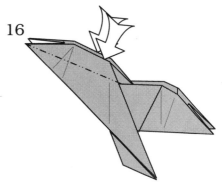

Closed-sink two layers.

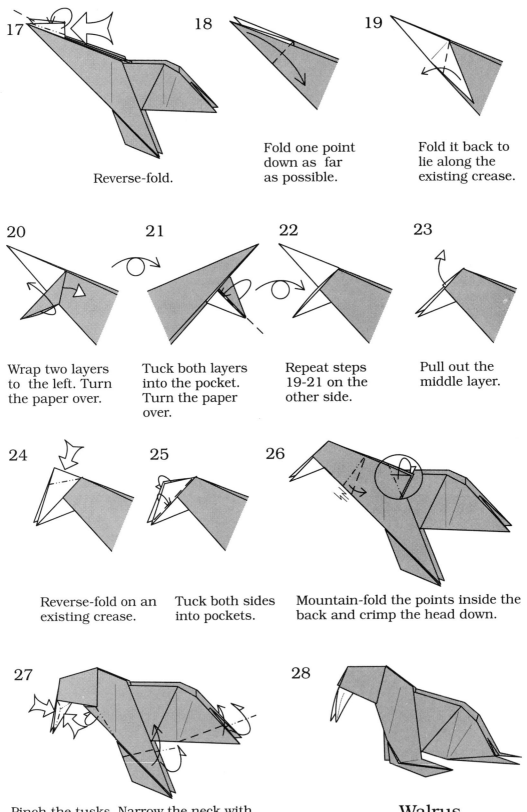

17

Reverse-fold.

18

Fold one point down as far as possible.

19

Fold it back to lie along the existing crease.

20

Wrap two layers to the left. Turn the paper over.

21

Tuck both layers into the pocket. Turn the paper over.

22

Repeat steps 19-21 on the other side.

23

Pull out the middle layer.

24

Reverse-fold on an existing crease.

25

Tuck both sides into pockets.

26

Mountain-fold the points inside the back and crimp the head down.

27

Pinch the tusks. Narrow the neck with mountain folds. Fold the flippers outwards.

28

Walrus

Sperm Whale

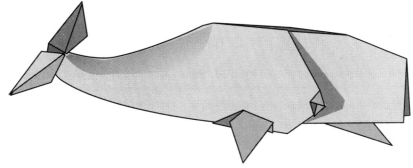

These 60-foot-long toothed whales have teeth only on their lower jaw.
Traveling in herds of 20 to 50, they migrate towards the equator in winter.
They feed mainly on giant squid which they can detect with their sonar
system. The sperm whale (*Physeter macrocephalus*) is dark gray. Often it is
found with white marks and scars on the head from fighting the giant squid.

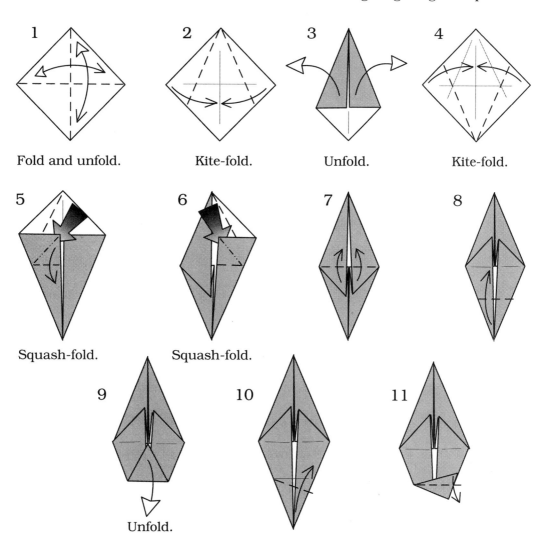

1
Fold and unfold.

2
Kite-fold.

3
Unfold.

4
Kite-fold.

5
Squash-fold.

6
Squash-fold.

7

8

9
Unfold.

10

11

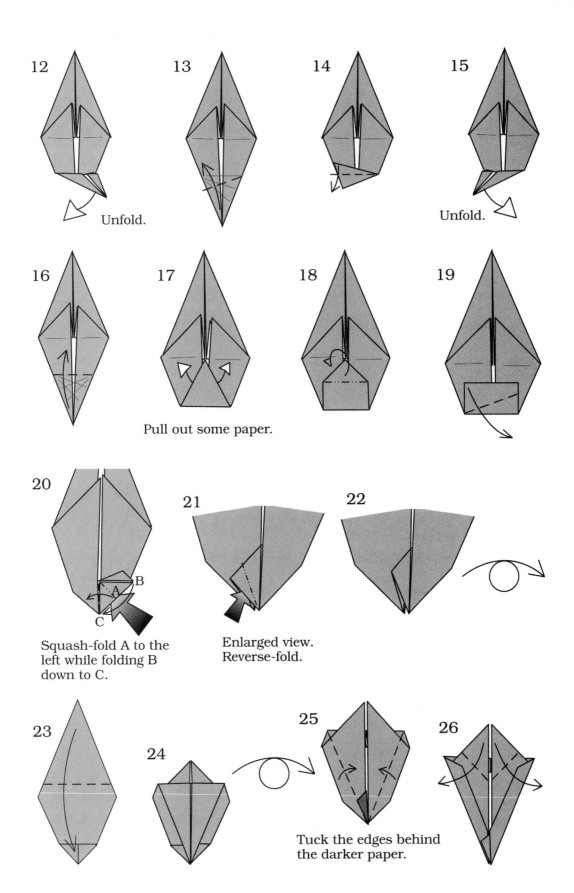

12

13

14

15

Unfold.

Unfold.

16

17

18

19

Pull out some paper.

20

Squash-fold A to the
left while folding B
down to C.

21

Enlarged view.
Reverse-fold.

22

23

24

25

Tuck the edges behind
the darker paper.

26

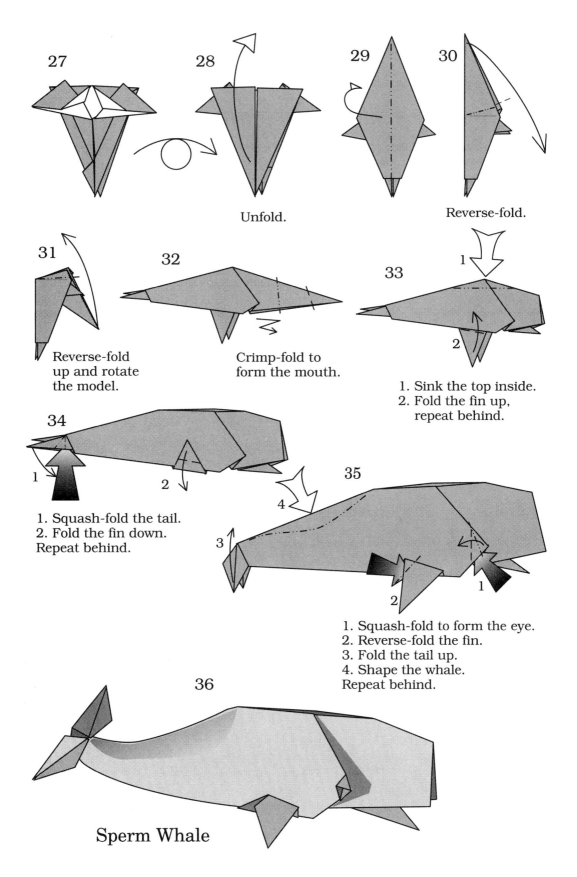

27

28

Unfold.

29

30

Reverse-fold.

31

Reverse-fold
up and rotate
the model.

32

Crimp-fold to
form the mouth.

33

1. Sink the top inside.
2. Fold the fin up,
   repeat behind.

34

1. Squash-fold the tail.
2. Fold the fin down.
Repeat behind.

35

1. Squash-fold to form the eye.
2. Reverse-fold the fin.
3. Fold the tail up.
4. Shape the whale.
Repeat behind.

36

Sperm Whale

Humpback Whale

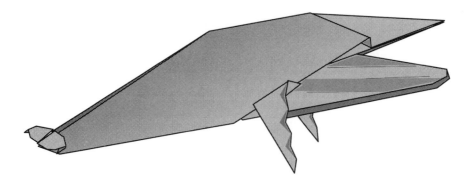

Named for the way it humps its back when it dives, the humpback whale (*Megaptera novaeangliae*) is about 50 feet long. It has large, ragged flippers with bumps along the front edge. This playful creature does somersaults while leaping out of the water. Humpbacks are famous for their long, haunting "songs," which are quite complex. These baleen whales feed on krill and small fish.

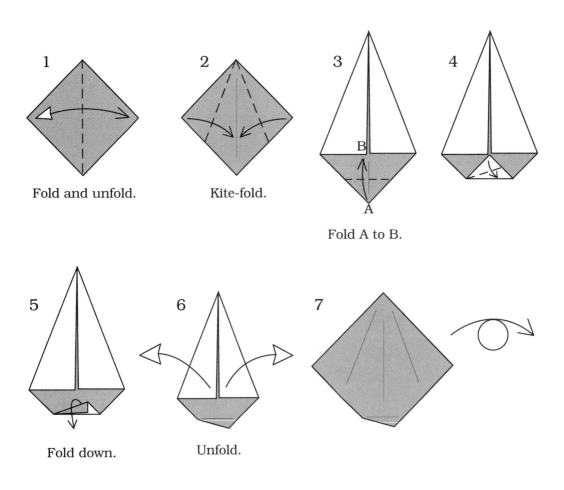

1
Fold and unfold.

2
Kite-fold.

3
Fold A to B.

4

5
Fold down.

6
Unfold.

7

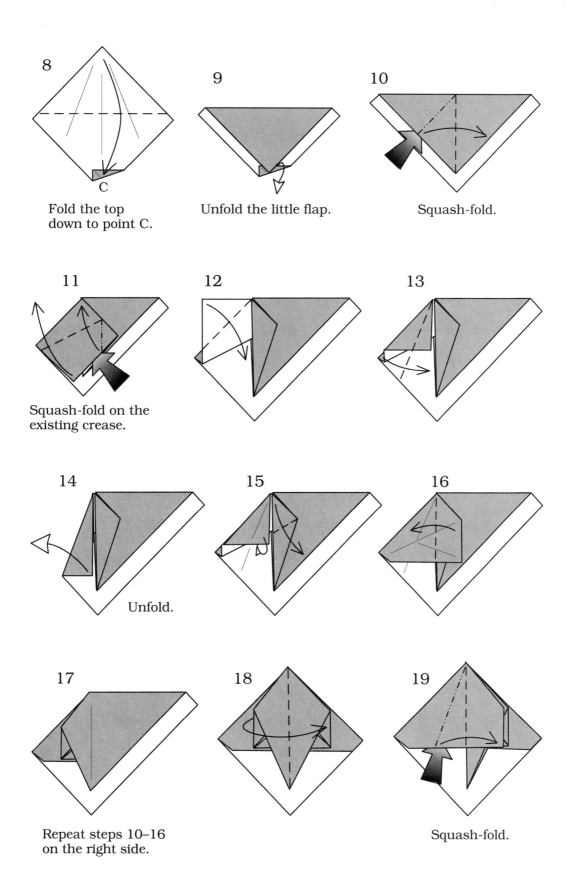

8

Fold the top
down to point C.

9

Unfold the little flap.

10

Squash-fold.

11

Squash-fold on the
existing crease.

12

13

14

Unfold.

15

16

17

Repeat steps 10–16
on the right side.

18

19

Squash-fold.

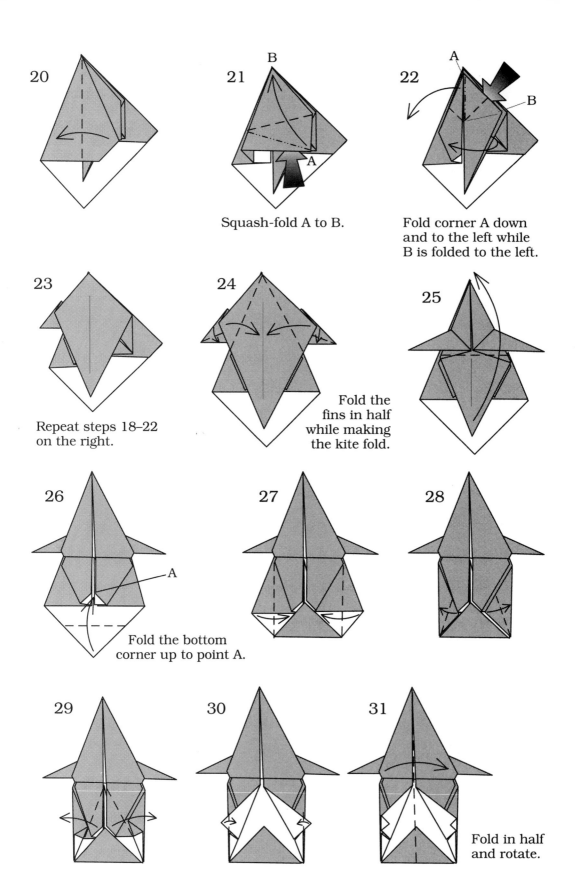

20

21

Squash-fold A to B.

22

Fold corner A down
and to the left while
B is folded to the left.

23

Repeat steps 18–22
on the right.

24

Fold the
fins in half
while making
the kite fold.

25

26

Fold the bottom
corner up to point A.

27

28

29

30

31

Fold in half
and rotate.

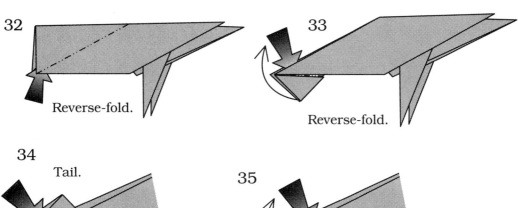

32 Reverse-fold.

33 Reverse-fold.

34 Tail.

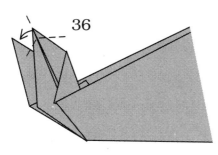

Reverse-fold.

35

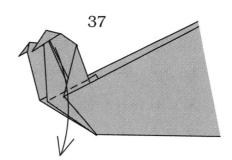

Form the tail with an asymmetric reverse fold. Repeat behind.

36

Form a tiny rabbit ear at the tip of the tail. Repeat behind.

37

Fold down, repeat behind.

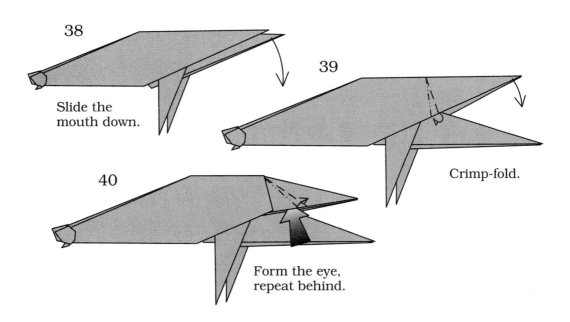

38 Slide the mouth down.

39 Crimp-fold.

40 Form the eye, repeat behind.

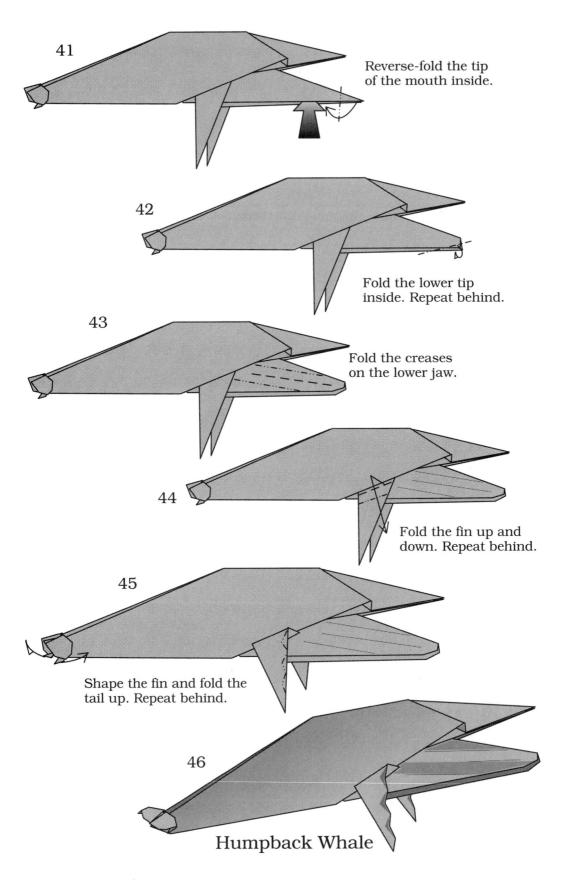

41

Reverse-fold the tip
of the mouth inside.

42

Fold the lower tip
inside. Repeat behind.

43

Fold the creases
on the lower jaw.

44

Fold the fin up and
down. Repeat behind.

45

Shape the fin and fold the
tail up. Repeat behind.

46

Humpback Whale

Killer Whale

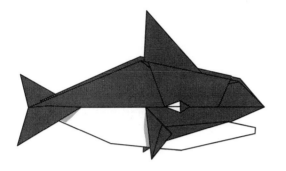

The killer whale (*Orcinus orca*) is not a whale at all, but rather a large dolphin, growing up to 30 feet long. Widely known as "the wolf of the seas," these whales roam in packs and have been known to attack the largest of whales, the blue whale; more commonly, however, they feed on fish, penguins, seals and squid, and have never been known to attack man. They are exceedingly intelligent creatures and are easily trained, and entertain at marine parks worldwide.

1

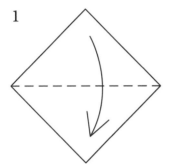

Fold the square in half along the diagonal.

2

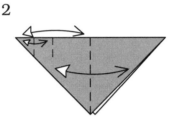

Fold and unfold three times.

3

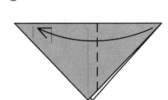

Fold the right corner over to touch the last crease you made.

4

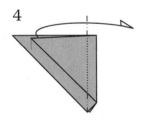

Fold the left corner behind on an existing crease.

5

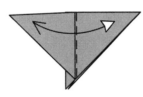

Fold and unfold.

6

Fold the left corner over to the right.

7

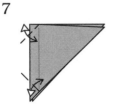

Fold and unfold.

8

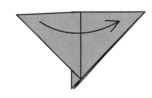

Fold and unfold.

9

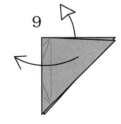

Unfold the paper completely.

10

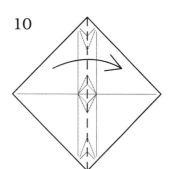

Fold the paper
in half.

11

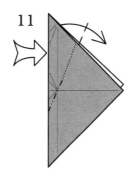

Reverse-fold, using existing
creases. Don't make the
crease sharp all the way.

12

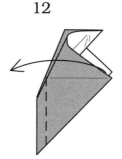

Fold one layer to
the left on an
existing crease.

13

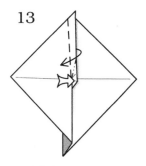

Fold the upper crease
to the left, using
existing creases to
make the zig-zag.

14

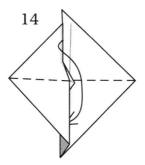

Fold the top half down
and tuck the indicated
flap into the lower pocket.

15

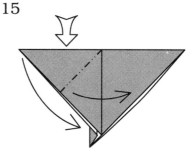

Squash-fold
the left flap.

16

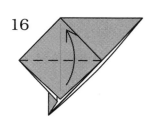

Fold the bottom
point up.

17

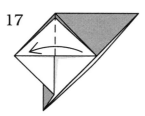

Close up.

18

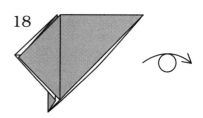

Like this. Turn
the paper over.

19

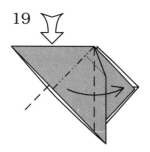

Squash-fold. The dotted
line shows hidden layers.

20

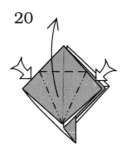

Petal-fold.

21

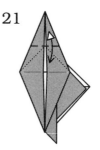

Fold and
unfold.

22

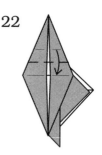

Fold the last crease
down to touch the
horizontal creases.

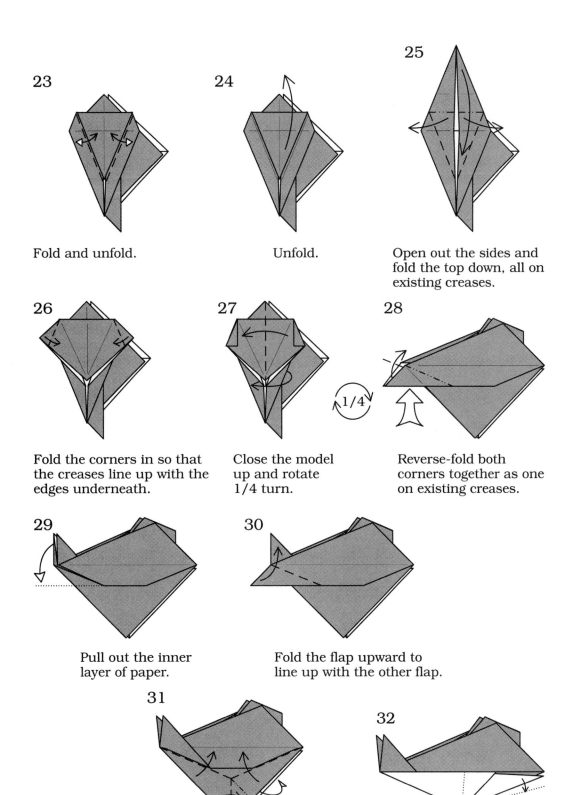

23

Fold and unfold.

24

Unfold.

25

Open out the sides and fold the top down, all on existing creases.

26

Fold the corners in so that the creases line up with the edges underneath.

27

Close the model up and rotate 1/4 turn.

28

Reverse-fold both corners together as one on existing creases.

29

Pull out the inner layer of paper.

30

Fold the flap upward to line up with the other flap.

31

Fold a rabbit ear; repeat behind.

32

Pull the white point down slightly.

33

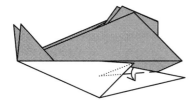

Valley-fold the white layer,
forming a reverse fold
where it goes under the
short flap. Repeat behind.

34

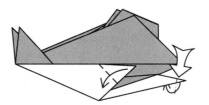

Fold the short flap down;
repeat behind. Reverse-fold
the tip of the white point.

35

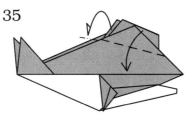

Fold the top flap down;
repeat behind.

36

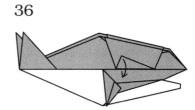

Unfold the corner.
Repeat behind.

37

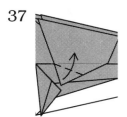

Fold the corner
upward. Repeat
behind.

38

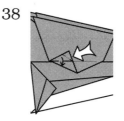

Squash-fold.
Repeat behind.

39

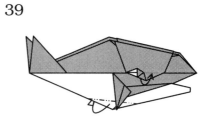

Mountain-fold the belly. Tuck
the corner below the white
spot under the lower layers,
but leave the white spot
showing. Repeat behind.

40

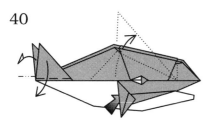

Fold the tail fins down. Open out the
pectoral fins. Reverse-fold the dorsal fin
up and out from the top of the body.

41

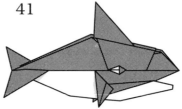

Killer Whale

Dolphin

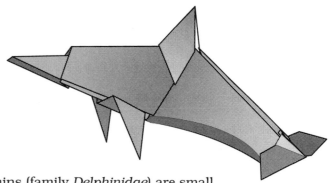

About 8 to 12 feet long, dolphins (family *Delphinidae*) are small, toothed whales. They are very playful and are often found near ships. They are known for their intelligence—dolphins can be taught many tricks—and for their ability to detect small objects with their sonar system. These noisy creatures can communicate by clicking and whistling through their blowholes.

1

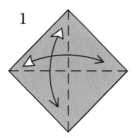

Fold and unfold along the diagonals.

2

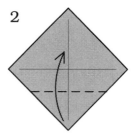

Crease lightly. There are no guides for this fold; in step 4 you will find out if it was correct.

3

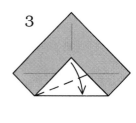

4

If the lines intersect where the circle is drawn then continue. Otherwise, go back to step 2 with a better guess.

5

Unfold.

6

Fold down along line A–B.

7

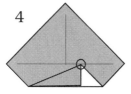

Fold C to D.

8

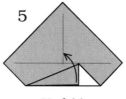

Fold up along line A–B.

9

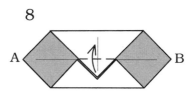

Unfold.

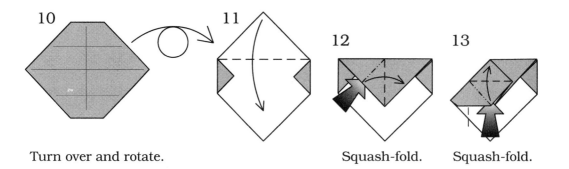

10 Turn over and rotate.

11

12 Squash-fold.

13 Squash-fold.

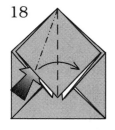

14

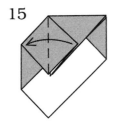

15

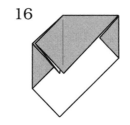

16

Repeat steps 12–15 on the right.

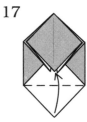

17

Fold up and tuck underneath the upper layers.

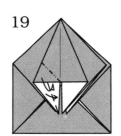

18 Squash-fold.

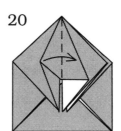

19

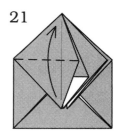

20

21

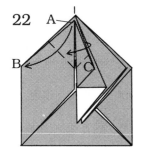

22 Fold A to B while folding C to the left.

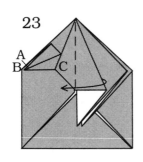

23

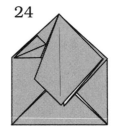

24 Repeat steps 18–23 on the right.

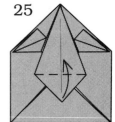

25

26

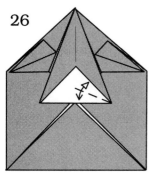

Fold and unfold.

27

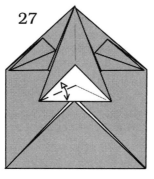

Fold and unfold.

28

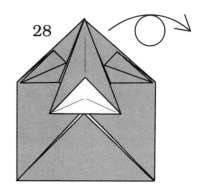

29

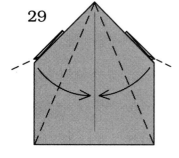

Fold the fins in half while making the kite fold.

30

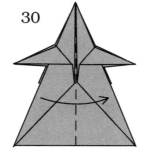

Fold in half and rotate.

31

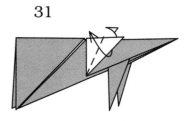

Outside-reverse-fold along the existing creases.

32

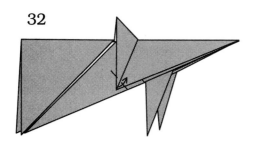

Make a small fold, repeat behind.

33

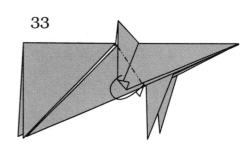

Tuck underneath, repeat behind.

34

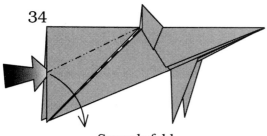

Squash-fold.

35

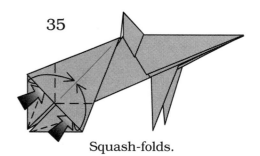

Squash-folds.

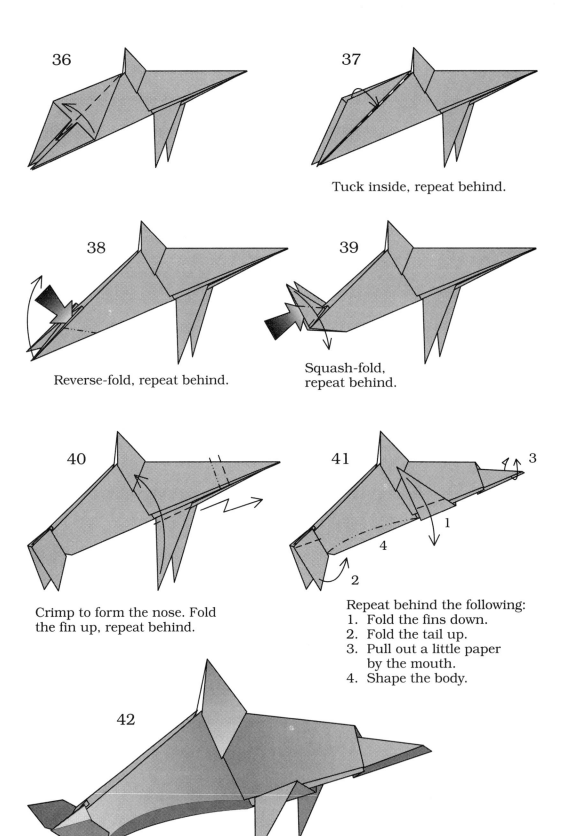

36

37

Tuck inside, repeat behind.

38

Reverse-fold, repeat behind.

39

Squash-fold,
repeat behind.

40

Crimp to form the nose. Fold
the fin up, repeat behind.

41

3

1

4

2

Repeat behind the following:
1. Fold the fins down.
2. Fold the tail up.
3. Pull out a little paper
   by the mouth.
4. Shape the body.

42

Dolphin

Mollusks

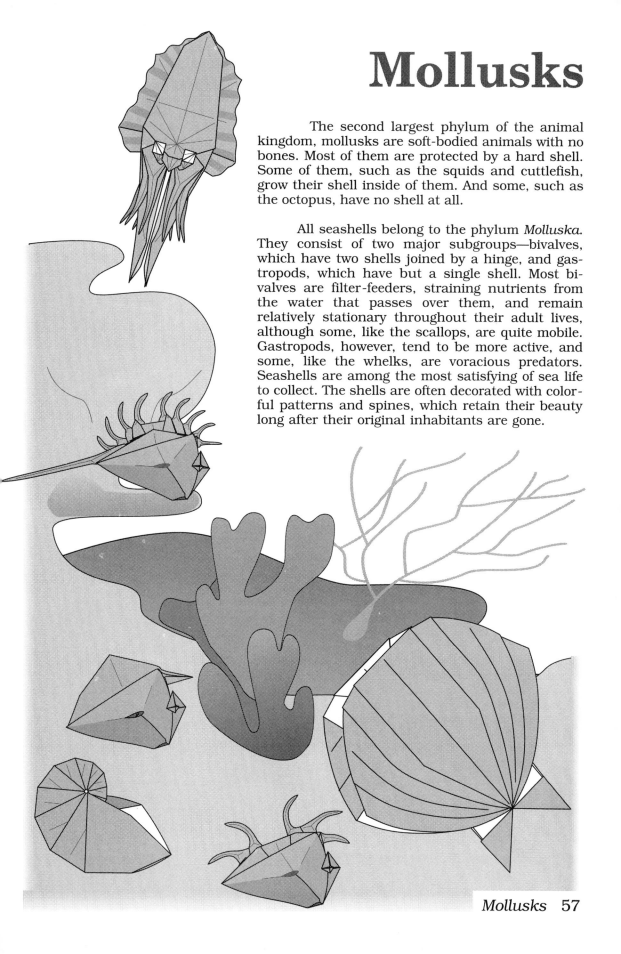

The second largest phylum of the animal kingdom, mollusks are soft-bodied animals with no bones. Most of them are protected by a hard shell. Some of them, such as the squids and cuttlefish, grow their shell inside of them. And some, such as the octopus, have no shell at all.

All seashells belong to the phylum *Molluska*. They consist of two major subgroups—bivalves, which have two shells joined by a hinge, and gastropods, which have but a single shell. Most bivalves are filter-feeders, straining nutrients from the water that passes over them, and remain relatively stationary throughout their adult lives, although some, like the scallops, are quite mobile. Gastropods, however, tend to be more active, and some, like the whelks, are voracious predators. Seashells are among the most satisfying of sea life to collect. The shells are often decorated with colorful patterns and spines, which retain their beauty long after their original inhabitants are gone.

Giant Clam

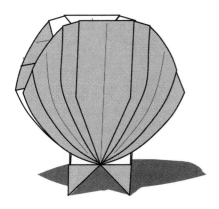

The Giant Clam (*Tridacna derasa*) produces the largest shell of any mollusk, ranging up to six feet across and weighing five hundred pounds. It anchors itself to the sea floor with its gape directed upward and its mantle protruding for maximum exposure to light. It derives its nutrition from symbiotic algae in the mantle tissue, and while it is famous from underwater B-movies in which an unwary diver, stepping into the open maw, becomes trapped and expires, the clam closes at the slightest disturbance in its vicinity, making such a scenario unlikely.

1

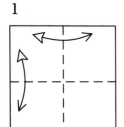

Crease the paper in half vertically and horizontally.

2

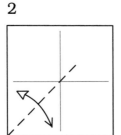

Crease the bottom left corner in half.

3

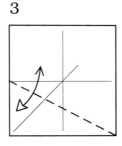

Make a crease that connects the two points shown.

4

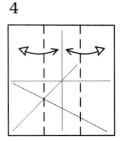

The crease from step 3 crosses the diagonal 1/3 of the way from left to right. Use this mark to divide the paper into thirds.

5

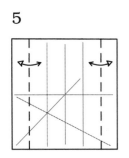

Fold the edges to the creases just made and unfold. Turn the paper over.

6

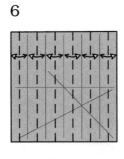

Divide the paper into 12ths with valley folds and turn the paper over.

7

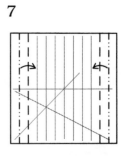

Pleat the sides.

8

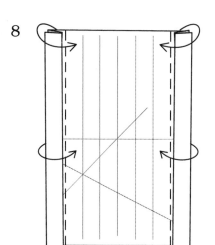

Fold all three layers together as one, on each side.

9

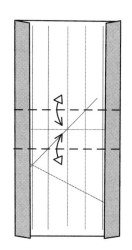

Crease through the inter-sections of the diagonal and vertical creases.

10

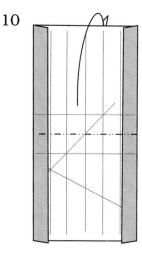

Mountain-fold the paper in half.

11

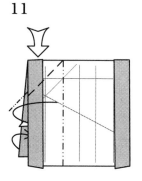

Crimp downward.

12

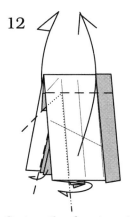

Swing the front and rear flaps upward.

13

Pull out all of the hidden layers of paper.

14

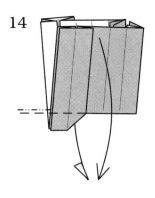

Fold the front and rear flaps back downward.

15

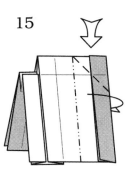

Repeat steps 11-14 on the right.

16

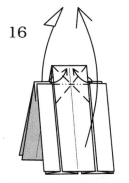

Fold the front and rear flaps back upward, incorporating the creases shown at the top.

17

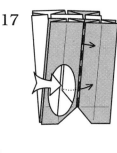

Closed-sink the hidden edge to the right.

Giant Clam 59

18

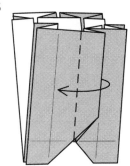

Fold the edge back to the left.

19

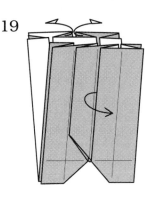

Repeat steps 17–18 on the right and on the back.

20

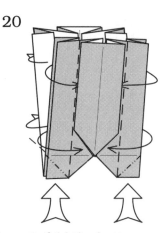

Squash-fold the bottom corners and tuck the layers symmetrically behind the middle edges.

21

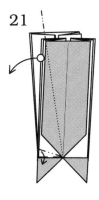

Crimp the bottom and swivel the layers of the top flap to the left as far as possible.

22

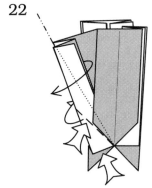

Valley-fold the remaining layers to the left and tuck the crimp underneath.

23

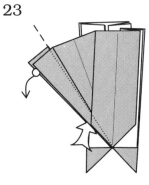

Stretch two more layers to the left.

24

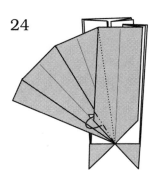

Mountain-fold the corner behind.

25

And again.

26

This is the direction all the pockets should be facing. Repeat steps 21–25 on the right side and behind.

27

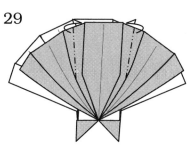

Pleat the sides in as shown; the middle of the paper will hump upward and the model will no longer lie flat.

28

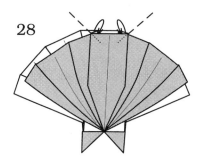

Valley-fold the pleats to lock them together.

29

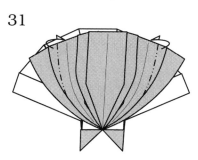

Pleat again. The middle will curve upward more and more with each set of pleats.

30

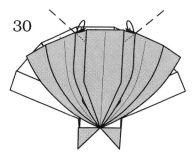

Valley-fold these pleats to lock them.

31

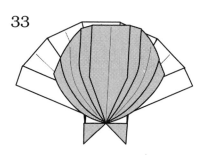

Pleat again.

32

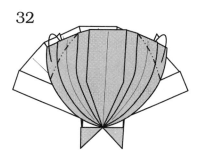

Valley-fold the corners underneath.

33

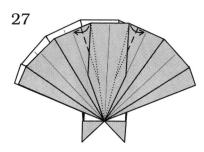

Repeat steps 27–32 on the other side of the model.

34

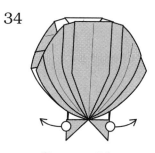

Giant Clam

Pull the two tabs away from each other and the shell will open and close.

Hawk-Wing Conch

 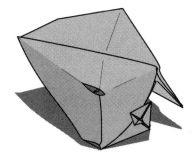

True conchs, family *Strombidae*, have large, heavy shells and inhabit tropical waters worldwide. Conchs are very mobile carnivores that move by pushing themselves along on a large, muscular foot. Their shells are large and robust, with a highly sculptured lip. This shell, the Hawk-Wing Conch (*Strombus raninus*), is further distinguished by a prominent tubular projection at the top of the mantle. It is found from Florida to the West Indies and Brazil.

1

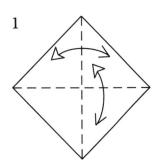

Crease the diagonals.

2

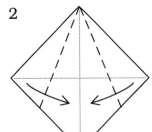

Fold the edges in to the center.

3

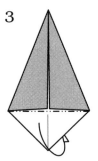

Fold the bottom corner up behind.

4

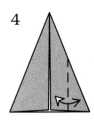

Fold the right corner in to the middle and back out again.

5

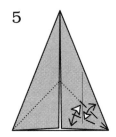

Crease the right corner into thirds. The upper crease lies on top of the hidden edge.

6

Fold a rabbit ear.

7

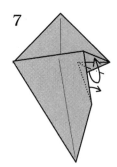

Swivel-fold.

8

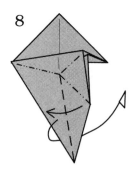

Pinch the flap in half and swing it over to the right. The model becomes three-dimensional.

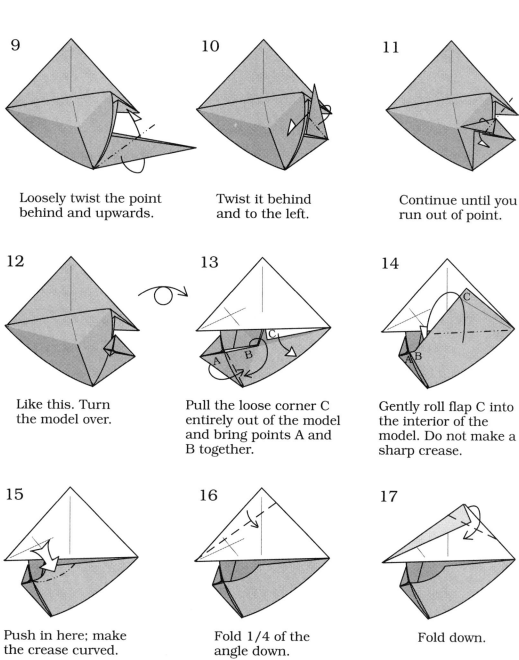

9

Loosely twist the point
behind and upwards.

10

Twist it behind
and to the left.

11

Continue until you
run out of point.

12

Like this. Turn
the model over.

13

Pull the loose corner C
entirely out of the model
and bring points A and
B together.

14

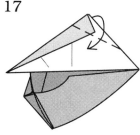

Gently roll flap C into
the interior of the
model. Do not make a
sharp crease.

15

Push in here; make
the crease curved.

16

Fold 1/4 of the
angle down.

17

Fold down.

18

Pinch the point and shape
the underside of the shell.
Turn the model over.

19

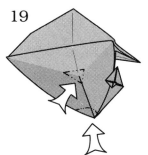

Push in these corners.

20

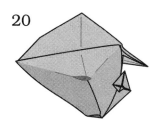

Hawk-Wing Conch

Spider Conch

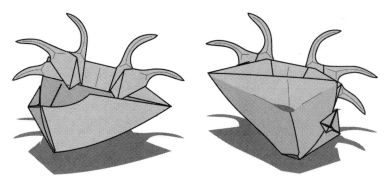

The spider conchs (genus *Lambis*) are large, conical shells distinguished by several long projections along the edge of their aperture lips, which may be long, short, knobby, or smooth, depending on the species. For this reason, spider conchs are popular among shell collectors. They range in size from four inches to about one foot in length and are predominantly tan on the outside with a pink inner surface. All members of the genus are found in the Indo-Pacific region, from southern Africa through Malaysia, Australia, and nearly to the coast of South America.

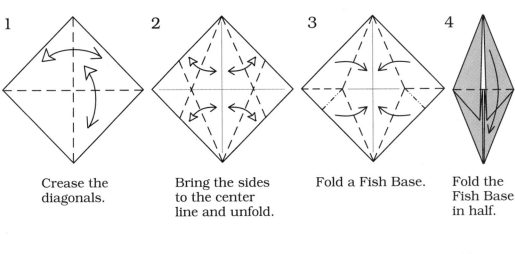

1

Crease the diagonals.

2

Bring the sides to the center line and unfold.

3

Fold a Fish Base.

4

Fold the Fish Base in half.

5

Fold one flap up so that the right edges are parallel.

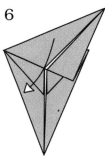

6

Unfold.

7

Fold the flap up so that the left edges are parallel.

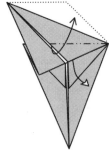

8

Pull out the trapped layers of paper.

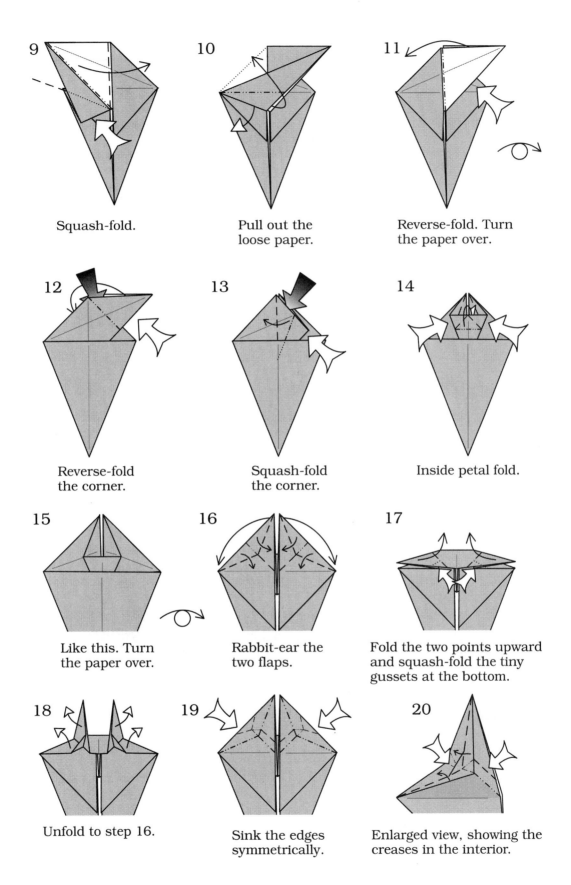

9 Squash-fold.

10 Pull out the loose paper.

11 Reverse-fold. Turn the paper over.

12 Reverse-fold the corner.

13 Squash-fold the corner.

14 Inside petal fold.

15 Like this. Turn the paper over.

16 Rabbit-ear the two flaps.

17 Fold the two points upward and squash-fold the tiny gussets at the bottom.

18 Unfold to step 16.

19 Sink the edges symmetrically.

20 Enlarged view, showing the creases in the interior.

Spider Conch 65

21

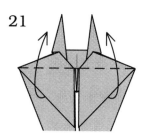

Fold two points up.

22

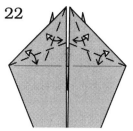

Crease.

23

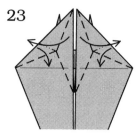

Rabbit-ear
both points.

24

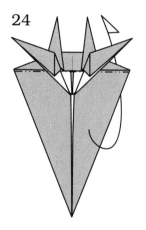

Fold the long point
up to the rear.

25

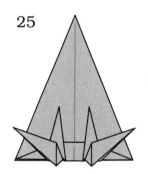

Like this.
Turn the
paper over.

26

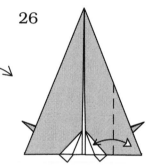

Fold the right
corner in to the
middle and
unfold.

27

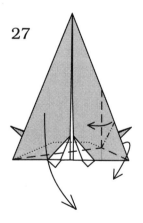

Rabbit-ear the flap
on existing creases.

28

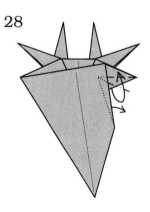

Swivel fold.

29

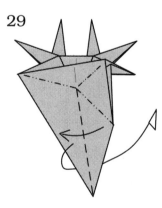

Pinch the bottom of
the point in half and
swing it up to the
right. The model
becomes three-
dimensional.

30

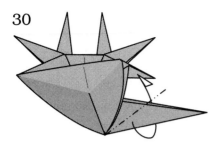

Mountain-fold the flap behind. This locks the folds from step 29 into place.

31

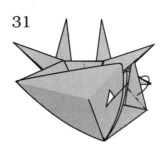

Mountain-fold the point behind again.

32

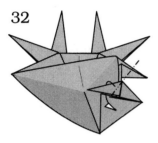

Continue until you run out of point.

33

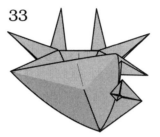

Like this. Turn the paper over.

34

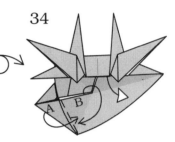

Pull the loose paper out from the interior as far as possible. Simultaneously bring points A and B together.

35

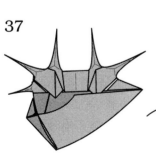

Push in the shell here to make the underside rounded.

36

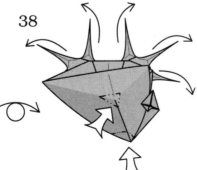

Pinch all the points.

37

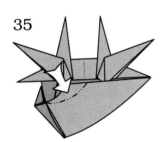

Like this. Turn the paper over.

38

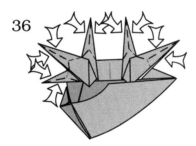

Sink the corners of the shell and curve the points.

39

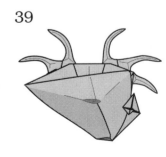

Spider Conch

Murex

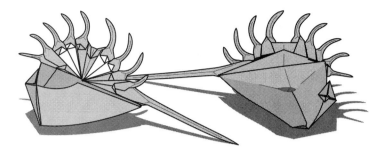

The murexes (family *Muricidae*) are one of the most beautiful and sought-after families by shell collectors. Many of them are covered in frills and needle-sharp projections. This shell, the Venus's comb, has a row of needles along the lip of the shell. Venus's combs are pure white outside and delicately pink inside, and are roughly five inches long. Murexes are found in tropical and temperate waters worldwide.

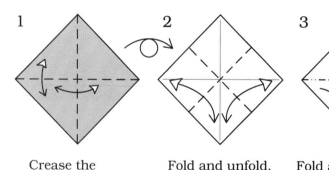

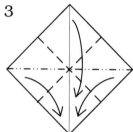

1 Crease the diagonals. Turn the model over.

2 Fold and unfold.

3 Fold a Preliminary Fold.

4 Reverse-fold four corners to make a Bird Base.

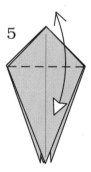

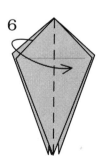

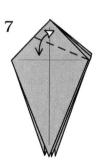

5 Enlarged view. Fold and unfold.

6 Fold one layer over from left to right.

7 Fold and unfold.

8 Open the top point out and sink it on the existing creases.

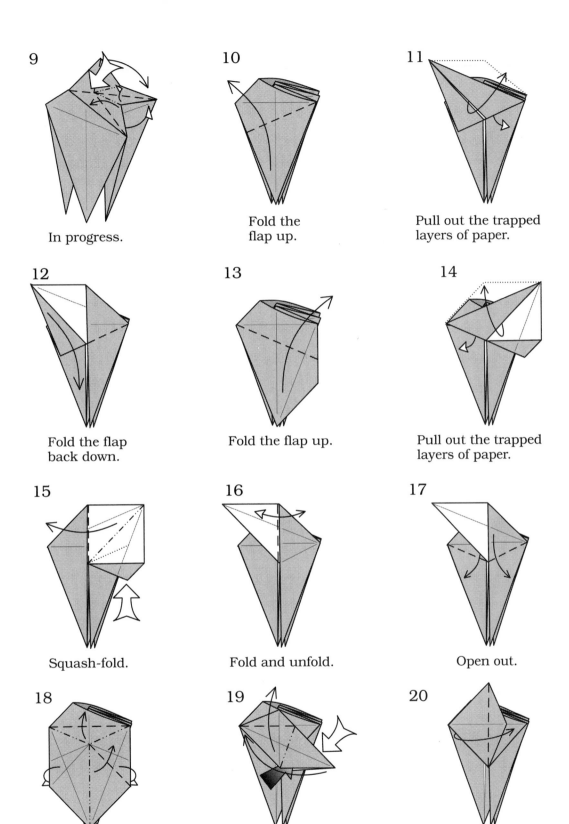

9

In progress.

10

Fold the
flap up.

11

Pull out the trapped
layers of paper.

12

Fold the flap
back down.

13

Fold the flap up.

14

Pull out the trapped
layers of paper.

15

Squash-fold.

16

Fold and unfold.

17

Open out.

18

Refold on existing
creases.

19

Squash-fold.

20

Fold a single layer
from left to right.

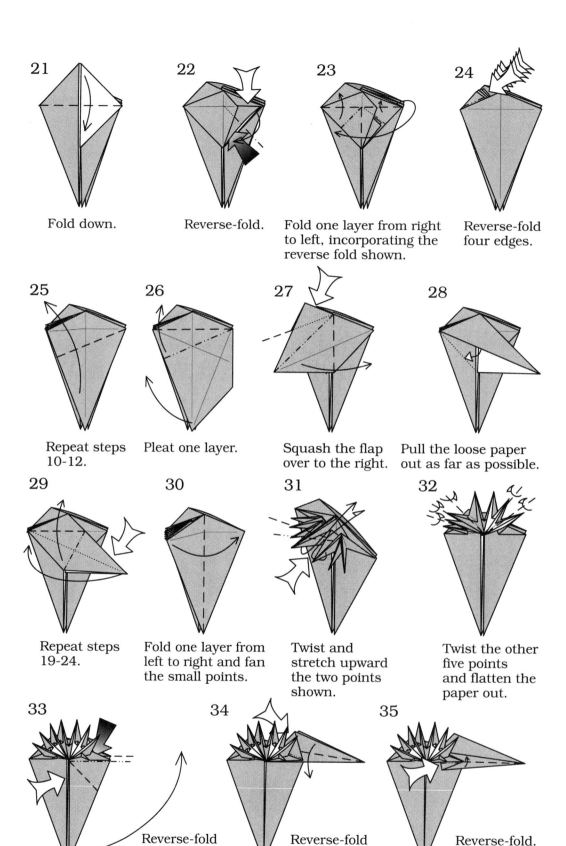

21 Fold down.

22 Reverse-fold.

23 Fold one layer from right to left, incorporating the reverse fold shown.

24 Reverse-fold four edges.

25 Repeat steps 10-12.

26 Pleat one layer.

27 Squash the flap over to the right.

28 Pull the loose paper out as far as possible.

29 Repeat steps 19-24.

30 Fold one layer from left to right and fan the small points.

31 Twist and stretch upward the two points shown.

32 Twist the other five points and flatten the paper out.

33 Reverse-fold the long point.

34 Reverse-fold one layer only.

35 Reverse-fold.

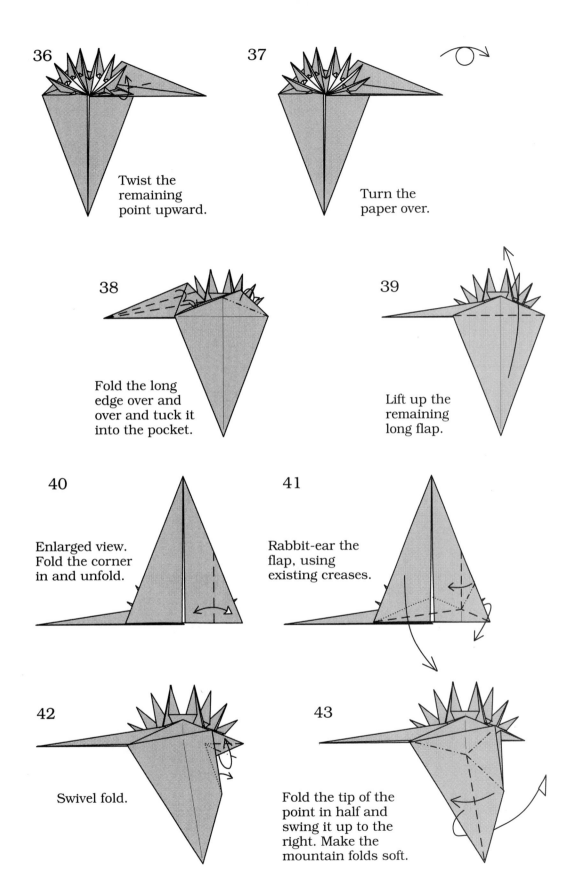

36 Twist the remaining point upward.

37 Turn the paper over.

38 Fold the long edge over and over and tuck it into the pocket.

39 Lift up the remaining long flap.

40 Enlarged view. Fold the corner in and unfold.

41 Rabbit-ear the flap, using existing creases.

42 Swivel fold.

43 Fold the tip of the point in half and swing it up to the right. Make the mountain folds soft.

44

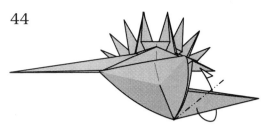

Mountain-fold the point behind.

45

Again.

46

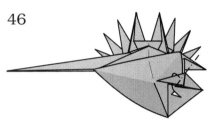

Continue until you run out of point.

47

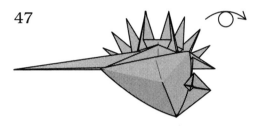

Like this. Turn the model over.

48

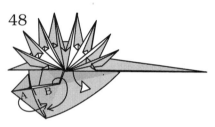

Pull the loose paper out as far as possible and bring points A and B together.

49

Push the shell in here.

50

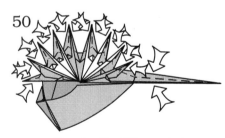

Pinch all of the points.

51

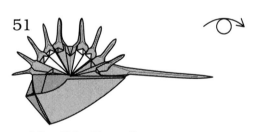

Like this. Turn the paper over.

52

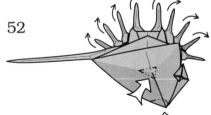

Curve the points. Sink the corners of the shell.

53

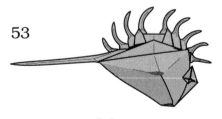

Murex

Chambered Nautilus Shell

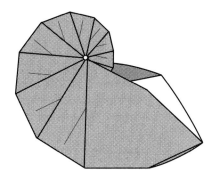

The Chambered Nautilus (*Nautilus pompilius*) is one of the oldest of the cephalopods, a group that includes the octopus and squid. It is highly valued for its symmetric shell, which forms a logarithmic spiral in cross section. The Nautilus is native to the Indian and Pacific Oceans.

1

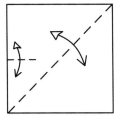

Crease the diagonal of the square and make a pinch mark along the left side halfway up.

2

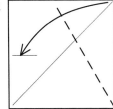

Fold the top right corner down to the pinch mark you just made.

3

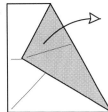

Unfold.

4

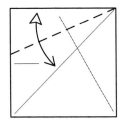

Fold the top edge down to lie along the diagonal.

5

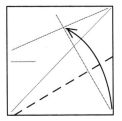

Fold the bottom right corner up to touch the intersection of the last two creases.

6

Fold the corner behind along the diagonal of the square.

7

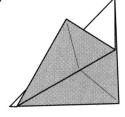

Like this. Turn the paper over.

8

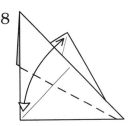

Fold the bottom left corner up to match the one behind and unfold.

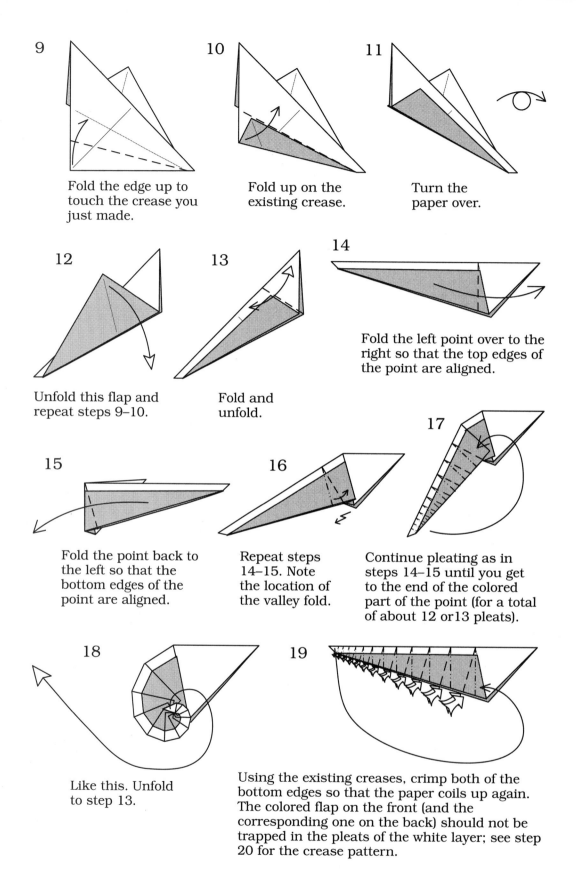

9

Fold the edge up to touch the crease you just made.

10

Fold up on the existing crease.

11

Turn the paper over.

12

Unfold this flap and repeat steps 9–10.

13

Fold and unfold.

14

Fold the left point over to the right so that the top edges of the point are aligned.

15

Fold the point back to the left so that the bottom edges of the point are aligned.

16

Repeat steps 14–15. Note the location of the valley fold.

17

Continue pleating as in steps 14–15 until you get to the end of the colored part of the point (for a total of about 12 or 13 pleats).

18

Like this. Unfold to step 13.

19

Using the existing creases, crimp both of the bottom edges so that the paper coils up again. The colored flap on the front (and the corresponding one on the back) should not be trapped in the pleats of the white layer; see step 20 for the crease pattern.

20

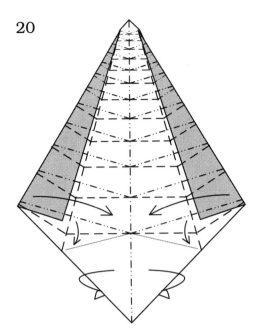

This shows the crease pattern for step 19.

21

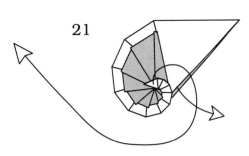

Unfold again to step 13 and open the model out flat.

22

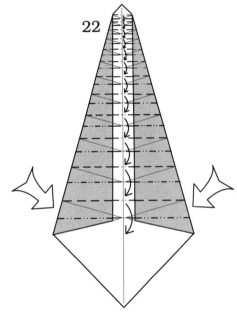

Using the existing creases as guides, crimp the point downward, folding it back and forth (push arrows are shown only for the first crimp).

23

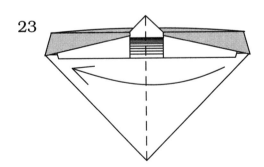

Like this. Fold the paper in half carefully (because of the many layers the model is quite thick). Rotate the model 90 degrees counterclockwise.

24

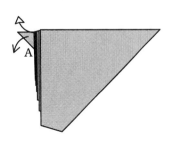

Carefully pull out the top of the protruding point and pivot it downward, taking point A as the axis of rotation. This has the effect of restoring a crimp we made in step 20.

25

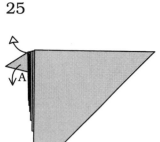

Like this. Now, carefully grasp that crimp and pull it out, again pivoting around point A; the result is to restore the next crimp.

26

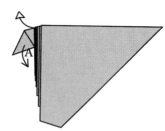

Continue pulling each crimp out and pivoting around point A. The paper remains locked together at point A at all crimps (except for an inevitable small amount of slippage). Continue until you've done them all (look ahead to step 27 to see what you're trying to accomplish).

27

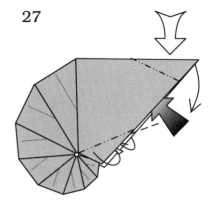

The paper should be securely locked together at the center of the rotation. Reverse-fold the top corner. Mountain-fold the corners shown. Repeat behind.

28

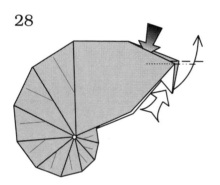

Reverse-fold the corner back up.

29

Sink the hidden corner.

30

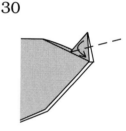

Fold the tip down.

31

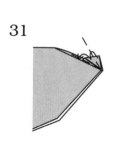

Fold the point over and over and tuck it into the pocket.

32

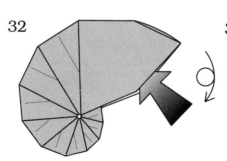

Open out the shell and turn it over.

33

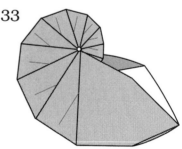

Chambered Nautilus Shell

Cuttlefish

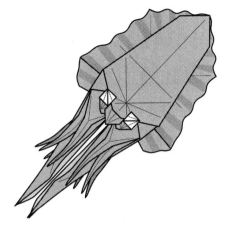

The Cuttlefish (*Sepia officinalis*), like other octopi and squid, possesses a reservoir of ink. When threatened by a predator, it ejects a blob of the ink and speeds away, leaving the predator to attack the squid-shaped globule. The ink of the cuttlefish is the original source of the dye sepia. The shell of the cuttlefish is an internal plate, which is harvested and sold as the "cuttlebone" often found in bird cages. It is found widely throughout the Atlantic Ocean and Mediterranean Sea.

1
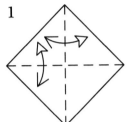

Fold and unfold.

2
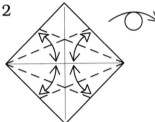

Fold and unfold.
Turn the paper over.

3
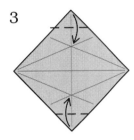

Fold the top and bottom corners to the intersections of the creases.

4
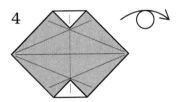

Like this. Turn the paper over.

5
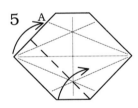

Fold the lower left edge up to point A.

6
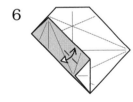

Fold and unfold, making a crease only where shown.

7
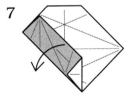

Unfold.

8
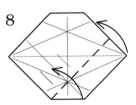

Repeat steps 5–7 on the right.

9

Repeat steps 5–7 on both sides of the top. Turn the paper over.

10

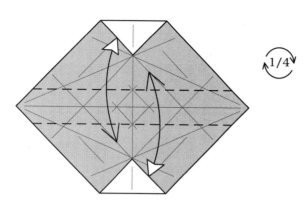

Fold and unfold
through the creases,
then rotate 1/4 turn.

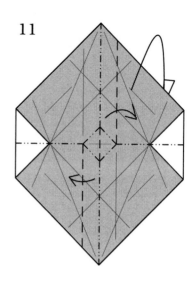

11

Fold, using the existing creases.

12

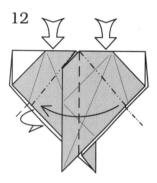

Squash-fold in
front and back.

13

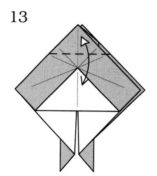

Fold and
unfold.

14

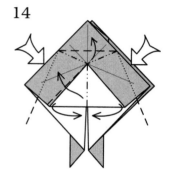

Swivel the sides in,
bring the bottom corners
of the white triangle
together, and swing it
over to one side.

15

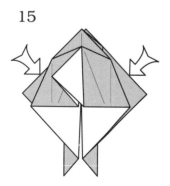

Repeat behind.

16

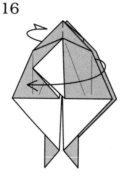

Fold one layer to the
left in front and one
to the right in back.

17

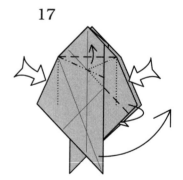

Swivel similarly
to step 14.

18

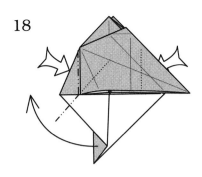

Repeat behind.

19

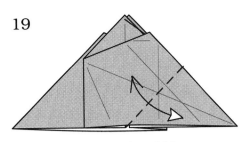

Fold and unfold.

20

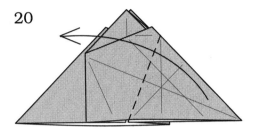

Fold the corner up to the left.

21

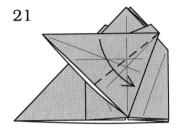

Fold the corner down to lie
along the crease you just made.

22

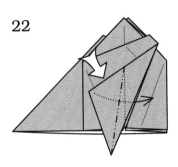

Reverse-fold both layers together.

23

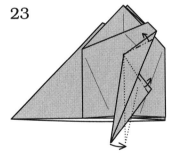

Shift the point so that its
left edge becomes vertical.

24

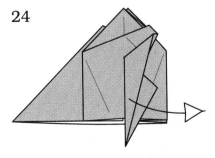

Unfold the flap.

25

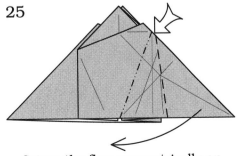

Crimp the flap symmetrically on
the creases made in step 23.

Cuttlefish 79

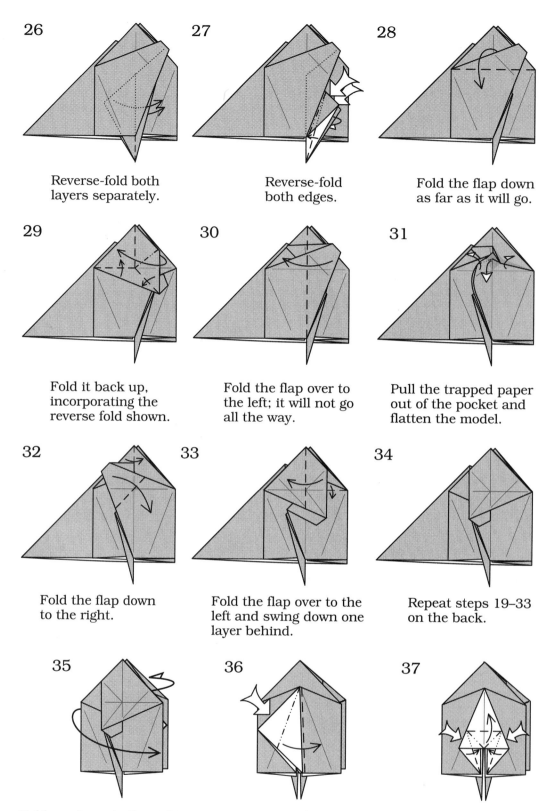

26

Reverse-fold both layers separately.

27

Reverse-fold both edges.

28

Fold the flap down as far as it will go.

29

Fold it back up, incorporating the reverse fold shown.

30

Fold the flap over to the left; it will not go all the way.

31

Pull the trapped paper out of the pocket and flatten the model.

32

Fold the flap down to the right.

33

Fold the flap over to the left and swing down one layer behind.

34

Repeat steps 19–33 on the back.

35

Fold one layer to the right in front and one to the left in back.

36

Squash-fold the white triangle.

37

Petal-fold.

38

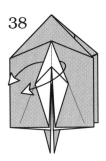

Unwrap the
loose paper.

39

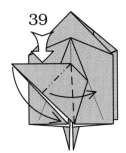

Squash-fold.

40

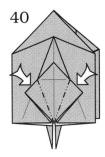

Reverse-fold
the edges.

41

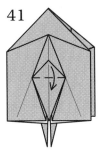

Fold the small
point down.

42

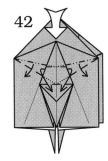

Pull the front layers down and
spread-squash the point.

43

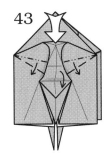

In progress.

44

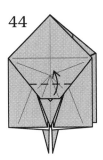

Fold a single flap up-
ward as far as possible.

45

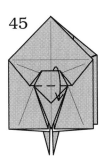

Fold the flap
down again.

46

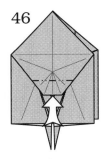

Sink the flap
inside the model.

47

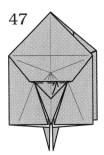

Tuck the flap up
inside the pocket.

48

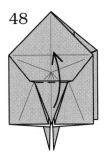

Fold the flap up.

49

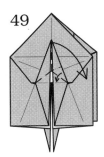

Fold a rabbit ear.

50

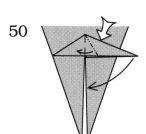

Enlarged view.
Squash-fold
the point.

51

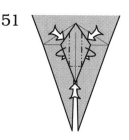

Reverse-fold the sides
so they are parallel, and
sink the tip of the point.

52

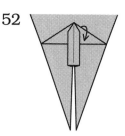

Tuck the top of the
point into the
pocket behind it.

53

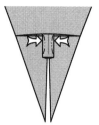

Squeeze the sides of
the funnel to round it.

54

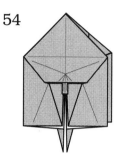

Like this. Turn
the paper over.

55

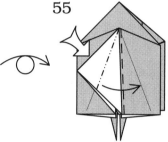

Repeat steps 36–40
on this side.

56

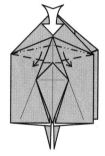

Spread-squash the point
similarly to step 42 (note that
the valley fold is higher here).

57

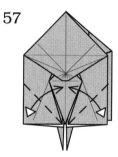

Fold and unfold.

58

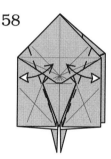

Fold and unfold.

59

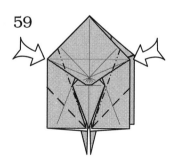

Reverse-fold each side in and
out, using the existing creases.

60

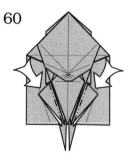

Reverse-fold
the edges.

61

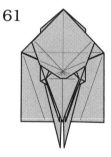

Repeat steps
57–60 behind.

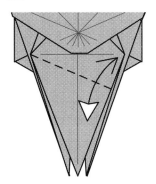

Fold and
unfold.

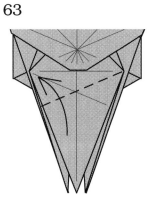

Enlarged view.
Fold the point up.

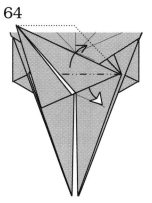

Pull out the
loose paper.

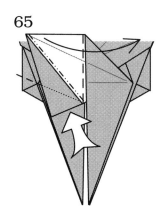

Squash-fold.

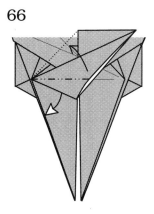

Pull out the
loose paper.

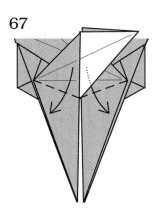

Spread the point
out and flatten it.

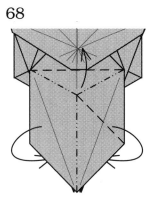

Squeeze the sides in
and swing the point
over to the right.

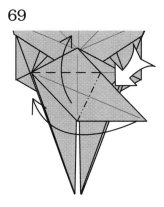

Squash-fold.

70

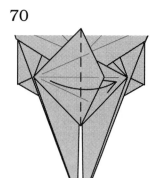

Fold one layer
over to the right.

71

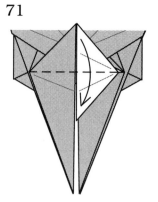

Fold the
point down.

72

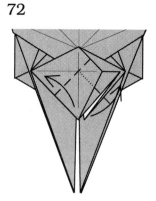

Spread the points
out to either side.

73

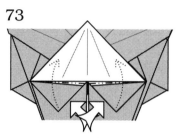

Reverse-fold the
edges upward.

74

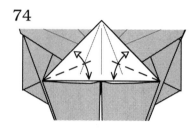

Fold and unfold.

75

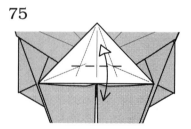

Fold and unfold.

76

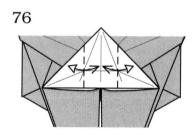

Fold and unfold.

77

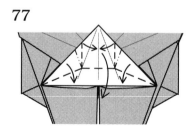

Fold two interlocking rabbit ear
folds using the existing creases.

78

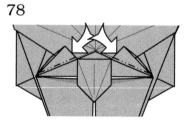

Reverse-fold
the two edges.

79

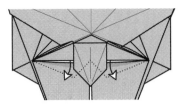

Pull out a single layer of paper on each side.

80

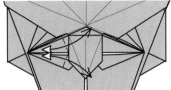

Fold and unfold.

81

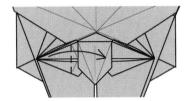

Fold over to the right.

82

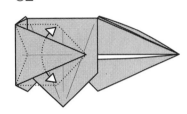

Enlarged view. Pull out the loose paper.

83

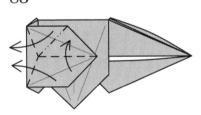

Fold a rabbit ear.

84

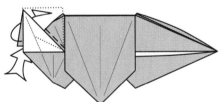

Reverse-fold.

85

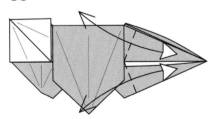

Repeat steps 80–84 on the right.

86

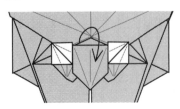

Bring the blunt point forward, but keep it behind the white eyes.

87

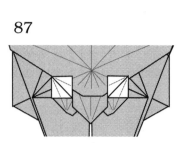

Like this.

88

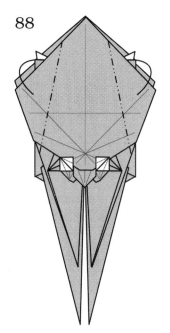

Mountain-fold the edges into the model; repeat behind.

89

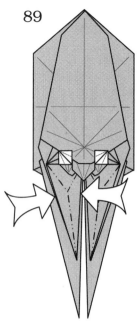

Pinch each of the eight short legs using rabbit ears.

90

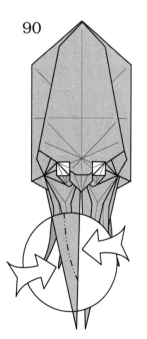

Flatten slightly the two longer legs.

91

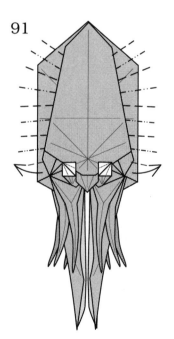

Pull the paper at the sides outward and upward a bit and curve it back and forth to make the edge ripple.

92

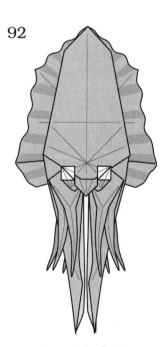

Cuttlefish

Fishes

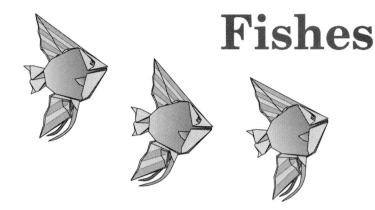

Probably the most diverse aquatic organisms in the water are the fishes. Superbly adaptable, they have found their way into every fresh and saltwater environment in the world. Fishes near the poles produce an antifreeze protein, while those living in oxygen-poor waters have developed primitive lungs and gulp air from the surface. Some species can even survive for long periods out of water altogether.

There are two major groups of fishes alive today—the cartilaginous and bony fishes. The cartilaginous fishes—sharks, rays, and skates—have no true bones but their skeletons are composed entirely of cartilage. All other fishes have true bone in their skeletons.

Seahorse

These small fish are mostly found in subtropical and tropical seas. They attach themselves to seaweed with their prehensile tails. Slowly and stiffly, they swim in an upright position. Their small scales form rings of hard protective covering around their bodies. Ranging in size from one and a half to twelve inches, seahorses (family *Hippocampus*) feed on small crustaceans and larvae.

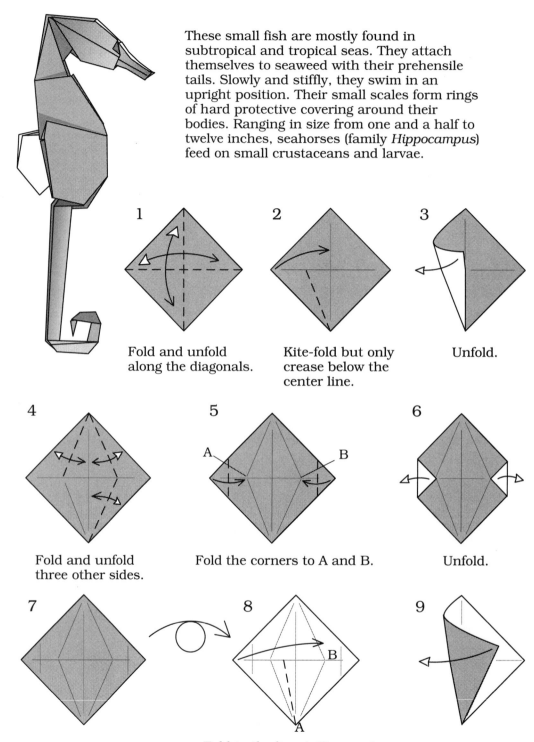

1

Fold and unfold along the diagonals.

2

Kite-fold but only crease below the center line.

3

Unfold.

4

Fold and unfold three other sides.

5

A   B

Fold the corners to A and B.

6

Unfold.

7

8

B

A

Fold to the line A–B, creasing only below the center line.

9

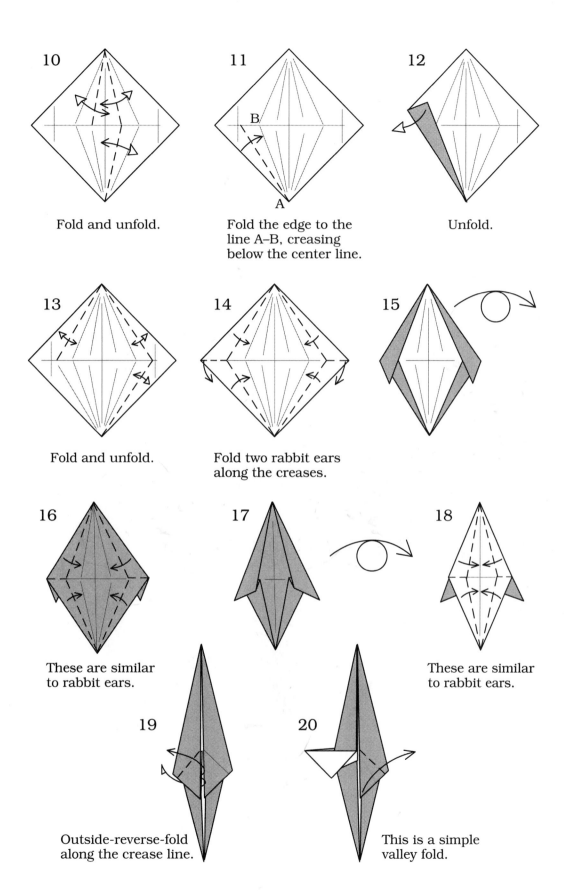

10

Fold and unfold.

11

B

A

Fold the edge to the
line A–B, creasing
below the center line.

12

Unfold.

13

Fold and unfold.

14

Fold two rabbit ears
along the creases.

15

16

These are similar
to rabbit ears.

17

18

These are similar
to rabbit ears.

19

Outside-reverse-fold
along the crease line.

20

This is a simple
valley fold.

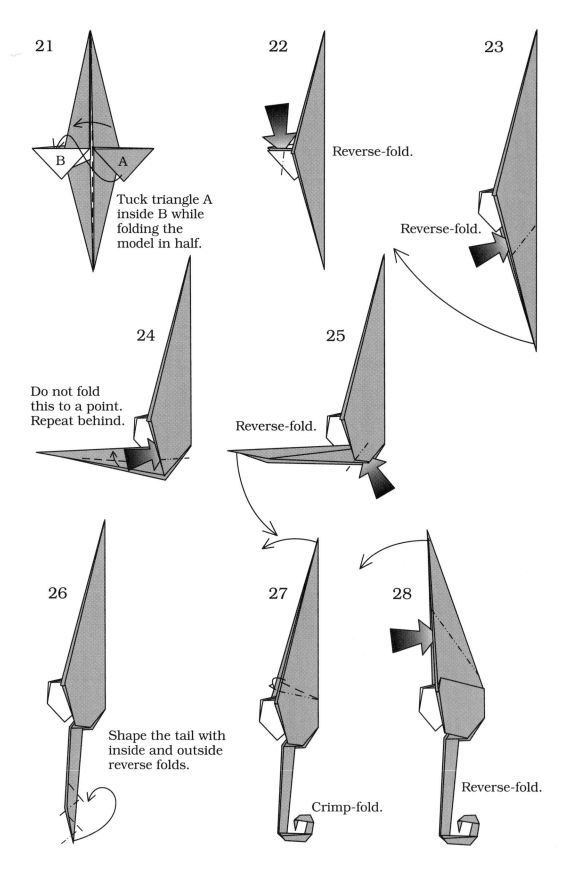

21

B   A

Tuck triangle A
inside B while
folding the
model in half.

22

Reverse-fold.

23

Reverse-fold.

24

Do not fold
this to a point.
Repeat behind.

25

Reverse-fold.

26

Shape the tail with
inside and outside
reverse folds.

27

Crimp-fold.

28

Reverse-fold.

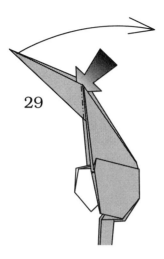

29

Reverse-fold.

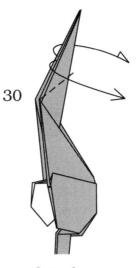

30

Outside-
reverse-fold.

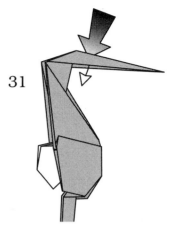

31

Pull out some paper to
form a wider head by
placing your finger into
the top of the head.

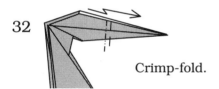

32

Crimp-fold.

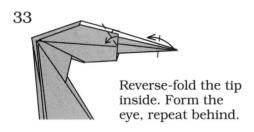

33

Reverse-fold the tip
inside. Form the
eye, repeat behind.

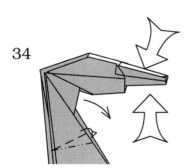

34

Crimp-fold the
neck. Squeeze the
tip of the head.

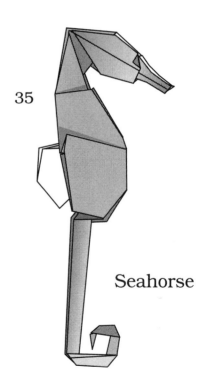

35

Seahorse

Carp

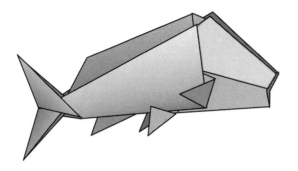

The carp or koi (*Cyprinos carpio*) has been genetically manipulated by the Japanese. These freshwater fish are found in Europe, North America, and Asia. They are most commonly found in ornamental pools and attain a length of two feet or more. These fish feed on tiny plants and animals in the mud.

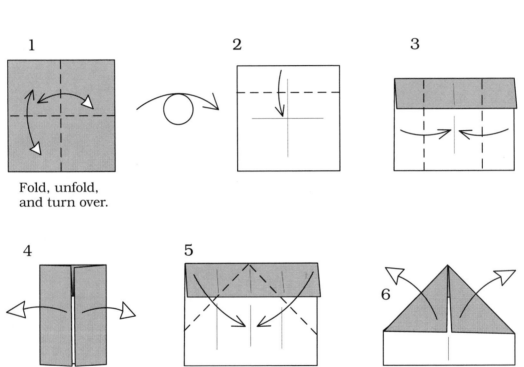

1

Fold, unfold, and turn over.

2

3

4

Unfold.

5

6

Unfold.

7

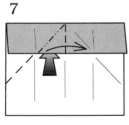

Squash-fold.

8

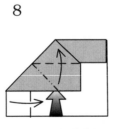

Squash-fold.

9

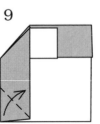

10

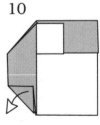

Unfold.

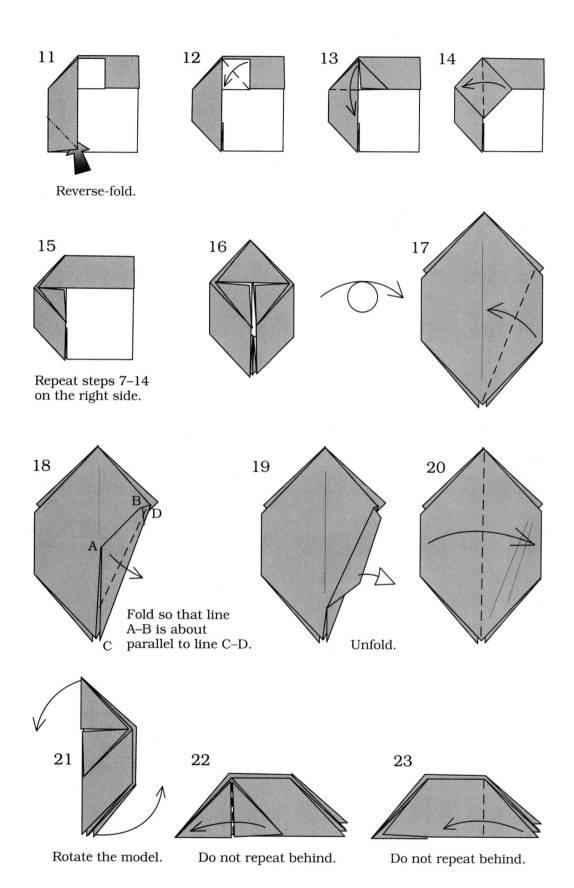

11

Reverse-fold.

12

13

14

15

Repeat steps 7–14
on the right side.

16

17

18

B
D
A
C

Fold so that line
A–B is about
parallel to line C–D.

19

Unfold.

20

21

Rotate the model.

22

Do not repeat behind.

23

Do not repeat behind.

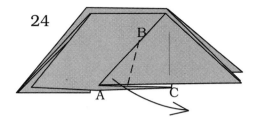

24

Fold so that some point between
line A–B touches point C.

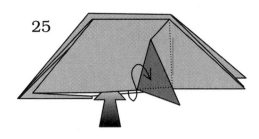

25

Place the paper above
the darker region.

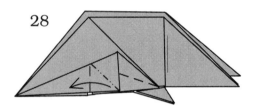

26

27

Repeat behind.

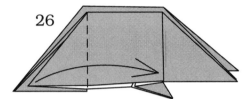

28

Squash-fold. Repeat behind.

29

Repeat behind.

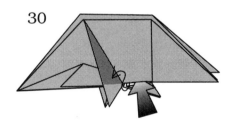

30

Place some paper over the
darker area. Repeat behind.

31

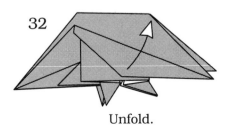

32

Unfold.

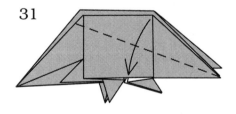

33

Sink. Push in corners A and
B but do not unfold them.

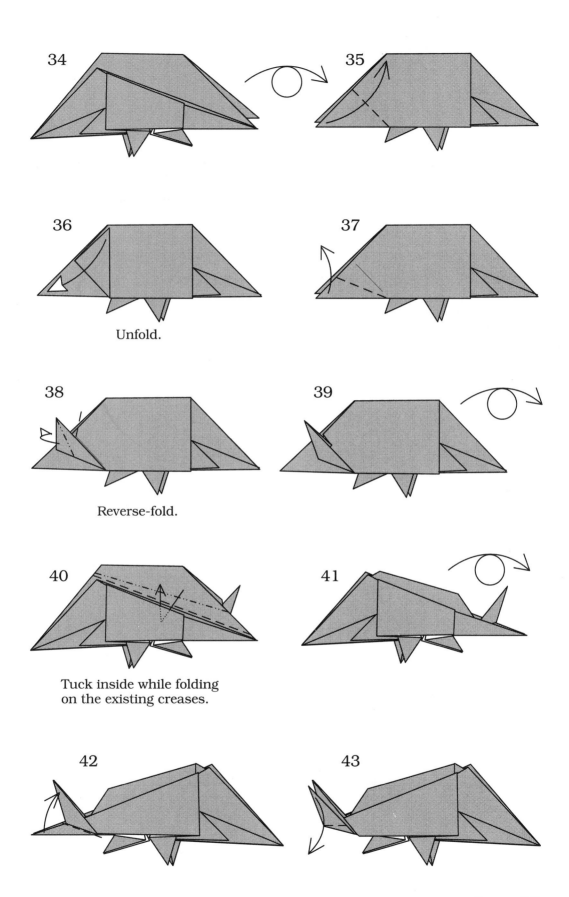

34

35

36

Unfold.

37

38

Reverse-fold.

39

40

Tuck inside while folding
on the existing creases.

41

42

43

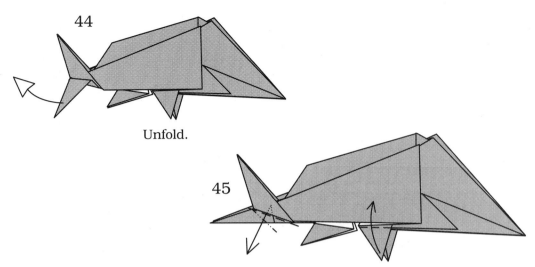

44

Unfold.

45

Tuck the tip of the base of the tail inside. Repeat behind for the fin.

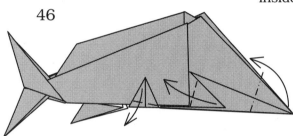

46

Reverse-fold the tip of the head. Repeat behind to form the other fins.

47

Make the mouth and body three-dimensional.

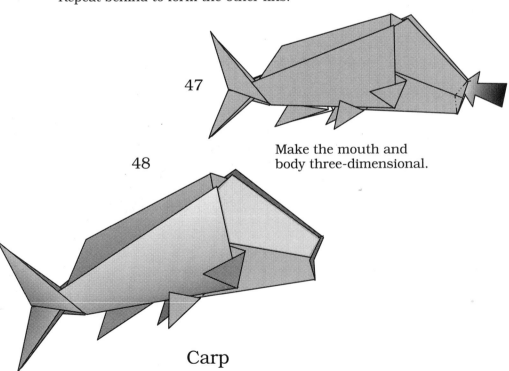

48

Carp

Brill

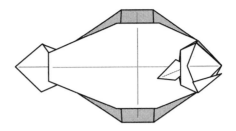

The Brill (*Scophthalamus rhombus*) is a variety of flatfish, a fish who, shortly after hatching, begins to lean to one side—the right side, in this case. As it leans, the right eye migrates to the upper side of the body, which assumes a dark coloration, and the fish eventually lies on the ocean's sandy bottom, its lighter side down. There are two groups of flatfishes—left-eyed and right-eyed—and by folding this model backwards, you can change this model to a fish of the opposite handedness.

1

Crease the diagonals.

2

Make pinch marks halfway down the sides.

3

Bring the bottom right corner to the crease, pinch, and unfold.

4

Fold the top and bottom corners to meet at the point where the crease crosses the diagonal.

5

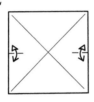

Connect the two pinch marks with a crease. Rotate the paper 1/8 turn counterclockwise.

6

Fold the left corner in front and the right corner behind.

7

Turn the paper over.

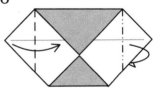

8

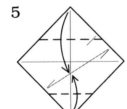

Fold the top edge down to the center line, allowing the point behind to flip up. Fold the bottom up similarly.

9

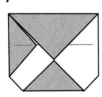

Fold down.

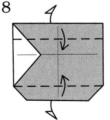
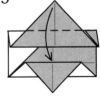

10

Turn the
paper over.

11

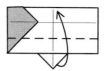

Fold the bottom
edge upward.

12

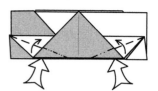

Reverse-fold.

13

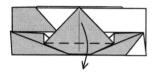

Fold down.

14

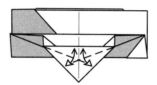

Crease the angle
bisectors.

15

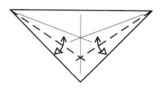

Enlarged view. Crease
the angle bisectors.

16

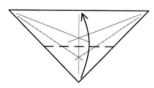

Fold the point up
to the top edge.

17

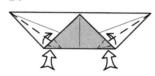

Valley-fold the edges and
squash-fold the corners.

18

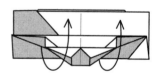

Fold the entire
assembly upward.

19

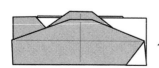

Turn the paper over.

20

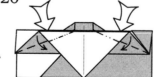

Reverse-fold the corners.

21

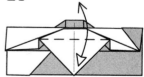

Fold and unfold.

22

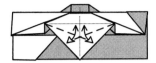

Repeat steps 14-17 on this flap.

23

Fold upward.

24

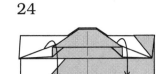

Fold the entire assembly downward.

25

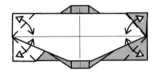

Fold and unfold.

26

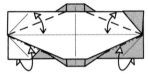

Fold and unfold.

27

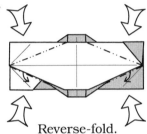

Reverse-fold.

28

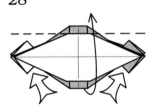

Lift up the top layers.

29

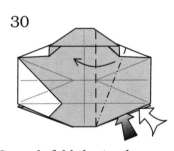

Fold and unfold.

30

Squash-fold the top layers.

31

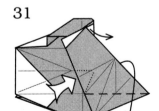

Swing the right side down, incorporating a hidden crimp. The model will not lie flat.

32

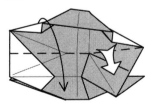

Close the model up and flatten it.

33

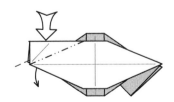

Reverse-fold (again).

34

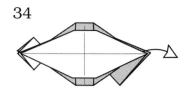

Undo steps 28-33.

35

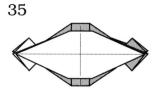

Turn over from top to bottom.

36

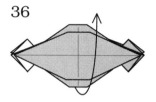

Repeat steps
28–33 on the left.

37

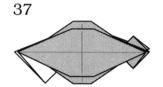

Refold the right
side to step 34.

38

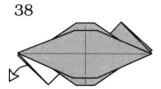

Pull out the
trapped paper.

39

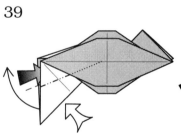

Reverse-fold.

40

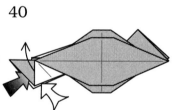

Reverse-fold a single
layer upward.

41

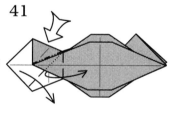

Squash-fold
asymmetrically.

42

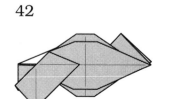

Turn the model over.

43

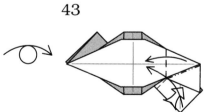

Squash-fold.

44

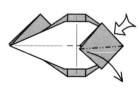

Squash-fold.

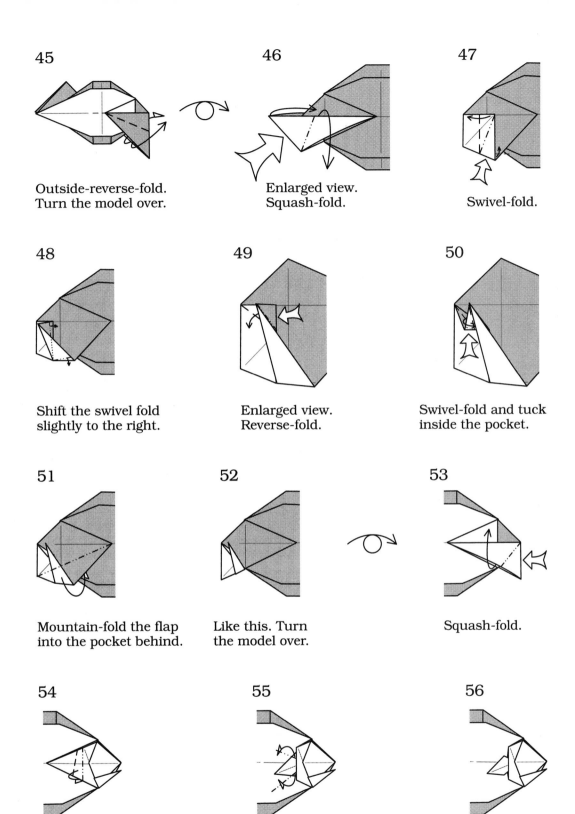

45

Outside-reverse-fold.
Turn the model over.

46

Enlarged view.
Squash-fold.

47

Swivel-fold.

48

Shift the swivel fold
slightly to the right.

49

Enlarged view.
Reverse-fold.

50

Swivel-fold and tuck
inside the pocket.

51

Mountain-fold the flap
into the pocket behind.

52

Like this. Turn
the model over.

53

Squash-fold.

54

Crimp. Repeat
behind.

55

Shape the fin.
Repeat behind.

56

Like this.

57

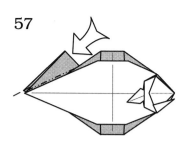

Reverse-fold.

58

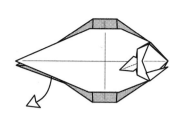

Pull out the trapped corner.

59

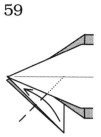

Valley-fold.

60

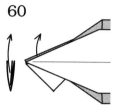

Fold one pair of layers
up from the inside.

61

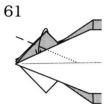

Valley-fold.

62

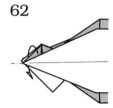

Fold one
layer down.

63

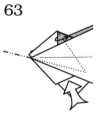

Enlarged view of tail.
Reverse-fold the edge.

64

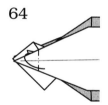

Mountain-fold the
point into the pocket.

65

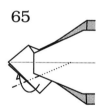

Repeat steps 61–64
on the bottom of the
other side.

66

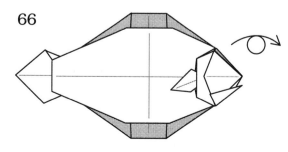

Turn the model over.

67

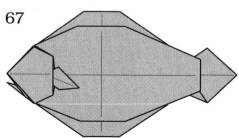

Brill

Ocean Sunfish

Ocean sunfishes (*Mola molas*) live in the open seas in temperate and tropical areas. They can grow to 13 feet and weigh 600 pounds. The young swim in a vertical position while adults often swim on their side. They feed on plankton, fish, and crustaceans.

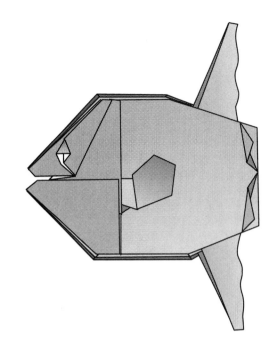

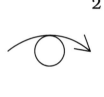

1

Fold and unfold.

2

Fold and unfold.

3

Collapse along the creases.

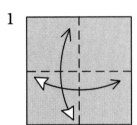

4

A three-dimensional intermediate step.

5

Squash-fold, repeat behind.

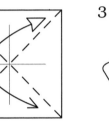

6

Unfold, repeat behind.

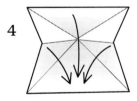

7

Fold up and unfold.

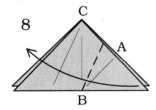

8

Fold so that A lies along line B–C.

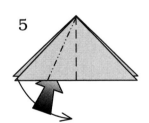

9

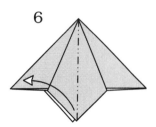

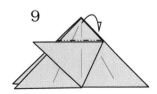

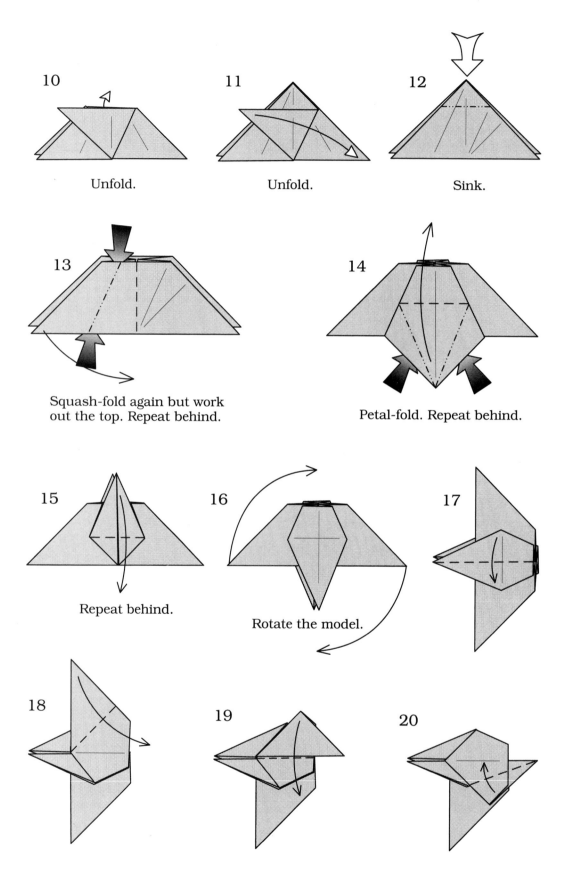

10

Unfold.

11

Unfold.

12

Sink.

13

Squash-fold again but work
out the top. Repeat behind.

14

Petal-fold. Repeat behind.

15

Repeat behind.

16

Rotate the model.

17

18

19

20

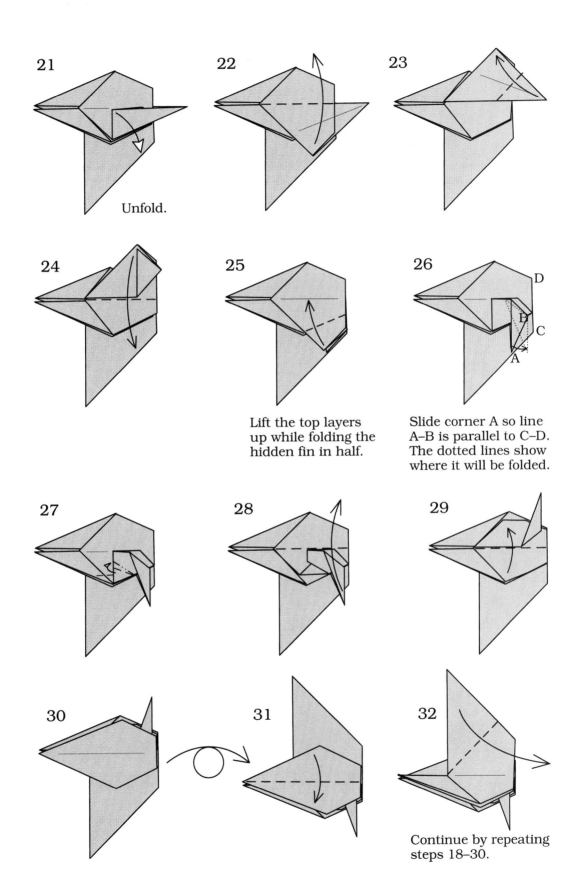

21

Unfold.

22

23

24

25

Lift the top layers up while folding the hidden fin in half.

26

D

B

C

A

Slide corner A so line A–B is parallel to C–D. The dotted lines show where it will be folded.

27

28

29

30

31

32

Continue by repeating steps 18–30.

33

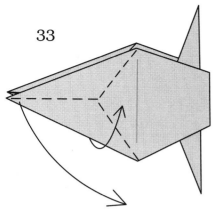

Rabbit-ear, repeat behind.

34

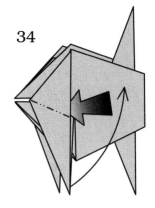

Reverse-fold, repeat behind.

35

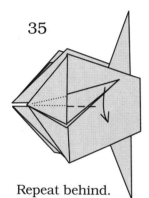

Repeat behind.

36

Squash-fold,
repeat behind.

37

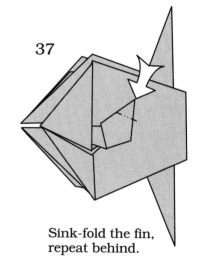

Sink-fold the fin,
repeat behind.

38

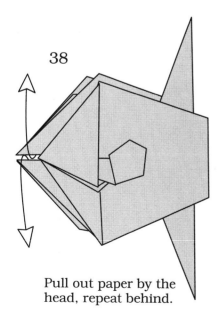

Pull out paper by the
head, repeat behind.

39

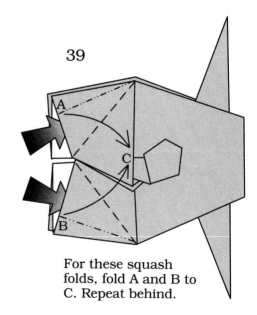

For these squash
folds, fold A and B to
C. Repeat behind.

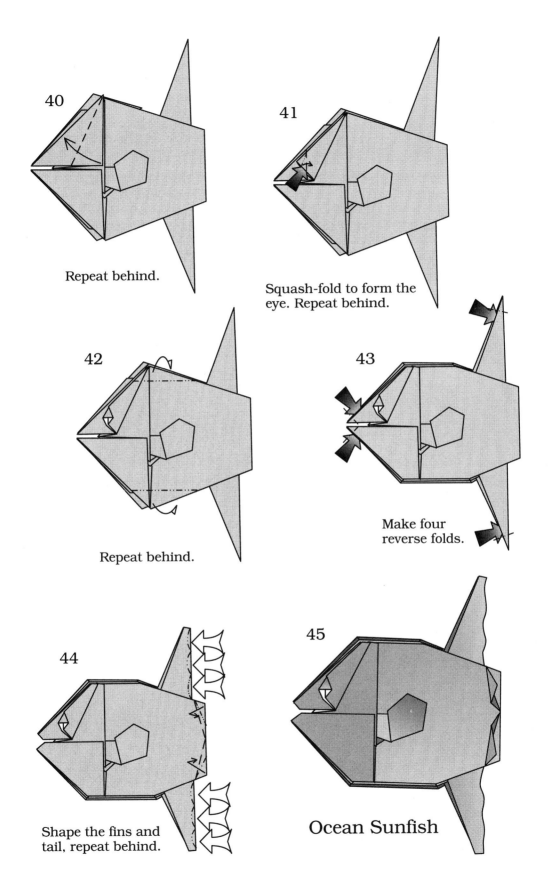

40

Repeat behind.

41

Squash-fold to form the eye. Repeat behind.

42

Repeat behind.

43

Make four reverse folds.

44

Shape the fins and tail, repeat behind.

45

Ocean Sunfish

Triggerfish

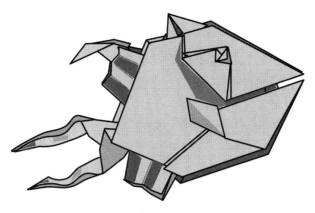

It is quite easy to tell where the triggerfish (*Balistes*) gets its name—the first three dorsal spines are thick and robust and resemble a trigger in shape. This apparatus is locked into place while the fish wedges itself into a crevice, making it almost impossible to extract, a very effective defense mechanism. These fish are found on tropical reefs world wide and are spectacularly colored. Their favorite food is sea urchin. Large specimens may reach a foot in length.

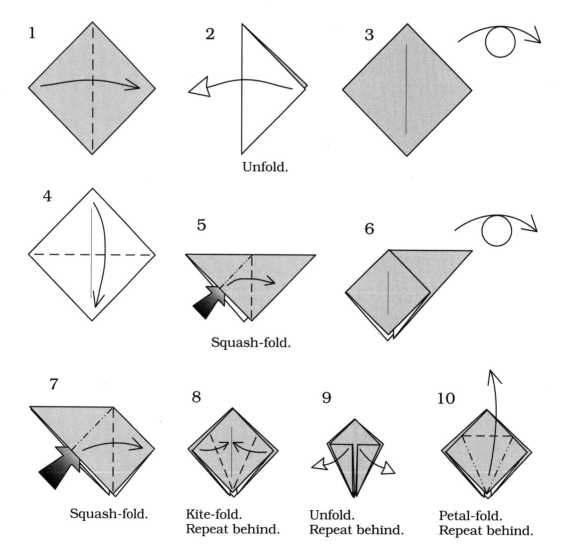

1

2

Unfold.

3

4

5

Squash-fold.

6

7

Squash-fold.

8

Kite-fold.
Repeat behind.

9

Unfold.
Repeat behind.

10

Petal-fold.
Repeat behind.

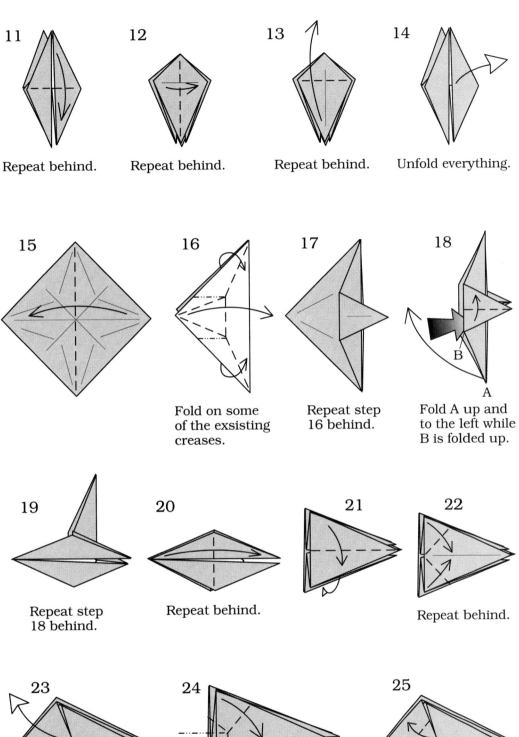

11

Repeat behind.

12

Repeat behind.

13

Repeat behind.

14

Unfold everything.

15

16

Fold on some
of the exsisting
creases.

17

Repeat step
16 behind.

18

B

A

Fold A up and
to the left while
B is folded up.

19

Repeat step
18 behind.

20

Repeat behind.

21

22

Repeat behind.

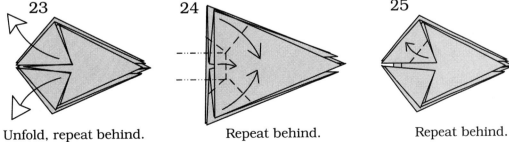

23

Unfold, repeat behind.

24

Repeat behind.

25

Repeat behind.

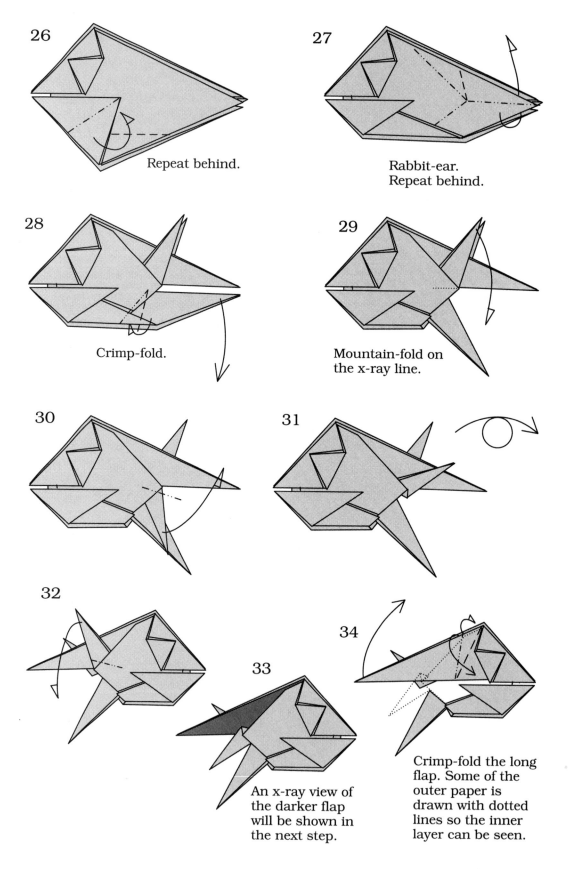

26

Repeat behind.

27

Rabbit-ear.
Repeat behind.

28

Crimp-fold.

29

Mountain-fold on
the x-ray line.

30

31

32

33

An x-ray view of
the darker flap
will be shown in
the next step.

34

Crimp-fold the long
flap. Some of the
outer paper is
drawn with dotted
lines so the inner
layer can be seen.

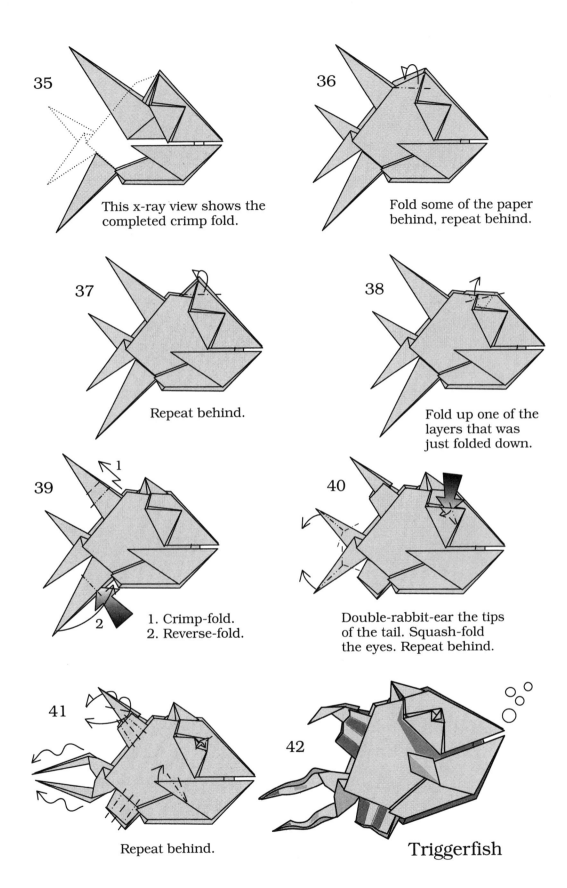

35 This x-ray view shows the completed crimp fold.

36 Fold some of the paper behind, repeat behind.

37 Repeat behind.

38 Fold up one of the layers that was just folded down.

39
1. Crimp-fold.
2. Reverse-fold.

40 Double-rabbit-ear the tips of the tail. Squash-fold the eyes. Repeat behind.

41 Repeat behind.

42

Triggerfish

Angelfish

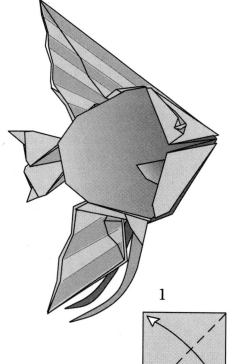

The angelfish (*Pterophyllum scalara*) belongs to the family known as cichlids. Only one color pattern occurs naturally—silver with black stripes and a red eye, but genetic manipulation has yielded pure silver, gold, calico, and marbled varieties. This fish is one of the most common types kept in the home aquarium. Found in the Amazon region in South America, angelfish are seldom longer than four inches.

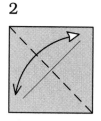

1

Fold and unfold.

2

Fold and unfold.

3

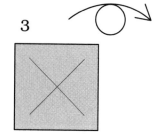

4

Fold and unfold.

5

6

Repeat behind.

7

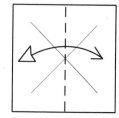

Squash-fold.

8

9

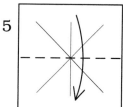

Squash-fold.

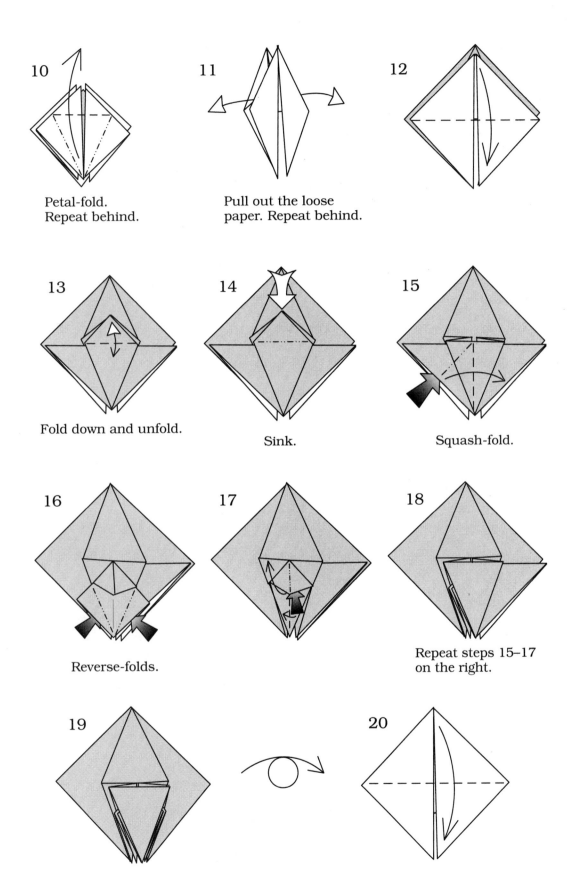

10
Petal-fold.
Repeat behind.

11
Pull out the loose
paper. Repeat behind.

12

13
Fold down and unfold.

14
Sink.

15
Squash-fold.

16
Reverse-folds.

17

18
Repeat steps 15–17
on the right.

19

20

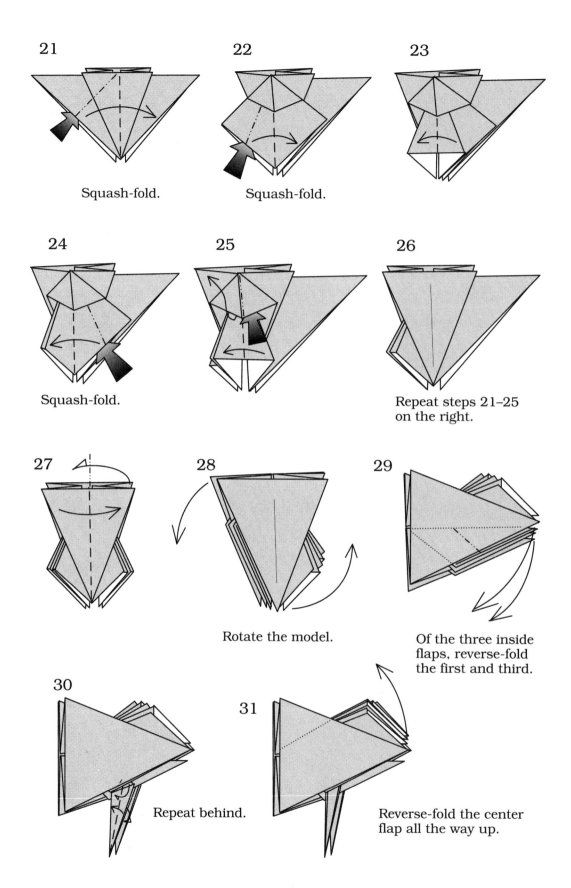

21

Squash-fold.

22

Squash-fold.

23

24

Squash-fold.

25

26

Repeat steps 21–25
on the right.

27

28

Rotate the model.

29

Of the three inside
flaps, reverse-fold
the first and third.

30

Repeat behind.

31

Reverse-fold the center
flap all the way up.

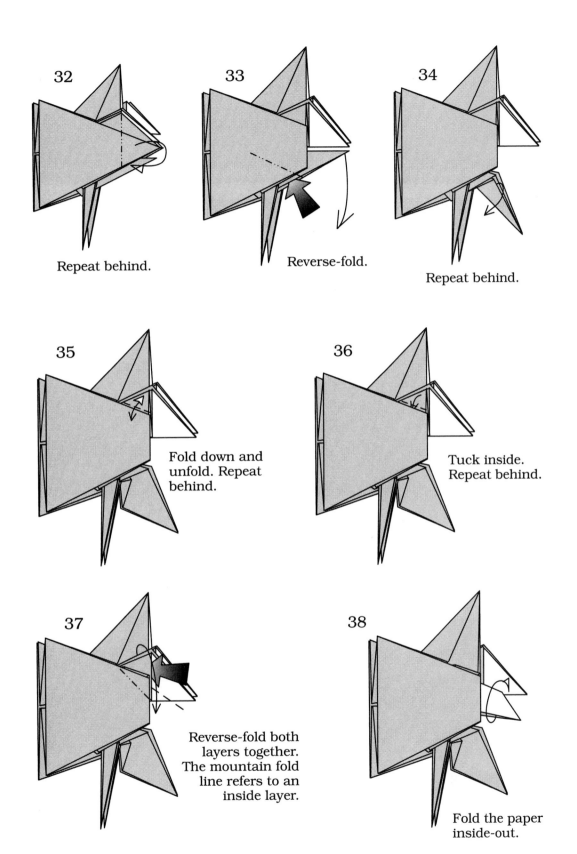

32

Repeat behind.

33

Reverse-fold.

34

Repeat behind.

35

Fold down and unfold. Repeat behind.

36

Tuck inside. Repeat behind.

37

Reverse-fold both layers together. The mountain fold line refers to an inside layer.

38

Fold the paper inside-out.

Angelfish 115

39

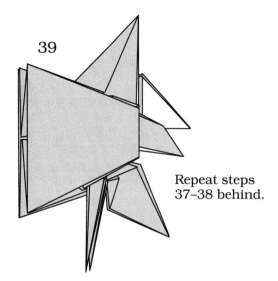

Repeat steps
37–38 behind.

40   Tail.

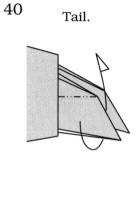

41

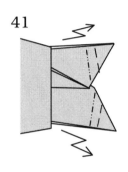

Crimp-folds.

42

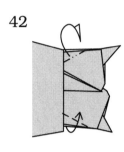

Shape the tail by folding
a little bit of the top part
behind and the bottom
part in front.

43

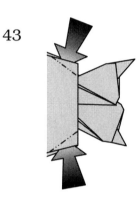

Reverse-folds.
Repeat behind.

44

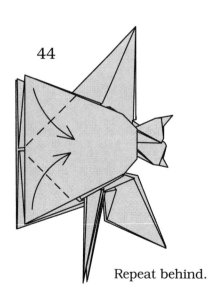

Repeat behind.

45

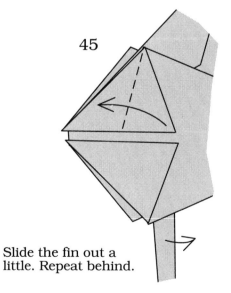

Slide the fin out a
little. Repeat behind.

46

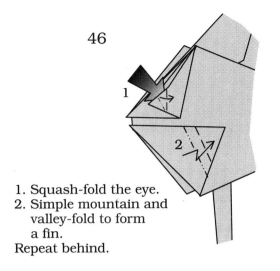

1. Squash-fold the eye.
2. Simple mountain and
   valley-fold to form
   a fin.
Repeat behind.

47

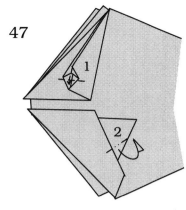

1. Fold part of the eye down.
2. Fold behind to shape the fin.
Repeat behind.

48

Make little
reverse folds
at the top and
bottom. Repeat
behind.

49

1. Mountain-fold.
2. Double-rabbit-ear
   the fins.
Repeat behind.

50

Pleat the fins.

51

Angelfish

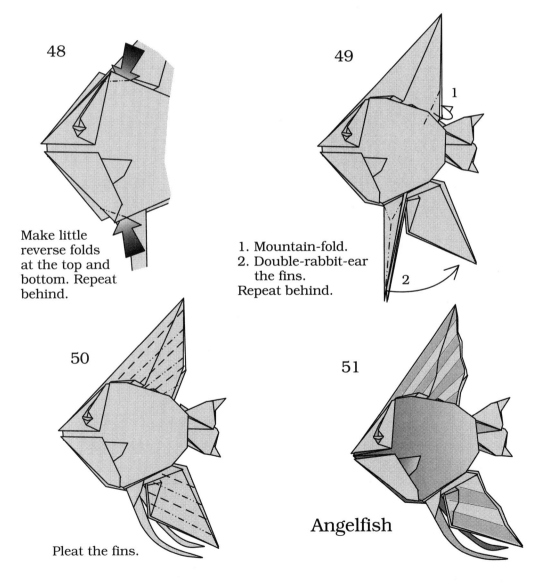

Goldfish

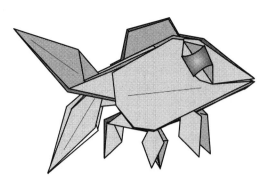

The goldfish, or oranda, (*Carassuis*) is one of the marvels of genetic manipulation. Originally developed in China from small species of carp, the modern goldfish can have as many as four separate tails, may or may not have a dorsal fin, and may have grotesque head growth or eye shape. Goldfish also come in a variety of colors from pure white to pure black to calico. Although suited to pond life, this fish is generally better displayed in an aquarium or fishbowl. Goldfish can reach a length of about eight inches, not including the tail.

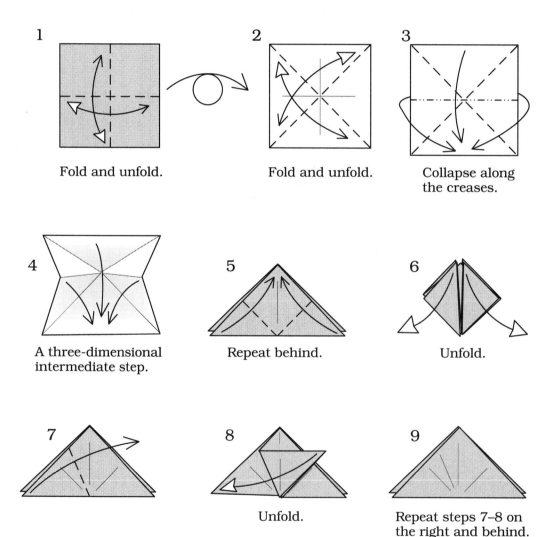

1

Fold and unfold.

2

Fold and unfold.

3

Collapse along the creases.

4

A three-dimensional intermediate step.

5

Repeat behind.

6

Unfold.

7

8

Unfold.

9

Repeat steps 7–8 on the right and behind.

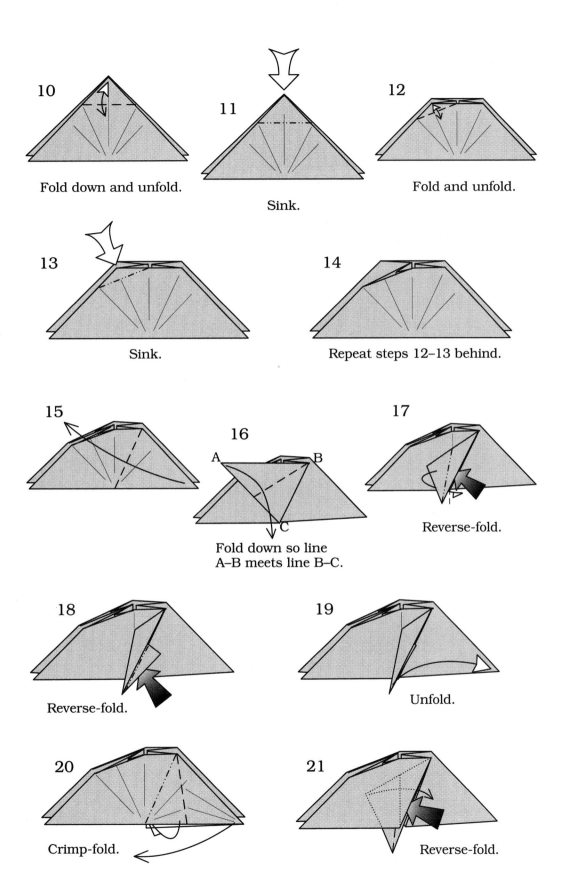

10 Fold down and unfold.

11 Sink.

12 Fold and unfold.

13 Sink.

14 Repeat steps 12–13 behind.

15

16 Fold down so line A–B meets line B–C.

17 Reverse-fold.

18 Reverse-fold.

19 Unfold.

20 Crimp-fold.

21 Reverse-fold.

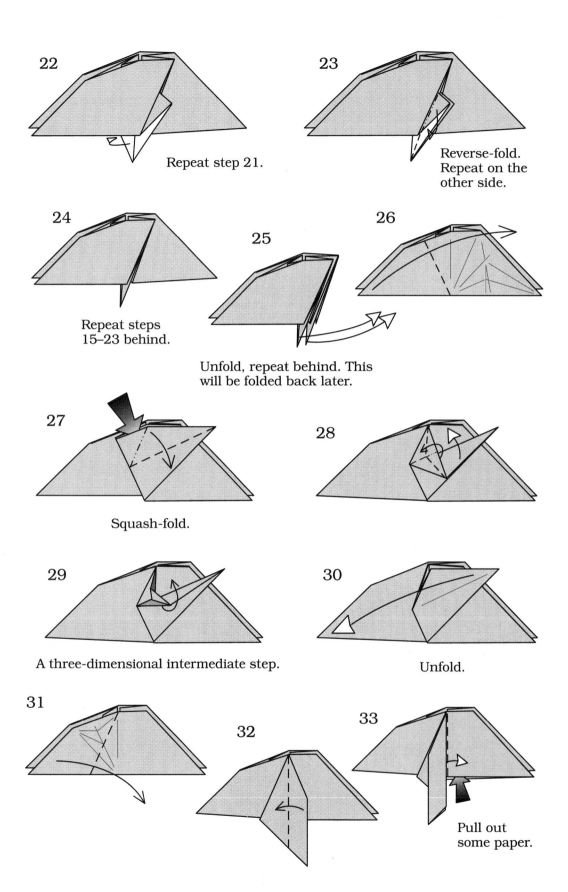

22

Repeat step 21.

23

Reverse-fold.
Repeat on the
other side.

24

Repeat steps
15–23 behind.

25

Unfold, repeat behind. This
will be folded back later.

26

27

Squash-fold.

28

29

A three-dimensional intermediate step.

30

Unfold.

31

32

33

Pull out
some paper.

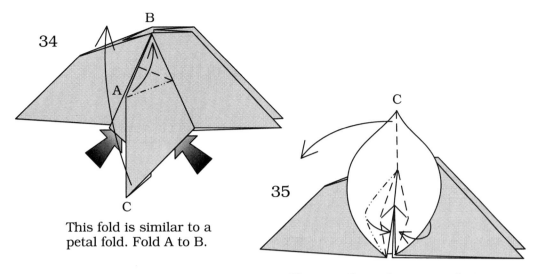

34 This fold is similar to a petal fold. Fold A to B.

35 This is a three-dimensional step.

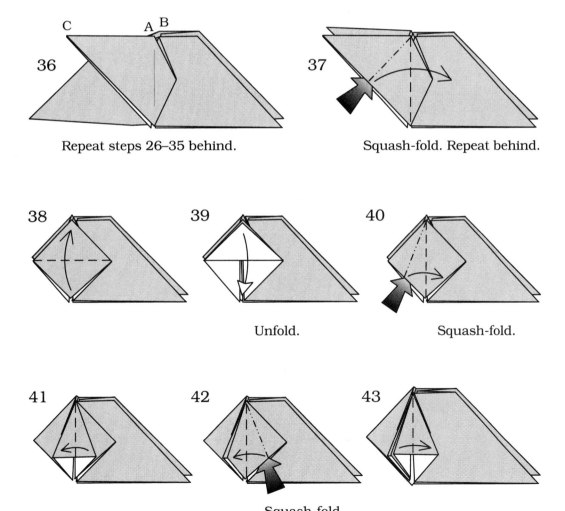

36 Repeat steps 26–35 behind.

37 Squash-fold. Repeat behind.

38

39 Unfold.

40 Squash-fold.

41

42 Squash-fold.

43

44

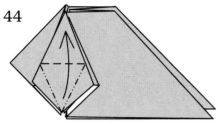

Petal-fold.

45

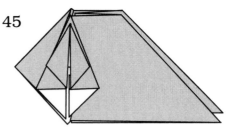

Repeat steps 38–44 behind.

46

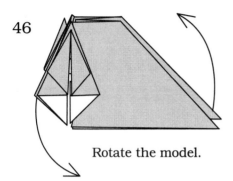

Rotate the model.

47

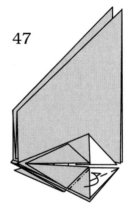

Reverse-fold, repeat behind.

48

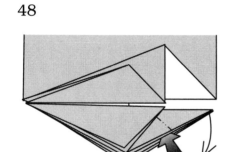

Only the bottom part of the figure is drawn. Reverse-fold.

49

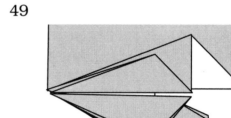

Spread the paper. Repeat behind.

50

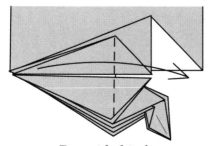

Repeat behind.

51

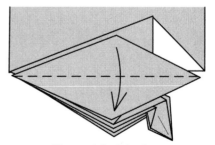

Repeat behind.

52

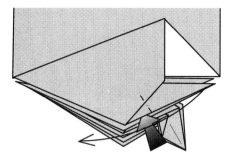

Reverse-fold, repeat behind.

53

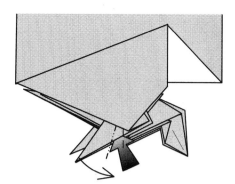

Squash-fold, repeat behind.

54

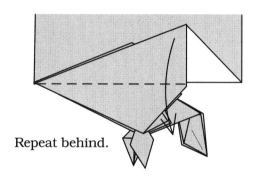

Repeat behind.

55

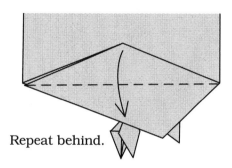

Repeat behind.

56

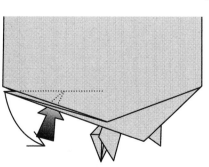

Squash-fold,
repeat behind.

57

Refold along the creases
formed in steps 20–24.
Repeat behind. Do
these folds slowly
and carefully.

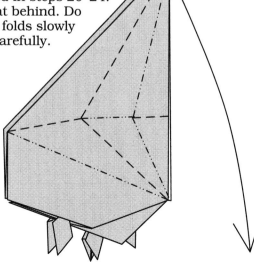

58

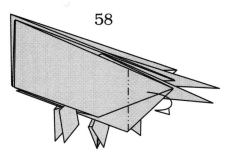

Tuck behind, repeat behind.

59

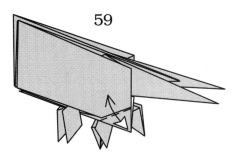

Fold up and unfold. Repeat behind.

60

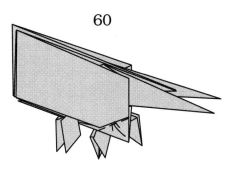

Tuck inside, repeat behind.

61

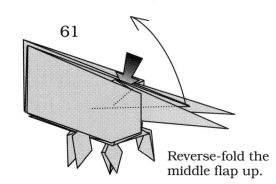

Reverse-fold the middle flap up.

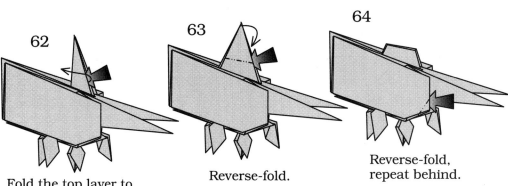

62

Fold the top layer to the left. Repeat behind.

63

Reverse-fold.

64

Reverse-fold, repeat behind.

65

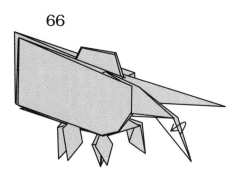

Place your finger inside the center layer for this reverse fold. Do not repeat behind.

66

Pull paper out from the inside of the tail. Repeat behind on this flap.

67

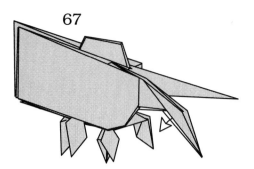

Pull out some paper. Repeat behind.

68

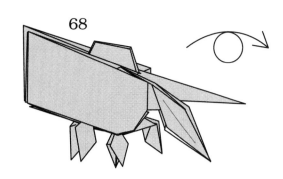

69

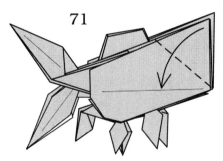

Place your finger inside the second pocket for this reverse fold.

70

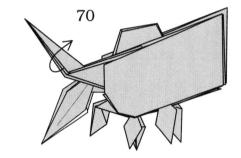

Slide the top layer up.

71

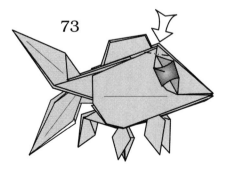

Repeat behind.

72

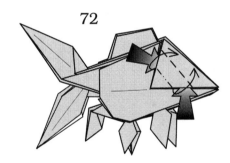

Spread-squash-fold to form a three-dimensional bulging eye. Repeat behind.

73

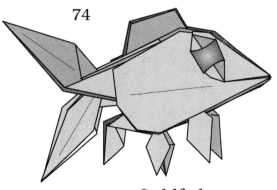

Reverse-fold at the top of the head. Repeat behind.

74

Goldfish

Cichlid

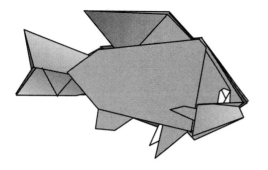

This family of fishes (family *Cichlidae*) is extremely diverse. One group of cichlids (pronounced 'SIK-lids') looks like a freshwater barracuda, while another is flat and disc shaped. They are small to medium in size and of all colors. They eat small marine animals. Many are found throughout Central and South America and Africa.

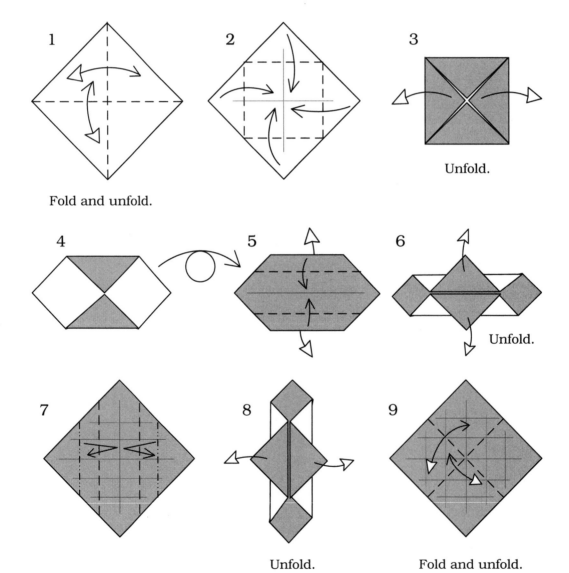

1

Fold and unfold.

2

3

Unfold.

4

5

6

Unfold.

7

8

Unfold.

9

Fold and unfold.

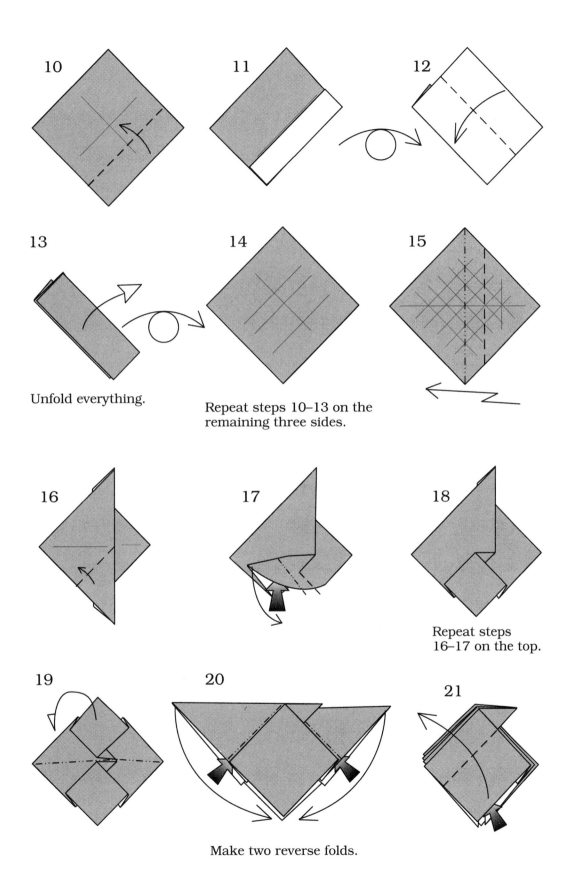

10

11

12

13

Unfold everything.

14

Repeat steps 10–13 on the remaining three sides.

15

16

17

18

Repeat steps 16–17 on the top.

19

20

Make two reverse folds.

21

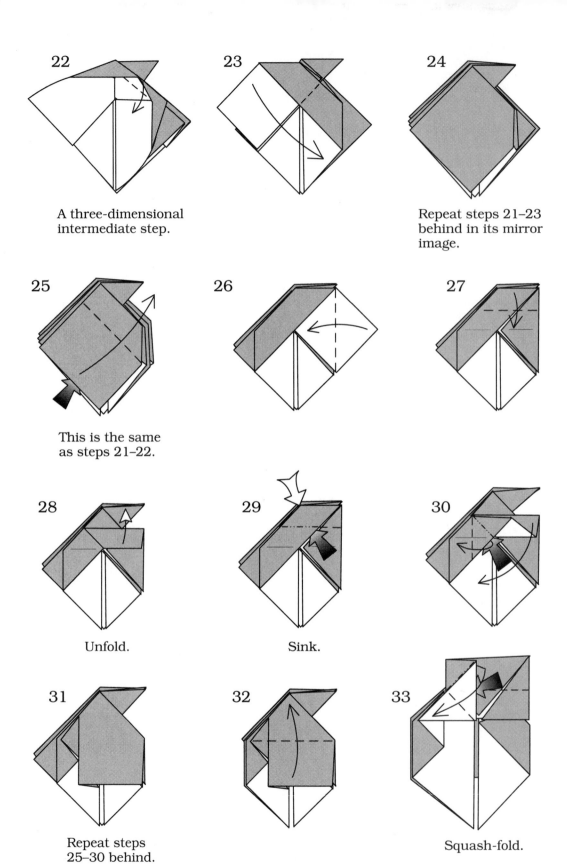

22

A three-dimensional
intermediate step.

23

24

Repeat steps 21–23
behind in its mirror
image.

25

This is the same
as steps 21–22.

26

27

28

Unfold.

29

Sink.

30

31

Repeat steps
25–30 behind.

32

33

Squash-fold.

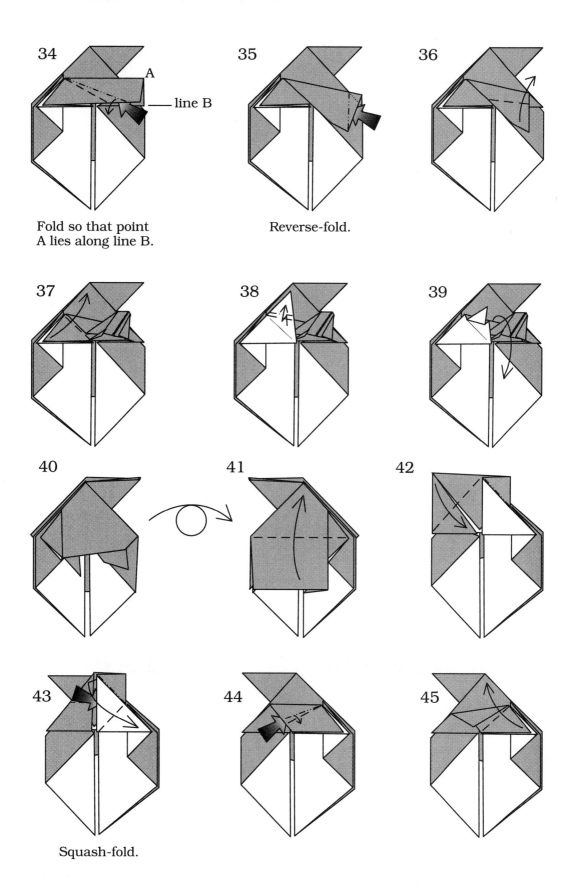

34

A

line B

Fold so that point
A lies along line B.

35

Reverse-fold.

36

37

38

39

40

41

42

43

Squash-fold.

44

45

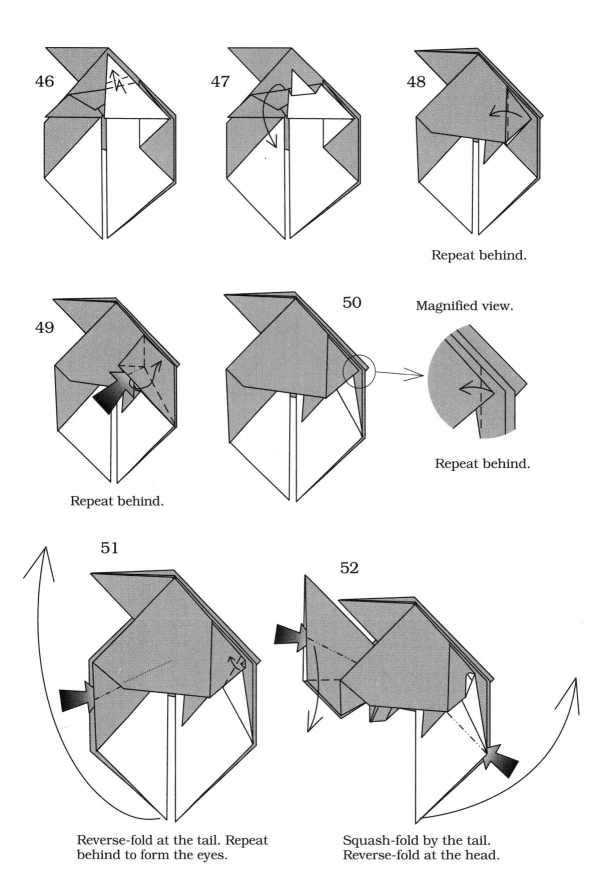

46

47

48

Repeat behind.

49

50

Magnified view.

Repeat behind.

Repeat behind.

51

Reverse-fold at the tail. Repeat
behind to form the eyes.

52

Squash-fold by the tail.
Reverse-fold at the head.

53

54

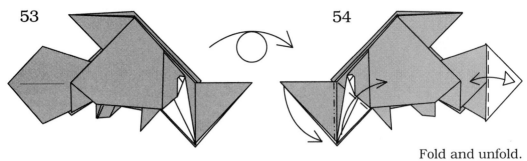

Fold and unfold.
Repeat behind.

55

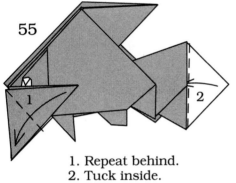

1. Repeat behind.
2. Tuck inside.

56

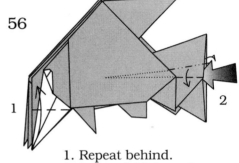

1. Repeat behind.
2. Crimp-fold the tail.

57

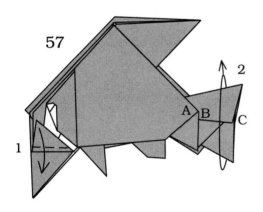

1. Repeat behind.
2. Slide the tail up so
   line B–C meets point A.

58

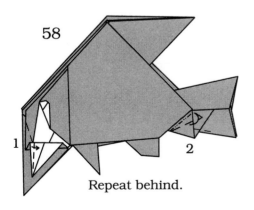

Repeat behind.

59

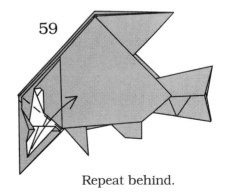

Repeat behind.

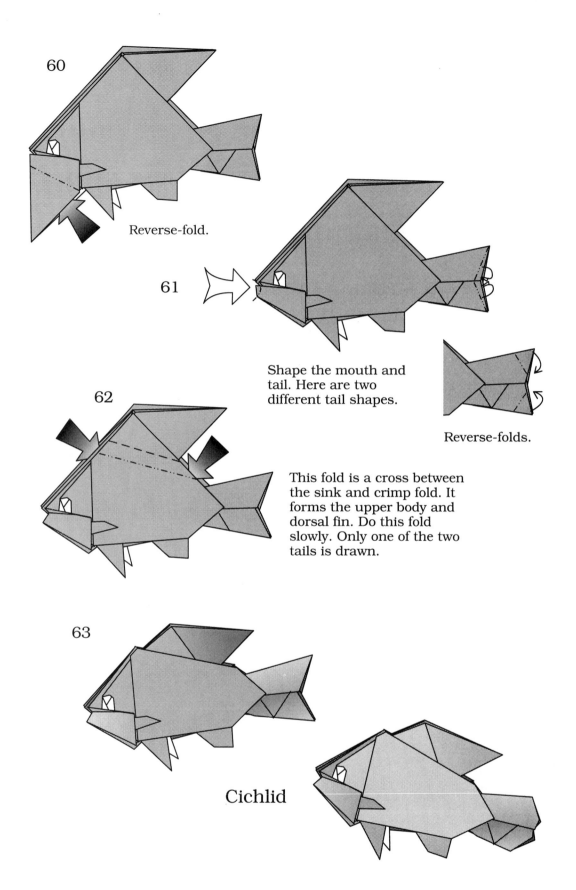

60

Reverse-fold.

61

Shape the mouth and
tail. Here are two
different tail shapes.

Reverse-folds.

62

This fold is a cross between
the sink and crimp fold. It
forms the upper body and
dorsal fin. Do this fold
slowly. Only one of the two
tails is drawn.

63

Cichlid

Sailfish

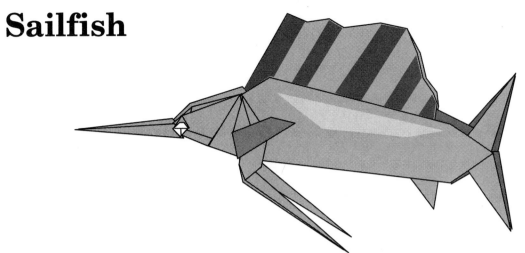

These fish are found worldwide in open oceans. They are 4 to 12 feet long. These agile fish can swim as fast as 60 miles an hour. Though they are toothless, they can catch fish with their swords. Hunting in groups, sailfish (*Istiophorus platypterus*) use their enlarged dorsal fins to trap smaller fish.

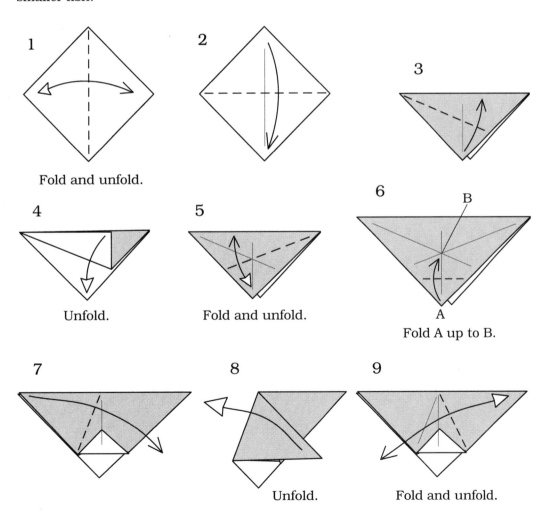

1

Fold and unfold.

2

3

4

Unfold.

5

Fold and unfold.

6

B

A

Fold A up to B.

7

8

Unfold.

9

Fold and unfold.

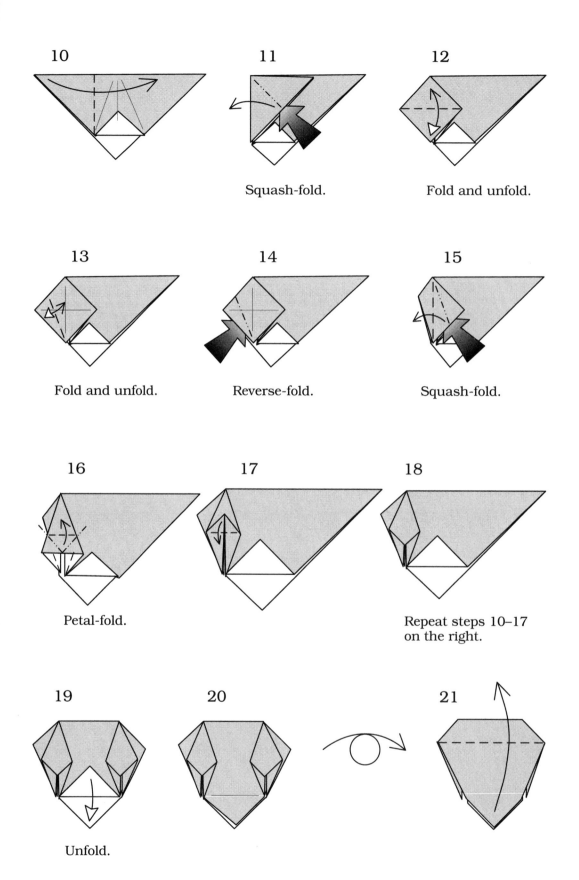

10

11

Squash-fold.

12

Fold and unfold.

13

Fold and unfold.

14

Reverse-fold.

15

Squash-fold.

16

Petal-fold.

17

18

Repeat steps 10–17 on the right.

19

Unfold.

20

21

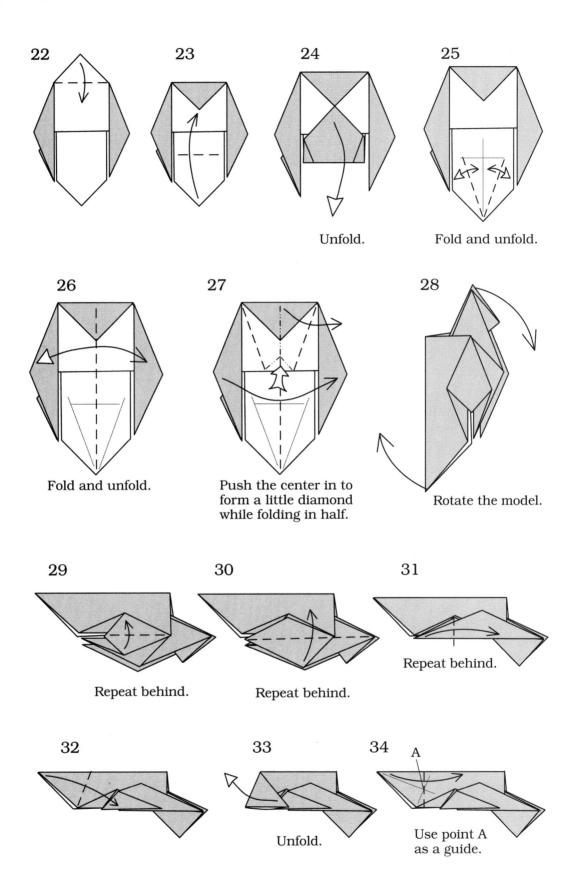

22

23

24

Unfold.

25

Fold and unfold.

26

Fold and unfold.

27

Push the center in to
form a little diamond
while folding in half.

28

Rotate the model.

29

Repeat behind.

30

Repeat behind.

31

Repeat behind.

32

33

Unfold.

34

A

Use point A
as a guide.

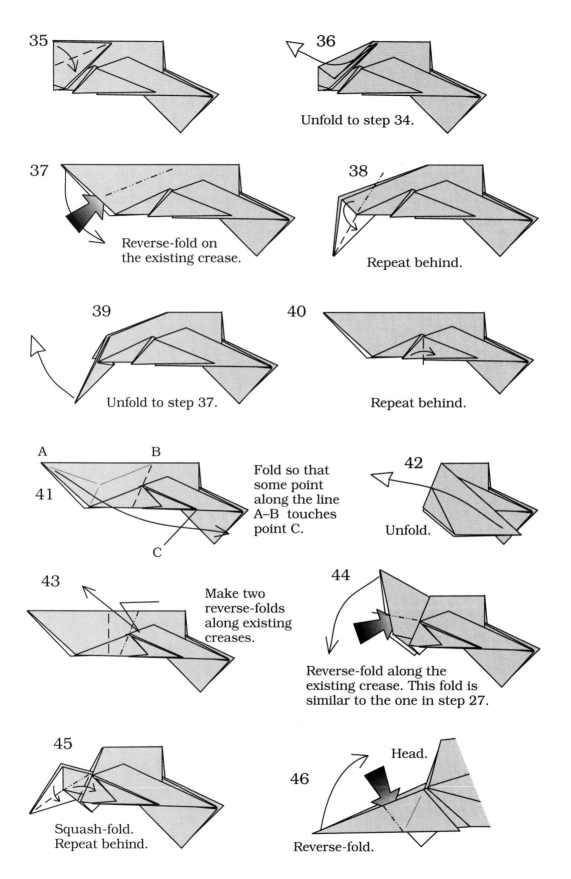

35

36

Unfold to step 34.

37 Reverse-fold on
the existing crease.

38 Repeat behind.

39 Unfold to step 37.

40 Repeat behind.

41 A B

Fold so that
some point
along the line
A–B touches
point C.

C

42 Unfold.

43

Make two
reverse-folds
along existing
creases.

44 Reverse-fold along the
existing crease. This fold is
similar to the one in step 27.

45 Squash-fold.
Repeat behind.

46 Head.

Reverse-fold.

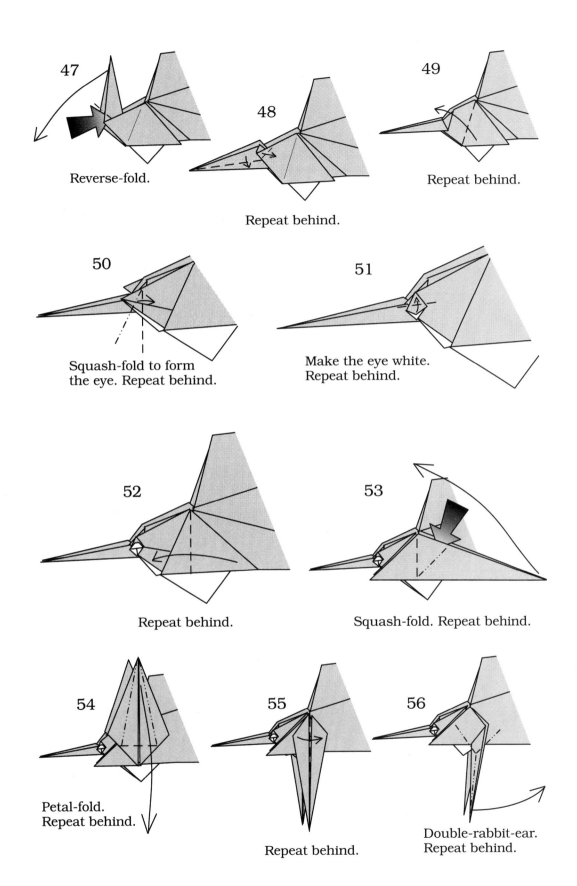

47

Reverse-fold.

48

Repeat behind.

Repeat behind.

49

Repeat behind.

50

Squash-fold to form
the eye. Repeat behind.

51

Make the eye white.
Repeat behind.

52

Repeat behind.

53

Squash-fold. Repeat behind.

54

Petal-fold.
Repeat behind.

55

Repeat behind.

56

Double-rabbit-ear.
Repeat behind.

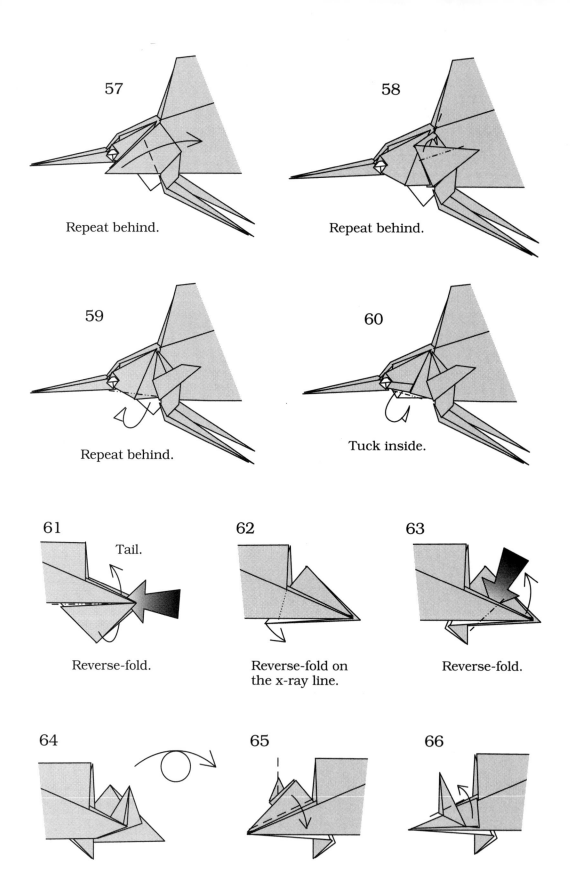

57

Repeat behind.

58

Repeat behind.

59

Repeat behind.

60

Tuck inside.

61

Tail.

Reverse-fold.

62

Reverse-fold on
the x-ray line.

63

Reverse-fold.

64

65

66

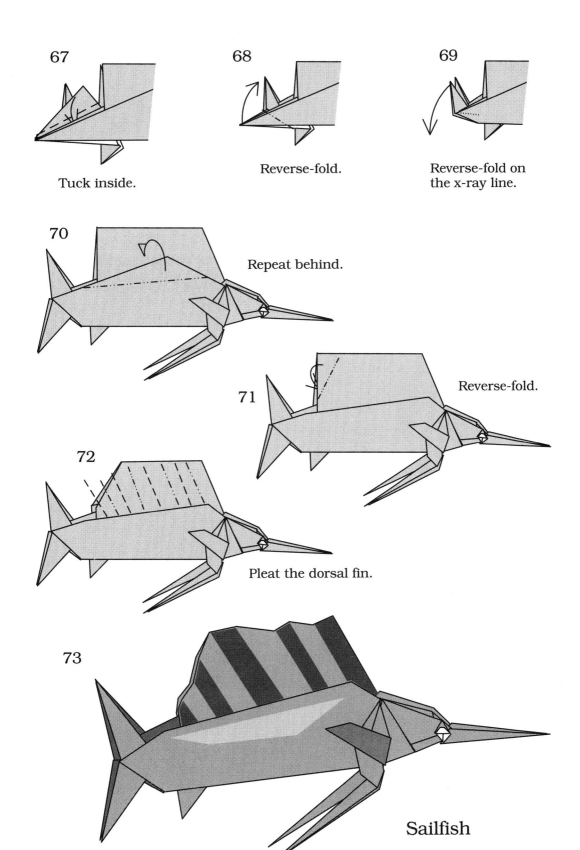

67

Tuck inside.

68

Reverse-fold.

69

Reverse-fold on the x-ray line.

70

Repeat behind.

71

Reverse-fold.

72

Pleat the dorsal fin.

73

Sailfish

Barracuda

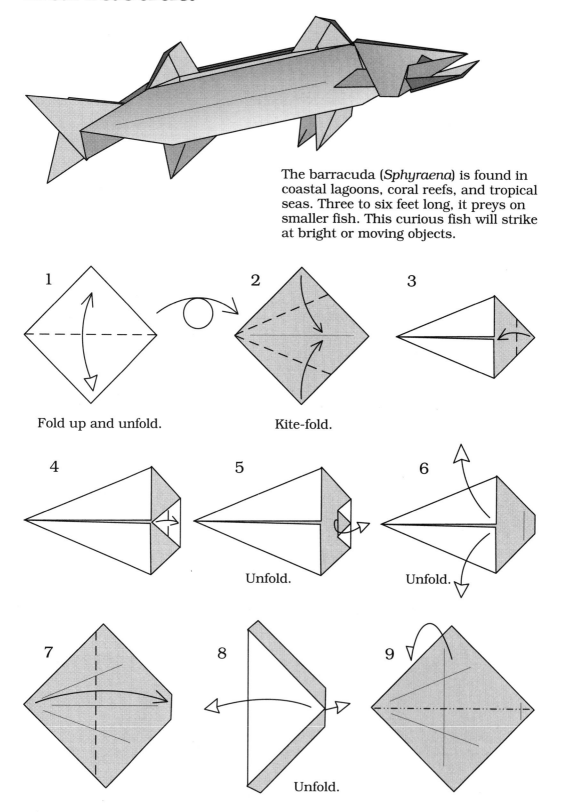

The barracuda (*Sphyraena*) is found in coastal lagoons, coral reefs, and tropical seas. Three to six feet long, it preys on smaller fish. This curious fish will strike at bright or moving objects.

1

Fold up and unfold.

2

Kite-fold.

3

4

5

Unfold.

6

Unfold.

7

8

Unfold.

9

10

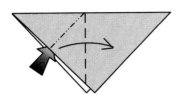

Squash-fold on the existing crease.

11

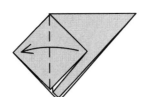

12

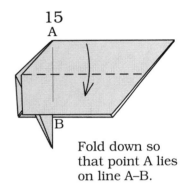

Squash-fold.
Repeat behind.

13

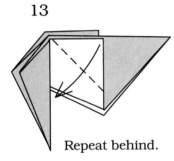

Repeat behind.

14

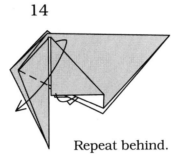

Repeat behind.

15

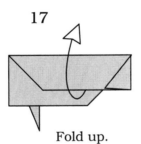

Fold down so that point A lies on line A–B.

16

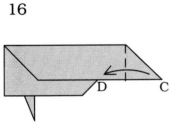

Fold C to D very accurately.

17

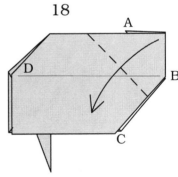

Fold up.

18

Fold so that
1. A lies on line D–B and
2. B lies on line B–C.

19

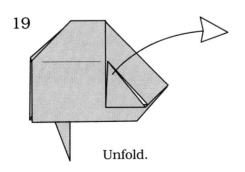

Unfold.

20

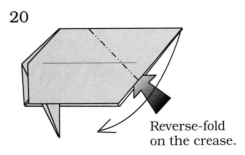

Reverse-fold on the crease.

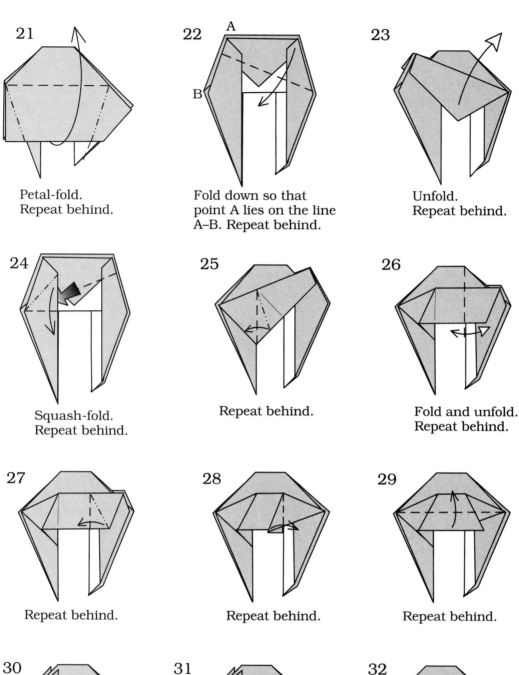

21

Petal-fold.
Repeat behind.

22

A

B

Fold down so that
point A lies on the line
A–B. Repeat behind.

23

Unfold.
Repeat behind.

24

Squash-fold.
Repeat behind.

25

Repeat behind.

26

Fold and unfold.
Repeat behind.

27

Repeat behind.

28

Repeat behind.

29

Repeat behind.

30

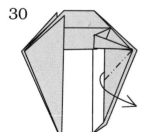

Pull some paper
out. Repeat behind.

31

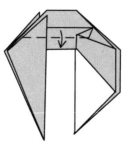

Repeat behind.

32

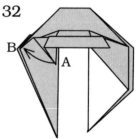

B

A

Open slightly to fold A
to B. Repeat behind.

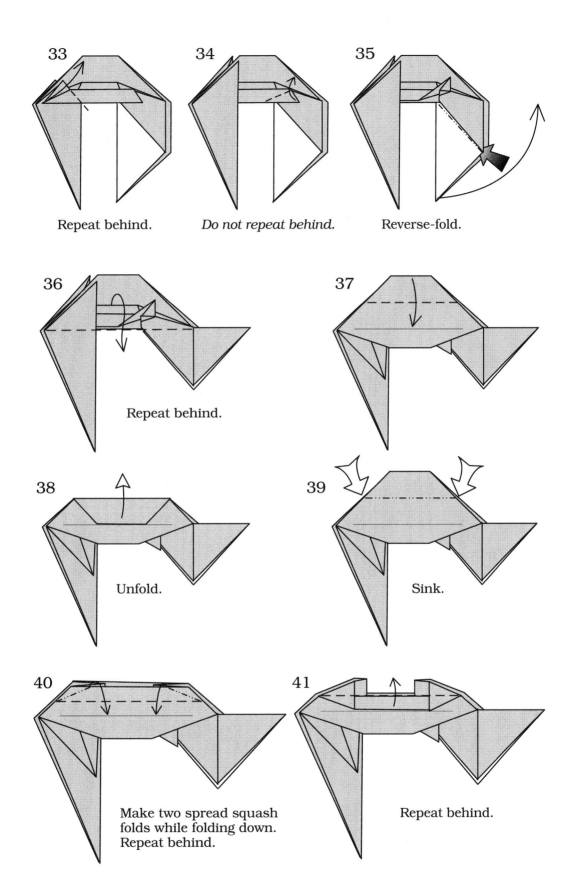

33

Repeat behind.

34

Do not repeat behind.

35

Reverse-fold.

36

Repeat behind.

37

38

Unfold.

39

Sink.

40

Make two spread squash folds while folding down. Repeat behind.

41

Repeat behind.

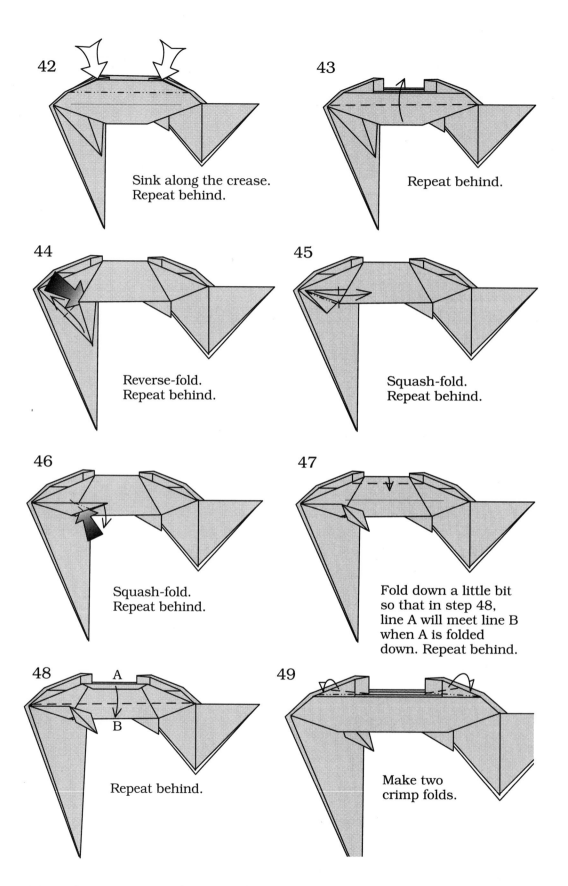

42 Sink along the crease.
Repeat behind.

43 Repeat behind.

44 Reverse-fold.
Repeat behind.

45 Squash-fold.
Repeat behind.

46 Squash-fold.
Repeat behind.

47 Fold down a little bit
so that in step 48,
line A will meet line B
when A is folded
down. Repeat behind.

48 A
B
Repeat behind.

49 Make two
crimp folds.

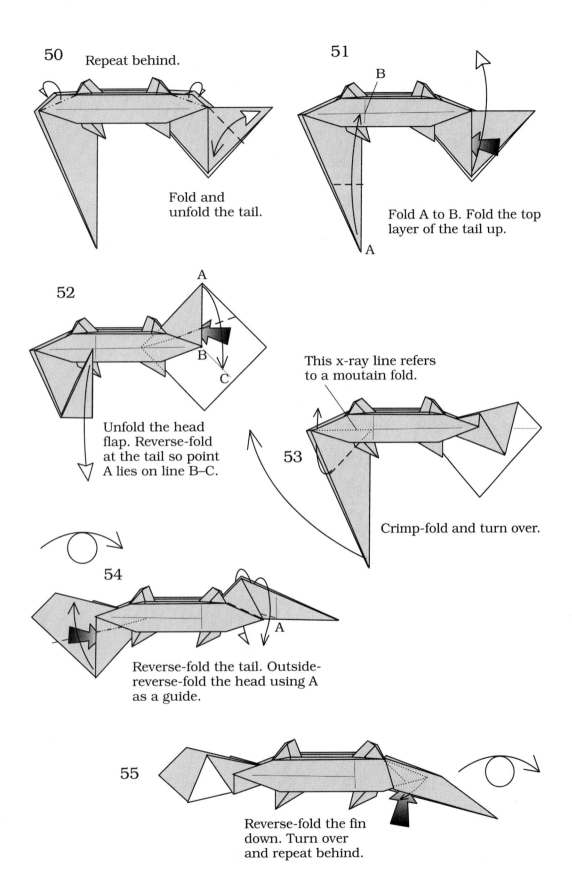

50 Repeat behind.

Fold and
unfold the tail.

51

B

Fold A to B. Fold the top
layer of the tail up.

A

52

A

B

C

Unfold the head
flap. Reverse-fold
at the tail so point
A lies on line B–C.

This x-ray line refers
to a moutain fold.

53

Crimp-fold and turn over.

54

A

Reverse-fold the tail. Outside-
reverse-fold the head using A
as a guide.

55

Reverse-fold the fin
down. Turn over
and repeat behind.

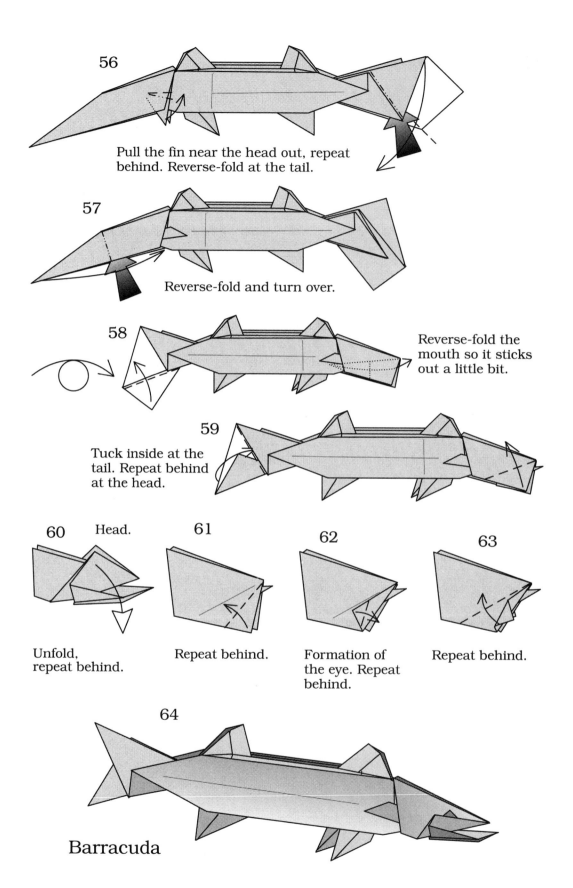

56

Pull the fin near the head out, repeat behind. Reverse-fold at the tail.

57

Reverse-fold and turn over.

58

Reverse-fold the mouth so it sticks out a little bit.

59

Tuck inside at the tail. Repeat behind at the head.

60 Head.

Unfold, repeat behind.

61

Repeat behind.

62

Formation of the eye. Repeat behind.

63

Repeat behind.

64

Barracuda

Blue Shark

Sharks are among the most primitive forms of fish and have changed little over millions of years. Their skeletons are made of cartilage, not bone. They have a good sense of smell. The blue shark (*Prionace glauca*) is about 10 feet long and weighs about 200 pounds. This big game fish is found in deep coastal waters and feeds on small fish.

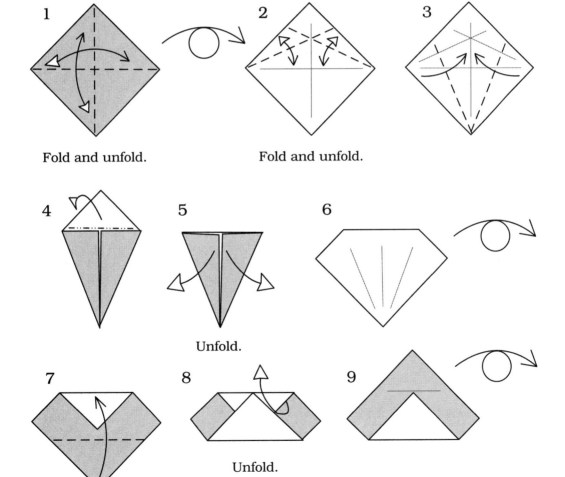

1

Fold and unfold.

2

Fold and unfold.

3

4

5

Unfold.

6

7

8

Unfold.

9

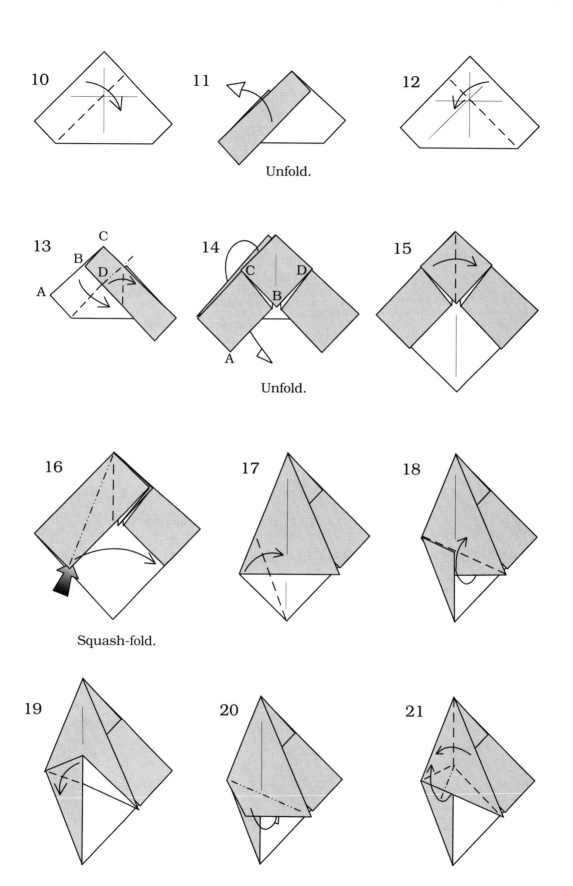

10

11

Unfold.

12

13

C

B

D

A

14

C

D

B

A

Unfold.

15

16

Squash-fold.

17

18

19

20

21

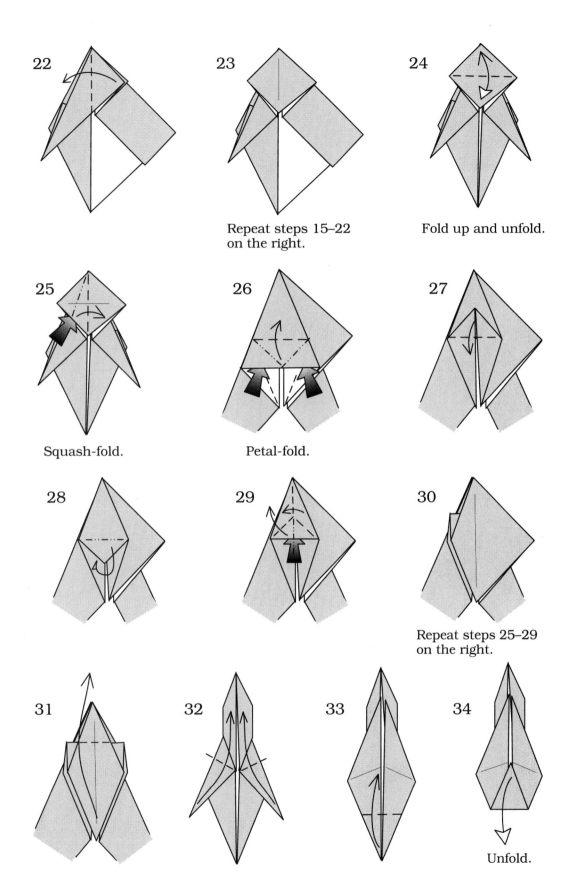

22

23

Repeat steps 15–22 on the right.

24

Fold up and unfold.

25

Squash-fold.

26

Petal-fold.

27

28

29

30

Repeat steps 25–29 on the right.

31

32

33

34

Unfold.

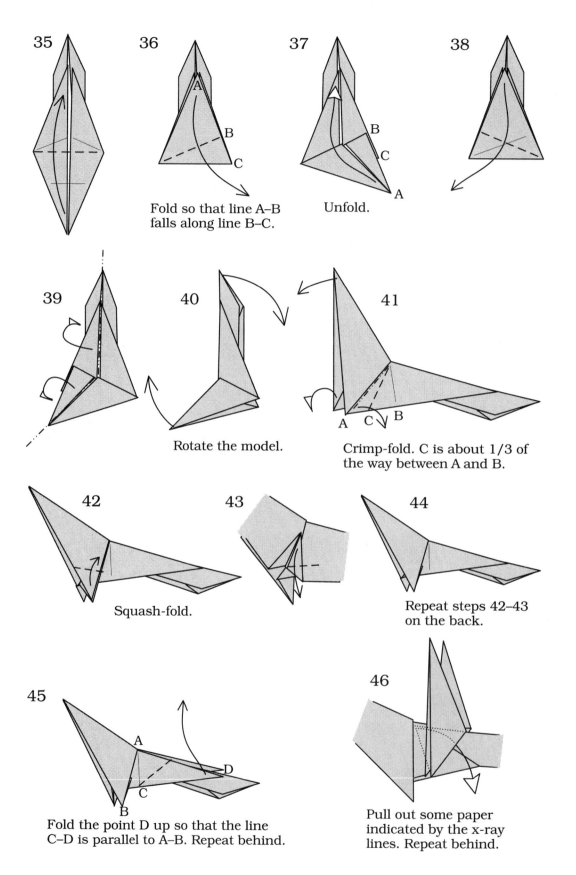

35

36

Fold so that line A–B
falls along line B–C.

37

Unfold.

38

39

40

Rotate the model.

41

Crimp-fold. C is about 1/3 of
the way between A and B.

42

Squash-fold.

43

44

Repeat steps 42–43
on the back.

45

Fold the point D up so that the line
C–D is parallel to A–B. Repeat behind.

46

Pull out some paper
indicated by the x-ray
lines. Repeat behind.

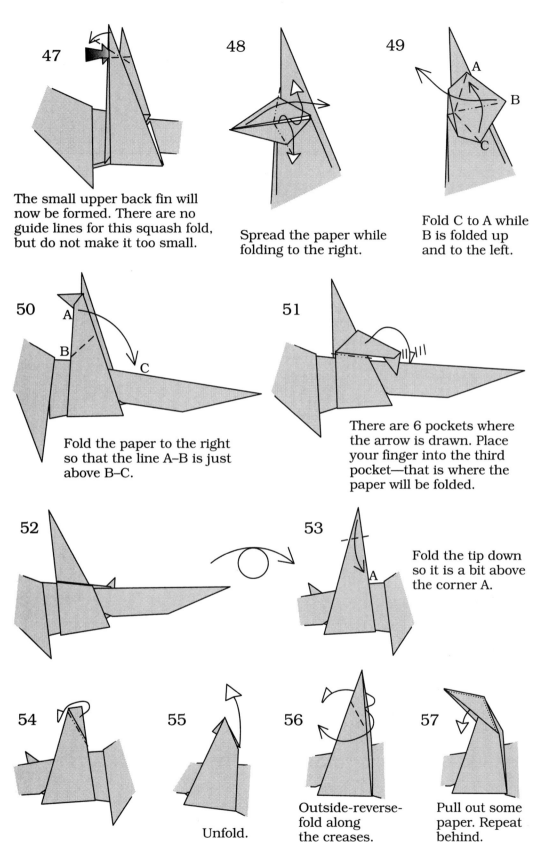

47 The small upper back fin will now be formed. There are no guide lines for this squash fold, but do not make it too small.

48 Spread the paper while folding to the right.

49 Fold C to A while B is folded up and to the left.

50 Fold the paper to the right so that the line A–B is just above B–C.

51 There are 6 pockets where the arrow is drawn. Place your finger into the third pocket—that is where the paper will be folded.

52

53 Fold the tip down so it is a bit above the corner A.

54

55 Unfold.

56 Outside-reverse-fold along the creases.

57 Pull out some paper. Repeat behind.

58

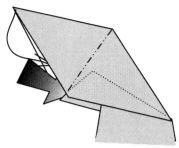

Reverse-fold the tip into the layer shown by the x-ray lines and large arrow. This will lock the fin.

59

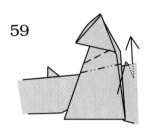

Pleat-fold to place the fin. Some of the paper is folded into the third layer. Give this fold a good, sharp crease.

60

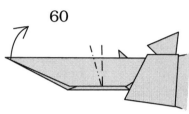

Crimp-fold the tail.

61

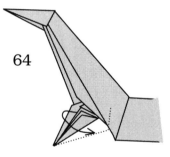

Crimp-fold the tip of the tail.

62

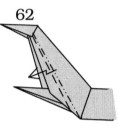

Repeat behind.

63

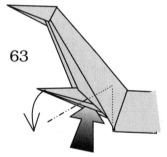

Place your finger into the most central layer to reverse-fold the lower part of the tail.

64

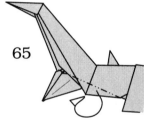

Pull out two layers to widen the tail. The dotted lines show where the paper will go. Repeat behind.

65

Repeat behind.

66

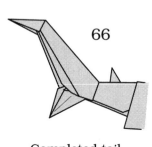

Completed tail.

67

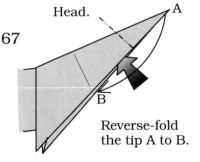

Head.

A

B

Reverse-fold the tip A to B.

68

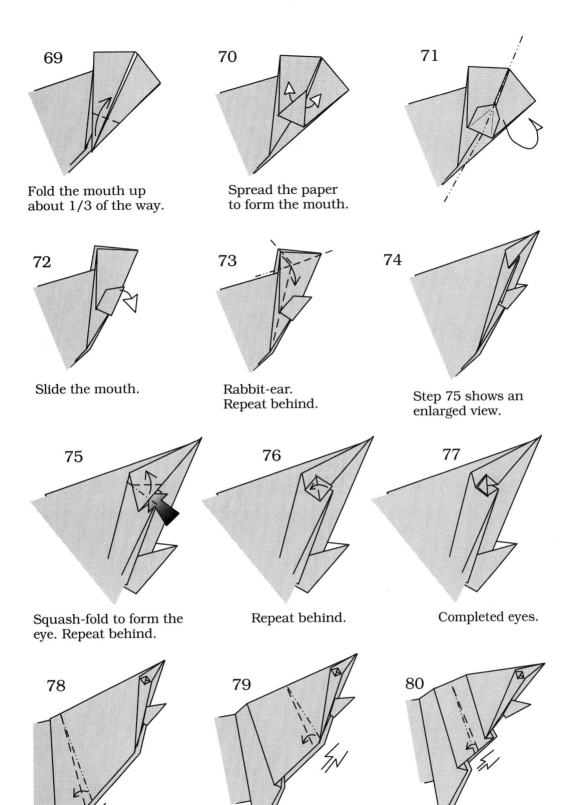

69 Fold the mouth up about 1/3 of the way.

70 Spread the paper to form the mouth.

71

72 Slide the mouth.

73 Rabbit-ear. Repeat behind.

74 Step 75 shows an enlarged view.

75 Squash-fold to form the eye. Repeat behind.

76 Repeat behind.

77 Completed eyes.

78 This is a very thin crimp fold.

79 Another thin crimp at the head.

80 One more crimp-fold between the others.

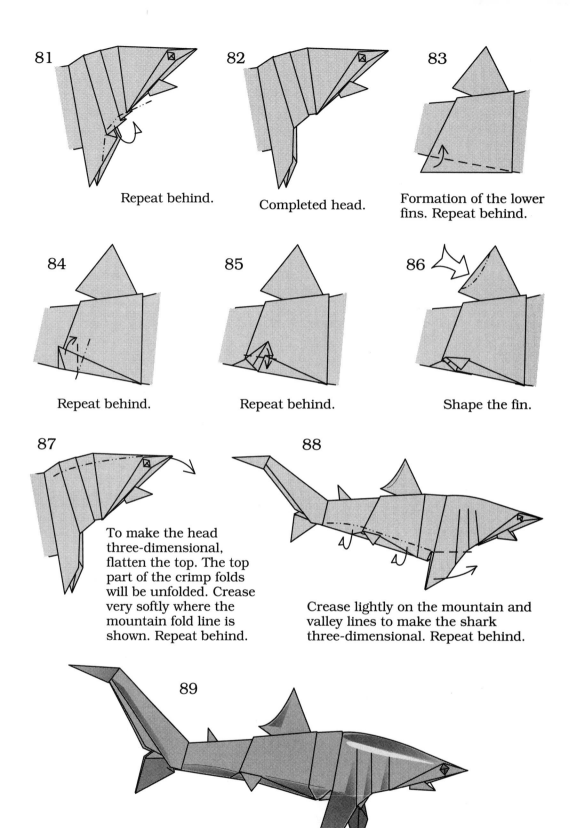

81 Repeat behind.

82 Completed head.

83 Formation of the lower fins. Repeat behind.

84 Repeat behind.

85 Repeat behind.

86 Shape the fin.

87 To make the head three-dimensional, flatten the top. The top part of the crimp folds will be unfolded. Crease very softly where the mountain fold line is shown. Repeat behind.

88 Crease lightly on the mountain and valley lines to make the shark three-dimensional. Repeat behind.

89

Blue Shark

Deep Sea Angler Fish

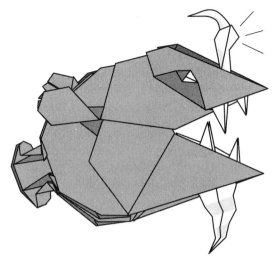

This scary looking fish lives in the deep sea at depths of two miles and more. It ranges in size from two inches to six feet. The majority of the fish is mouth and stomach, both of which are expandable and allow the fish to swallow a meal up to twice its own size. Because no light penetrates to the depth where this fish lives, many of the creatures use bioluminescence. The deep sea angler (*Linophryne arborifer*) uses light to its advantage by having a small "lamp" on the top of its head. Other fish are attracted to the light without noticing the waiting jaws of death. For obvious reasons, this fish has been called the devil's lantern.

1

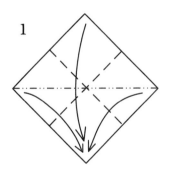

Begin with the
Preliminary Fold.

2

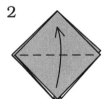

Fold up,
repeat behind.

3

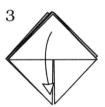

Unfold, repeat
behind.

4

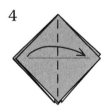

Repeat behind.

5

Fold up and unfold.
Repeat behind.

6

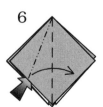

Squash-fold.
Repeat behind.

7

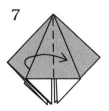

Repeat behind.

8

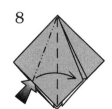

Squash-fold.
Repeat behind.

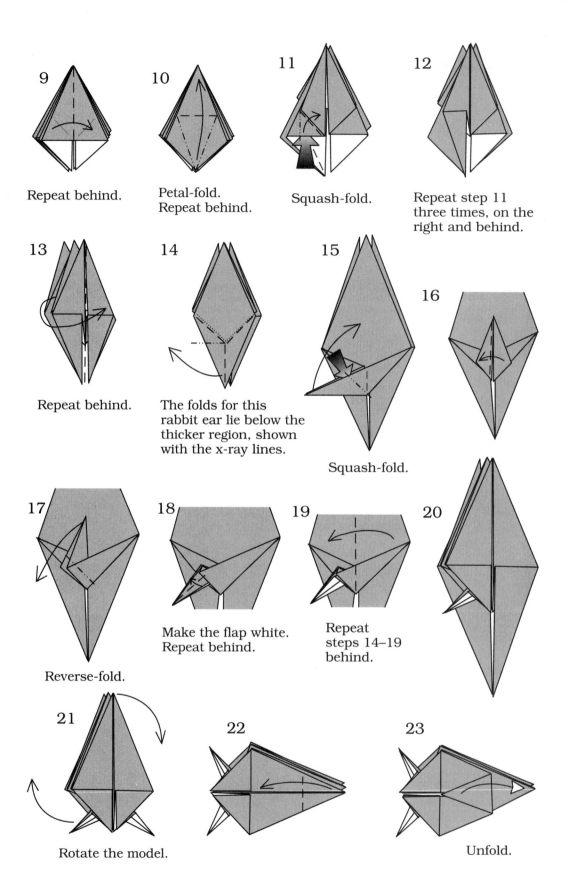

9 Repeat behind.

10 Petal-fold. Repeat behind.

11 Squash-fold.

12 Repeat step 11 three times, on the right and behind.

13 Repeat behind.

14 The folds for this rabbit ear lie below the thicker region, shown with the x-ray lines.

15 Squash-fold.

16

17 Reverse-fold.

18 Make the flap white. Repeat behind.

19 Repeat steps 14–19 behind.

20

21 Rotate the model.

22

23 Unfold.

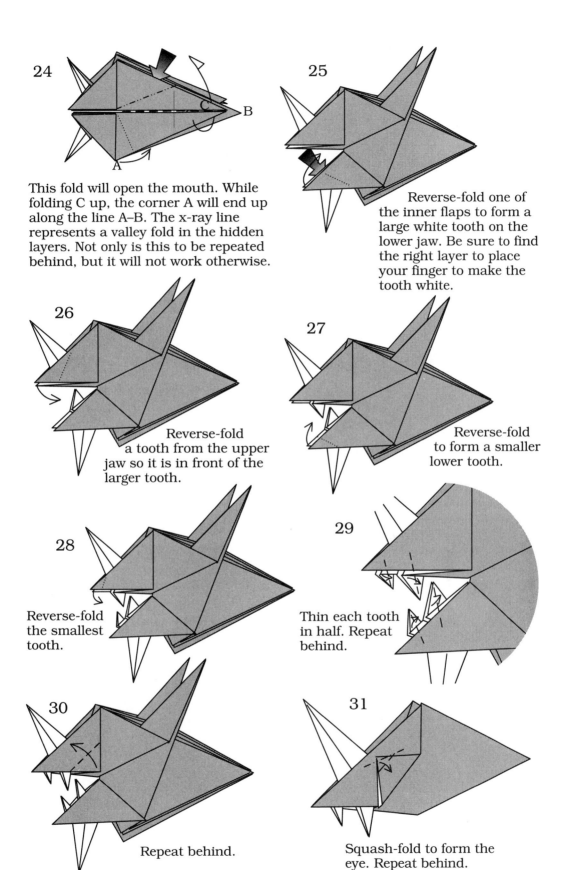

24 This fold will open the mouth. While folding C up, the corner A will end up along the line A–B. The x-ray line represents a valley fold in the hidden layers. Not only is this to be repeated behind, but it will not work otherwise.

25 Reverse-fold one of the inner flaps to form a large white tooth on the lower jaw. Be sure to find the right layer to place your finger to make the tooth white.

26 Reverse-fold a tooth from the upper jaw so it is in front of the larger tooth.

27 Reverse-fold to form a smaller lower tooth.

28 Reverse-fold the smallest tooth.

29 Thin each tooth in half. Repeat behind.

30 Repeat behind.

31 Squash-fold to form the eye. Repeat behind.

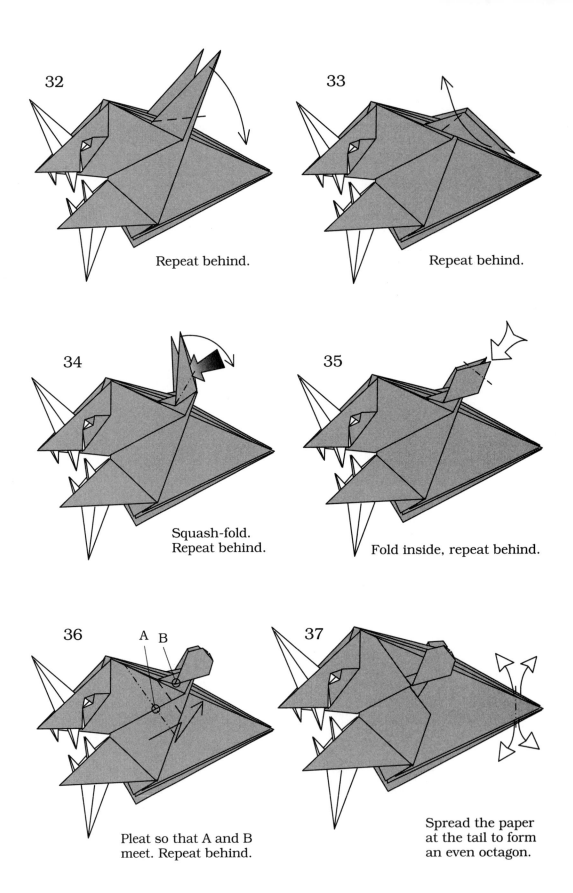

32

Repeat behind.

33

Repeat behind.

34

Squash-fold.
Repeat behind.

35

Fold inside, repeat behind.

36

A B

Pleat so that A and B
meet. Repeat behind.

37

Spread the paper
at the tail to form
an even octagon.

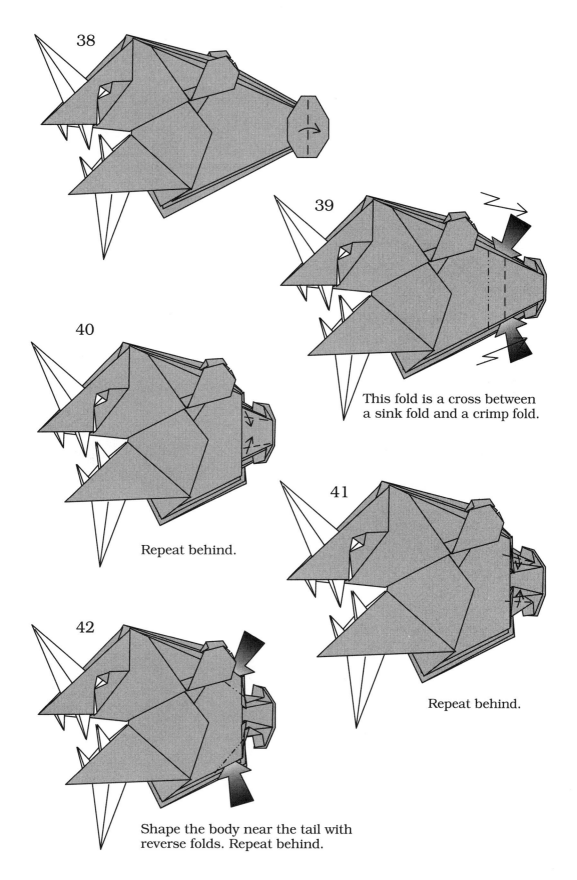

38

39

This fold is a cross between
a sink fold and a crimp fold.

40

Repeat behind.

41

Repeat behind.

42

Shape the body near the tail with
reverse folds. Repeat behind.

43

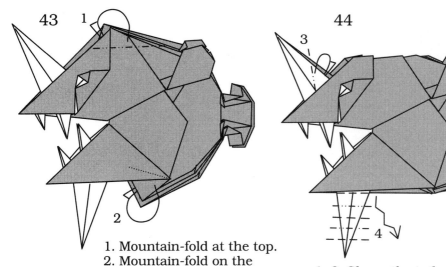

1. Mountain-fold at the top.
2. Mountain-fold on the
   x-ray line.
Repeat behind.

44

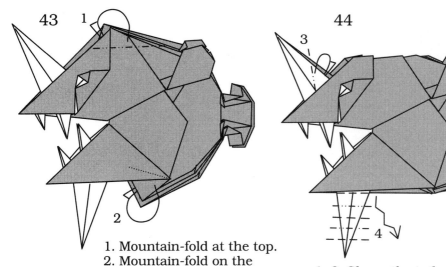

1, 2. Shape the tail with
   reverse folds.
3. Mountain-fold, repeat behind.
4. Valley and mountain folds.

45

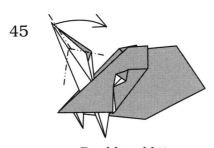

Double-rabbit-ear.

46

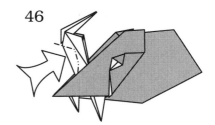

Make the lure three-dimensional.

47

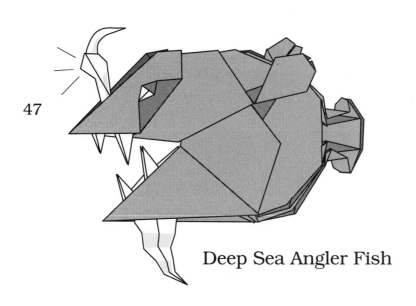

Deep Sea Angler Fish

Blackdevil Angler

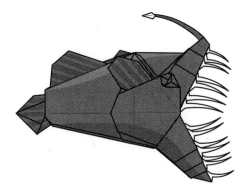

The Blackdevil Angler (*Melanocetus niger*) may well be one of the most scary fishes in the world. But despite their ferocious appearance, deep sea anglers rarely reach six inches in length. They are black and tend to have warty growths over their body. The female is much larger than the male, which lives its life parasitically attached to the female's body. This greatly enhances the chances for reproduction in an environment where individuals might otherwise never meet another of their own species.

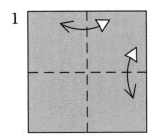

1

Crease. Turn the paper over.

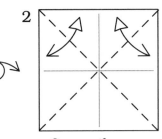

2

Crease the diagonals.

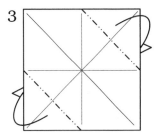

3

Fold the corners behind.

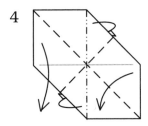

4

Fold a hybrid Waterbomb Base-Preliminary Fold.

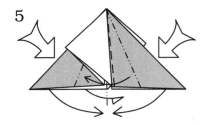

5

Squash-fold. Repeat behind.

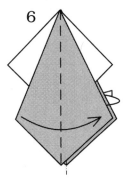

6

Fold one layer to the right in front and one to the left in back.

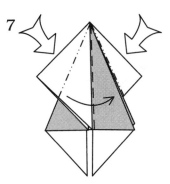

7

Squash-fold. Repeat behind.

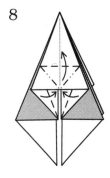

8

Petal-fold. Repeat behind.

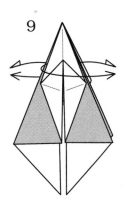

9

Unwrap the trapped
layer of paper.
Repeat behind.

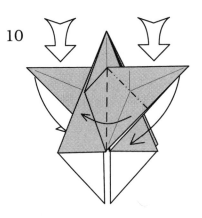

10

Squash-fold.
Repeat behind.

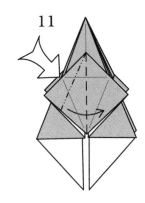

11

Squash-fold.

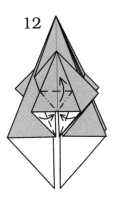

12

Petal-fold.

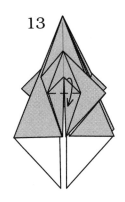

13

Fold the
point down.

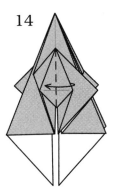

14

Fold one layer
to the left.

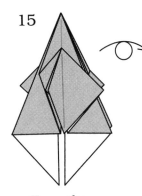

15

Turn the
paper over.

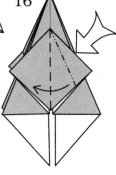

16

Repeat steps
11–14
on this flap.

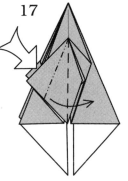

17

Repeat
steps 11–13
on this flap.

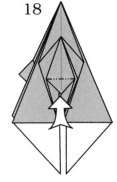

18

Reverse-fold the
point up inside
the model.

19

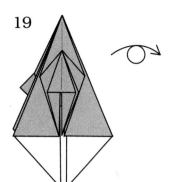

Turn the model over.

20

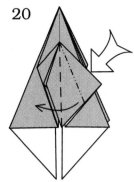

Repeat steps 11–13 and 18 on this flap.

21

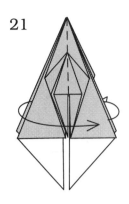

Rearrange the layers as shown.

22

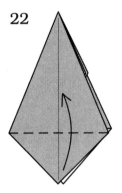

Fold one layer up.

23

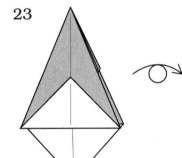

Turn the paper over.

24

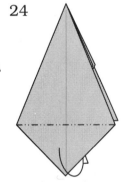

Mountain-fold the point up into the inside of the model.

25

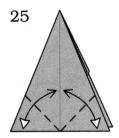

Fold and unfold.

26

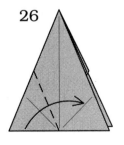

Fold the edge to lie along the crease.

27

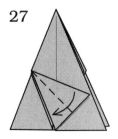

Fold down.

28

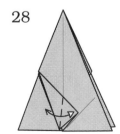

Fold and unfold.

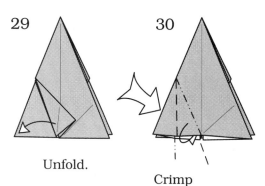

29

Unfold.

30

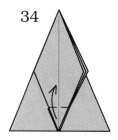

Crimp
symmetrically.

31

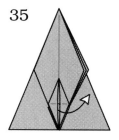

Reverse-fold both
corners back to the
outside on existing
creases.

32

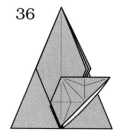

Reverse-fold
both corners.

33

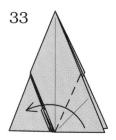

Repeat steps
26–32 on the
right.

34

Fold one point up
as far as possible.

35

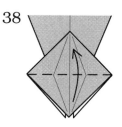

Pull the trapped
layers of paper
entirely out.

36

Like this.

37

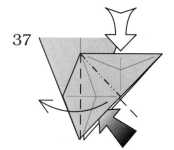

Enlarged view.
Squash-fold the flap.

38

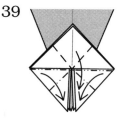

Fold one
layer up.

39

Form a Preliminary Fold.

40

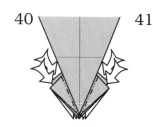

Reverse-fold
four corners.

41

Fold one point up
as far as possible.

42

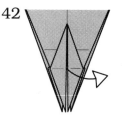

Pull the trapped
layer out from
the interior.

43

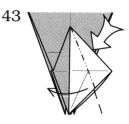

Squash-fold.

44

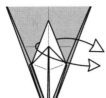

Petal-fold.

45

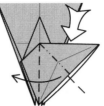

Unwrap the loose
layer of paper.

46

Squash-fold.

47

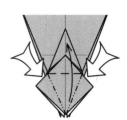

Petal-fold.

48

Like this.

49

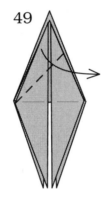

Enlarged view of
the tip. Fold the tip
down so that the
crease lines up
with the edge
underneath.

50

Unfold.

51

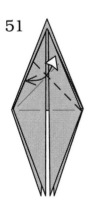

Fold and
unfold.

52

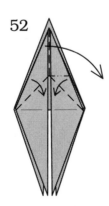

Rabbit-ear the flap
using the creases
you just made.

53

Wrap one layer
of paper from
inside to the
outside.

54

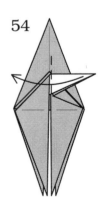

Fold the point
over to the left.

55

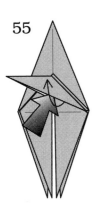

Repeat step 53.

56

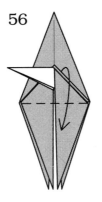

Fold all layers
downward.

57

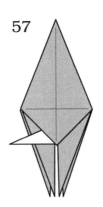

Like this.

58

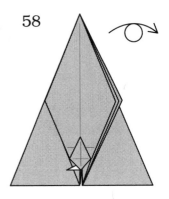

This is the entire model.
Turn the paper over.

59

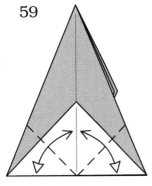

Repeat steps 25–33 on
this side.

60

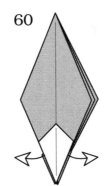

Pull out the
loose paper.

61

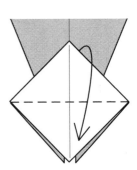

Fold one layer down.

62

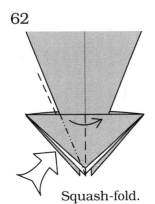

Squash-fold.

63

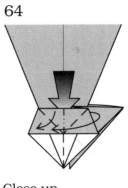

Squash-fold
again.

64

Close up,
incorporating the
reverse fold shown.

65

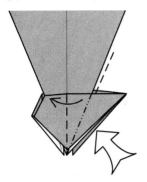

Repeat steps 62–64 on this side.

66

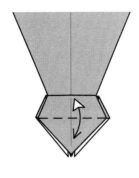

Fold and unfold the top.

67

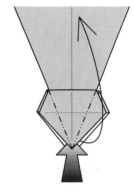

Grasp a single layer and pull it as far upward as you can.

68

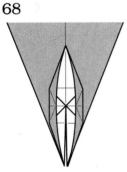

A white pyramid forms between the colored layers.

69

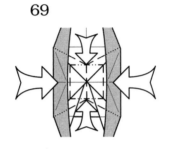

Enlarged view. Collapse the pyramid on the creases shown.

70

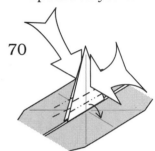

Crimp it symmetrically downward.

71

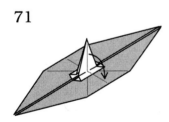

Swing the white point over to one side.

72

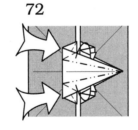

Enlarged view. Swivel-fold the edges inside.

73

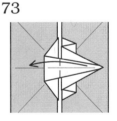

Fold the point back to the left.

74

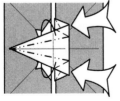

Repeat step 72 on this side.

75

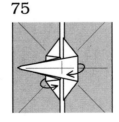

Tuck the edges under the colored layers.

76

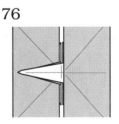

Like this.

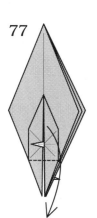

77

78

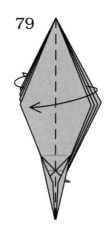

79

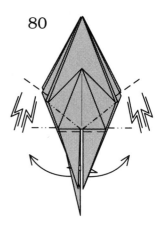

80

Fold the point downward.

Fold the edges in to the center.

Fold two layers to the left in front and two to the right behind.

Crimp symmetrically through all layers.

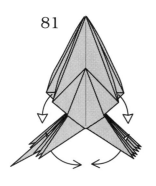

81

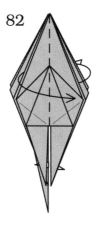

82

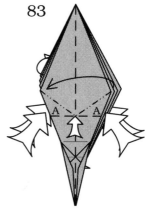

83

Undo the crimps.

Return the paper to the configuration of step 79.

Refold the crimps of step 80 with this change; on the top and bottom single layers of paper, change valley folds to mountain folds and vice-versa. The effect is to sink the edges marked A into themselves (similarly behind).

84

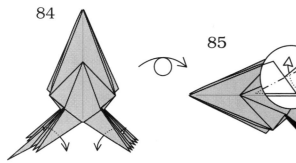

85

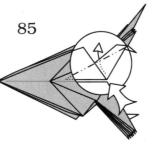

86

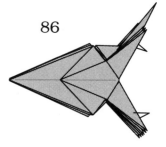

Swing the two white points (the results of steps 57 and 76) downward. Turn the paper over.

Sink the inside corner upward as far as possible.

Like this.

87

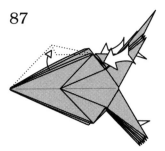

Pull out as much paper as possible; crimps at the white arrows disappear in the process.

88

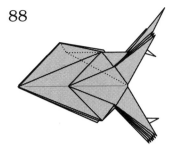

Like this. X-ray lines show hidden edges.

89

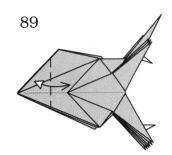

Fold and unfold (there's no reference point).

90

Enlarged view of tail. Crease the angle bisector.

91

Pleat through all layers.

92

Swivel-fold.

93

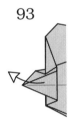

Unfold to step 90.

94

Spread the bottom layers symmetrically to form a three-sided pyramid.

95

Carefully collapse the pyramid on the creases shown.

96

Sink this corner.

97

Swivel-fold the hidden corner.

98

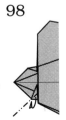

Repeat behind.

99

Fold upwards.

100

Sink.

101

Like this.

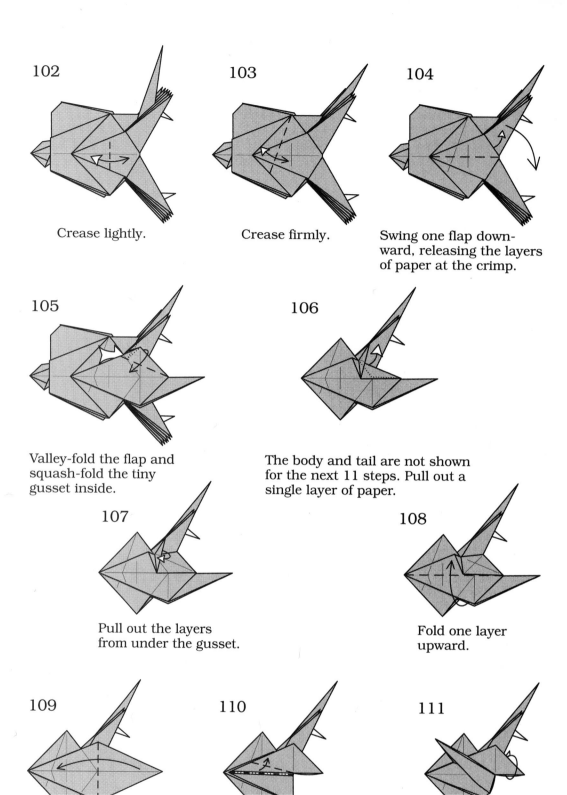

102

Crease lightly.

103

Crease firmly.

104

Swing one flap down-
ward, releasing the layers
of paper at the crimp.

105

Valley-fold the flap and
squash-fold the tiny
gusset inside.

106

The body and tail are not shown
for the next 11 steps. Pull out a
single layer of paper.

107

Pull out the layers
from under the gusset.

108

Fold one layer
upward.

109

Fold the point
over to the left.

110

Pleat the top portion of
the point; the bottom
will not lie flat.

111

With the pleat in place,
wrap one layer of paper
from front to back.

112

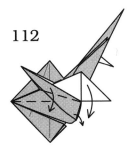

Close the model up, adding a second pleat.

113

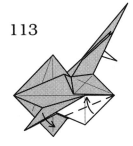

Shift the point slightly downward and fold the white edge upward.

114

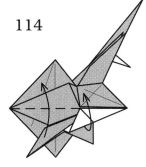

Close up the flap.

115

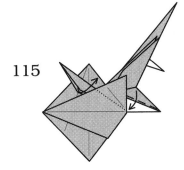

Open out the colored point and fold the single layer over the white point.

116

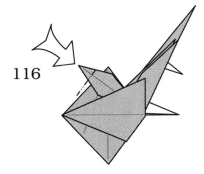

Sink the tip. This will be a fin.

117

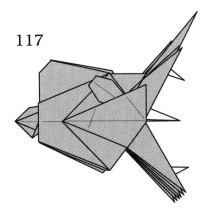

Repeat steps 102–116 on the other side of the model.

118

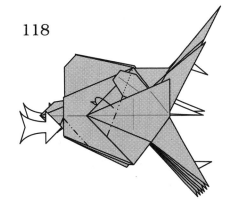

Reverse-fold the corner at the base of the tail. Mountain-fold the flap next to the fin. Repeat behind.

119

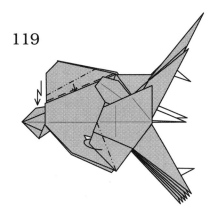

Pleat the top of the model and tuck it into the pocket shown. Mountain-fold the bottom of the model. Repeat behind.

120

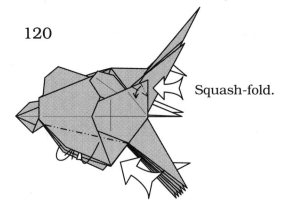

Squash-fold.

Reverse-fold a single layer.

121

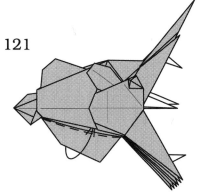

Tuck the remaining layers into the pocket you just made.

122

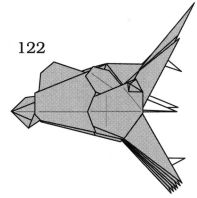

Like this.

123

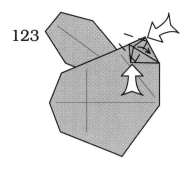

Enlarged view of fin and eye. Petal-fold. Repeat behind.

124

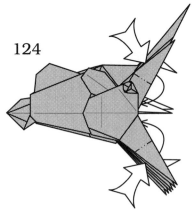

Reverse-fold the two front points into the model.

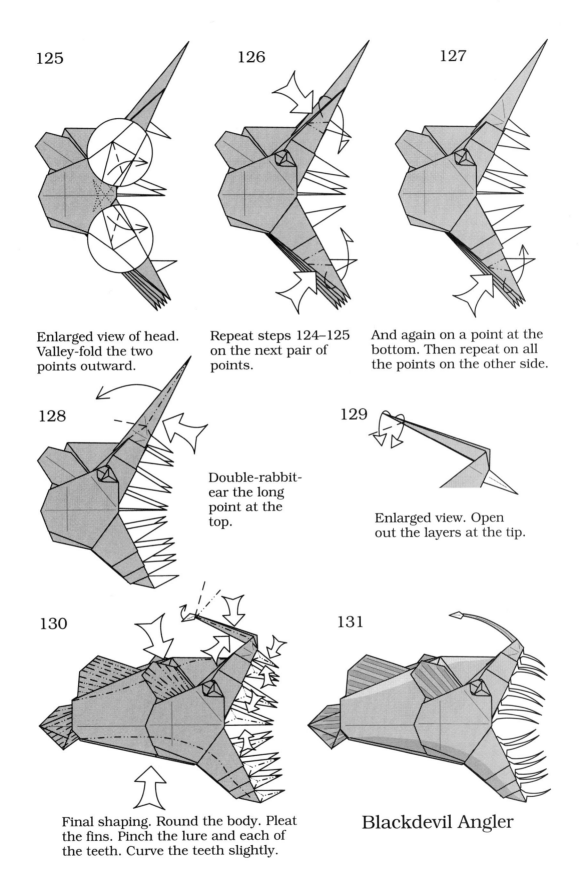

125

Enlarged view of head. Valley-fold the two points outward.

126

Repeat steps 124–125 on the next pair of points.

127

And again on a point at the bottom. Then repeat on all the points on the other side.

128

Double-rabbit-ear the long point at the top.

129

Enlarged view. Open out the layers at the tip.

130

Final shaping. Round the body. Pleat the fins. Pinch the lure and each of the teeth. Curve the teeth slightly.

131

Blackdevil Angler

Lionfish

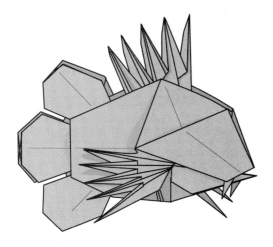

There are several species of lionfish (genus *Pterois*); they belong to the family *Scorpionidae*, which also includes the stonefish and scorpionfish. The lionfish lives in deep water but close to shore in the region along the Atlantic shore, where it ambushes smaller fish from its rocky hiding places. The lionfish is distinctively colored with red and white stripes, making it highly visible on the reefs where it makes its home. However, its long dorsal spines are tipped with a powerful toxin, making it as deadly as it is beautiful.

1

Crease the diagonals of the square.

2

Crease it vertically and horizontally.

3

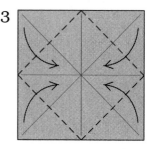

Fold the four corners to the center.

4

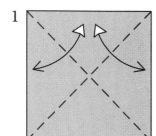

Mountain-fold the square in half.

5

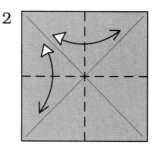

Reverse-fold the corners down to make a Preliminary Fold.

6

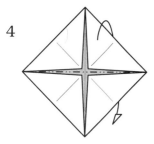

Petal-fold the model to make a Bird Base.

7

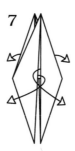

Unfold the paper completely.

8

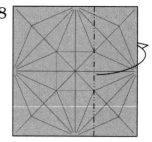

Fold the right side of the model behind.

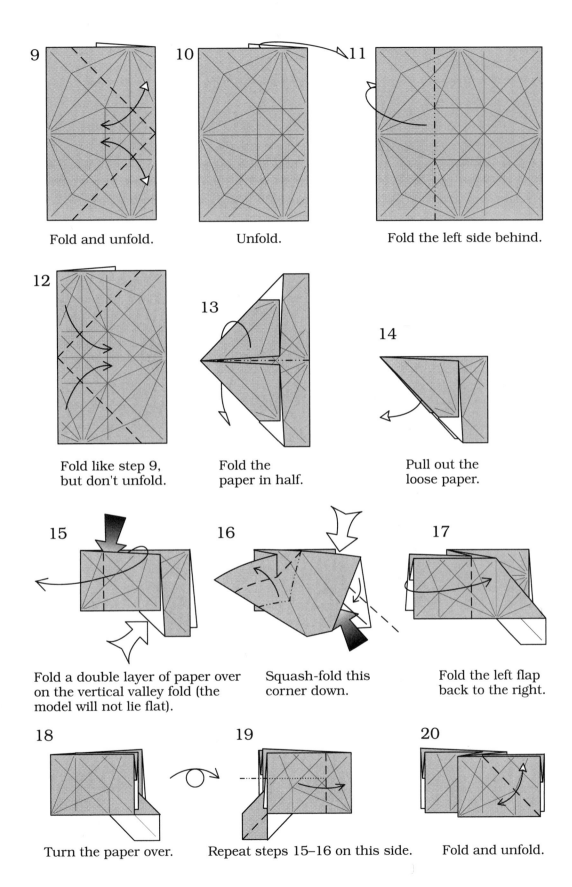

9 Fold and unfold.

10 Unfold.

11 Fold the left side behind.

12 Fold like step 9, but don't unfold.

13 Fold the paper in half.

14 Pull out the loose paper.

15 Fold a double layer of paper over on the vertical valley fold (the model will not lie flat).

16 Squash-fold this corner down.

17 Fold the left flap back to the right.

18 Turn the paper over.

19 Repeat steps 15–16 on this side.

20 Fold and unfold.

21

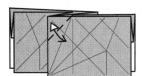

Fold and unfold.

22

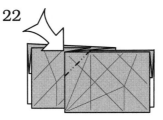

Open-sink the corner.

23

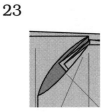

Close-up view of the sink.

24

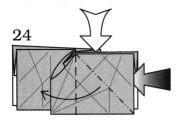

Squash-fold the right flap, letting the extra interior layers of paper lie on the right.

25

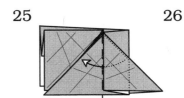

Invert the hidden corner, as if making a closed sink.

26

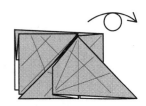

Like this. Turn the paper over.

27

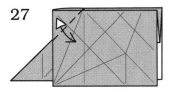

Repeat steps 21–25.

28

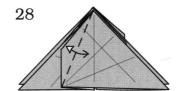

Fold and unfold.

29

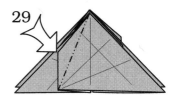

Open-sink the corner.

30

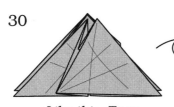

Like this. Turn the paper over.

31

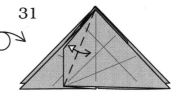

Repeat steps 28–29.

32

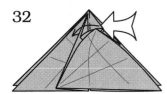

Reverse-fold a double layer of paper to the left.

33

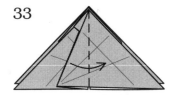

Fold one flap to the right.

34

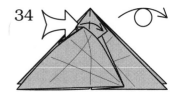

Repeat step 32 here and turn the paper over.

35

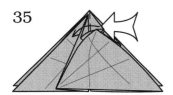

Repeat steps 32–34 on this side.

36

Fold one layer over to the right in front and one to the left in back.

37

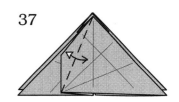

Repeat steps 28–29 here and behind.

38

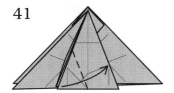

Squash-fold.

39

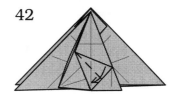

Mountain-fold the flap inside.

40

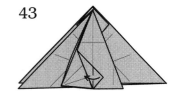

Fold and unfold.

41

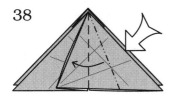

Fold this corner up to the right.

42

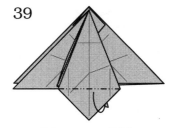

Fold it back down to the bottom.

43

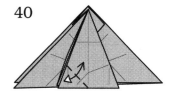

Fold the corner over to the side.

44

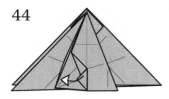

Unfold to step 40.

45

Fold the corner in to the center.

46

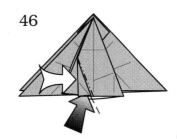

Reverse-fold.

47

Reverse-fold both hidden corners back out.

48

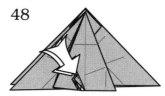

Reverse-fold all layers.

49

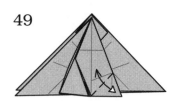

Repeat steps 40–48 on the right.

50

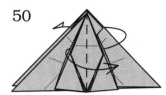

Fold all of the short flaps to the right in front and all of the long flaps to the left in back. Then rotate 1/4 turn counterclockwise.

51

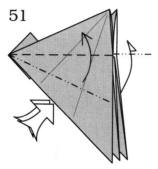

Squash-fold. Repeat behind.

52

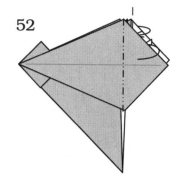

Fold into the interior.

53

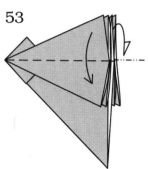

Fold one flap down on each side.

54

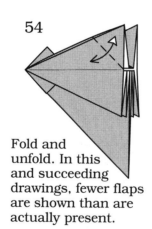

Fold and unfold. In this and succeeding drawings, fewer flaps are shown than are actually present.

55

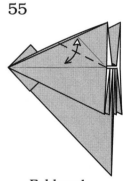

Fold and unfold.

56

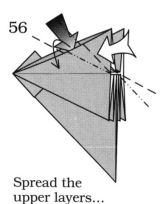

Spread the upper layers...

57

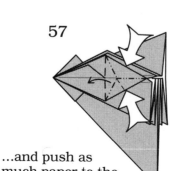

...and push as much paper to the left (from the inside) as possible. Flatten the paper.

58

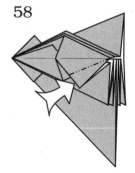

Reverse-fold.

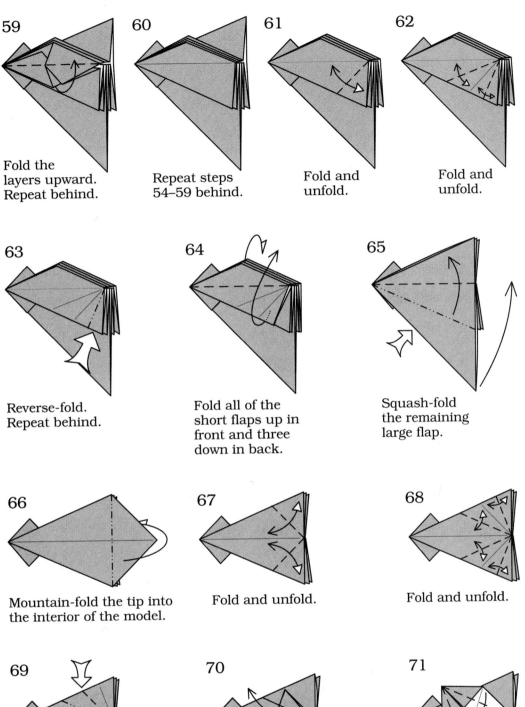

59

Fold the layers upward. Repeat behind.

60

Repeat steps 54–59 behind.

61

Fold and unfold.

62

Fold and unfold.

63

Reverse-fold. Repeat behind.

64

Fold all of the short flaps up in front and three down in back.

65

Squash-fold the remaining large flap.

66

Mountain-fold the tip into the interior of the model.

67

Fold and unfold.

68

Fold and unfold.

69

Crimp, using the existing creases.

70

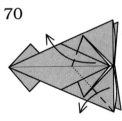

Fold the right point upward, opening out the model.

71

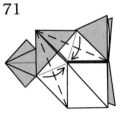

Fold the edges in to the diagonal.

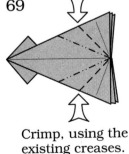

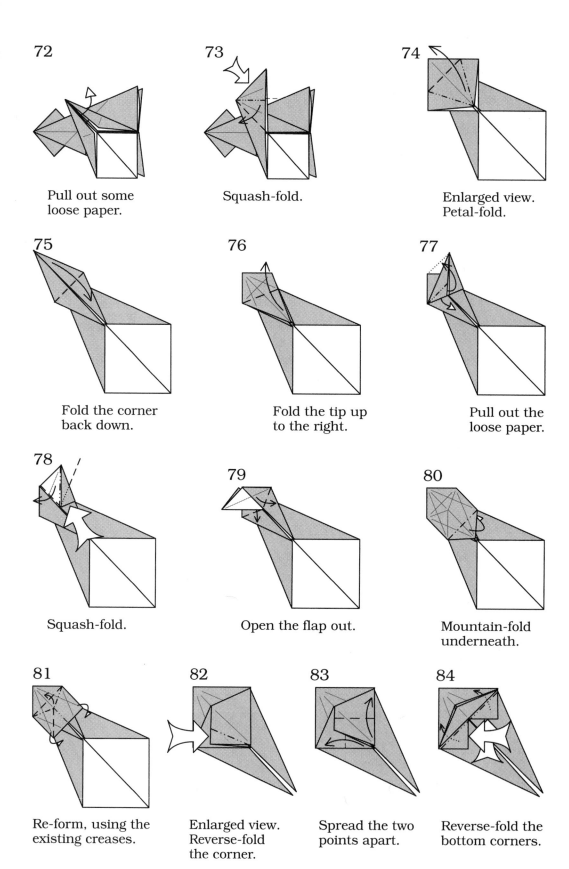

72

Pull out some
loose paper.

73

Squash-fold.

74

Enlarged view.
Petal-fold.

75

Fold the corner
back down.

76

Fold the tip up
to the right.

77

Pull out the
loose paper.

78

Squash-fold.

79

Open the flap out.

80

Mountain-fold
underneath.

81

Re-form, using the
existing creases.

82

Enlarged view.
Reverse-fold
the corner.

83

Spread the two
points apart.

84

Reverse-fold the
bottom corners.

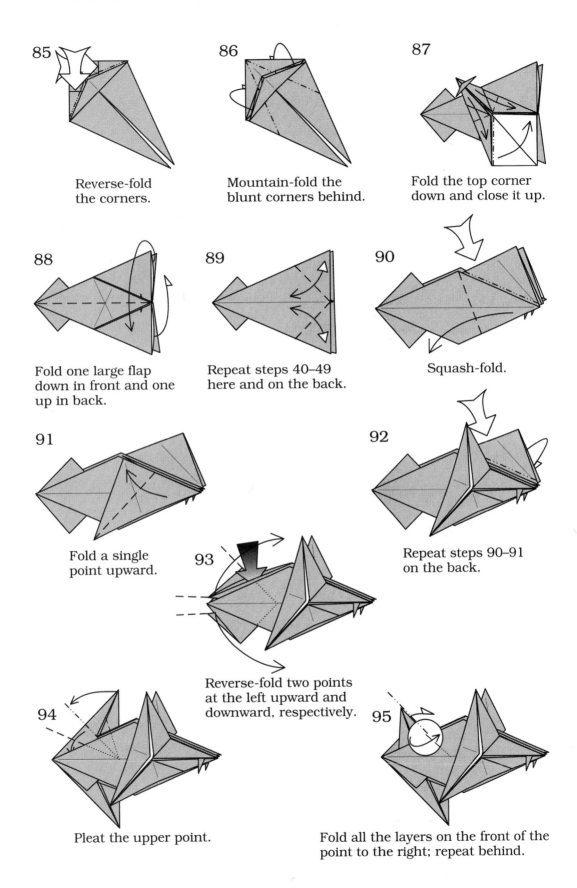

85 Reverse-fold the corners.

86 Mountain-fold the blunt corners behind.

87 Fold the top corner down and close it up.

88 Fold one large flap down in front and one up in back.

89 Repeat steps 40–49 here and on the back.

90 Squash-fold.

91 Fold a single point upward.

92 Repeat steps 90–91 on the back.

93 Reverse-fold two points at the left upward and downward, respectively.

94 Pleat the upper point.

95 Fold all the layers on the front of the point to the right; repeat behind.

Lionfish 181

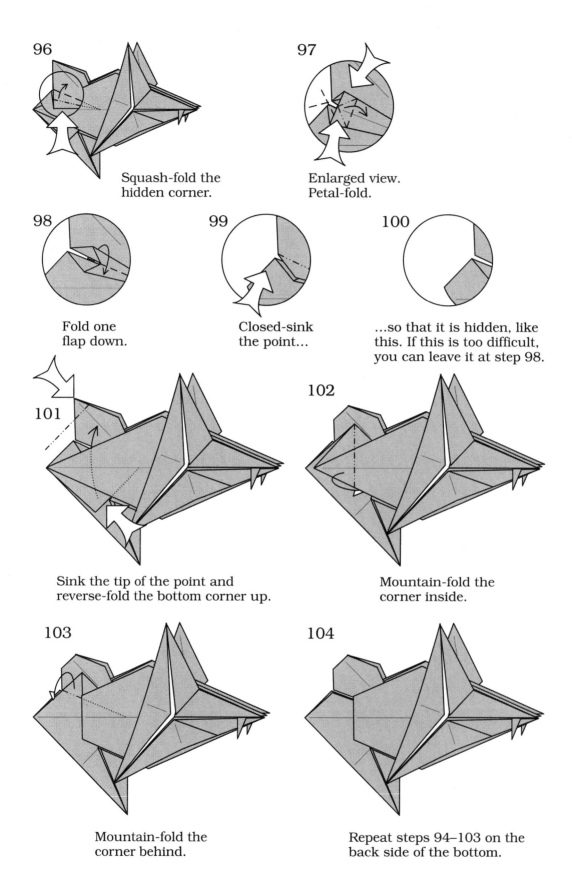

96 Squash-fold the hidden corner.

97 Enlarged view. Petal-fold.

98 Fold one flap down.

99 Closed-sink the point...

100 ...so that it is hidden, like this. If this is too difficult, you can leave it at step 98.

101 Sink the tip of the point and reverse-fold the bottom corner up.

102 Mountain-fold the corner inside.

103 Mountain-fold the corner behind.

104 Repeat steps 94–103 on the back side of the bottom.

105

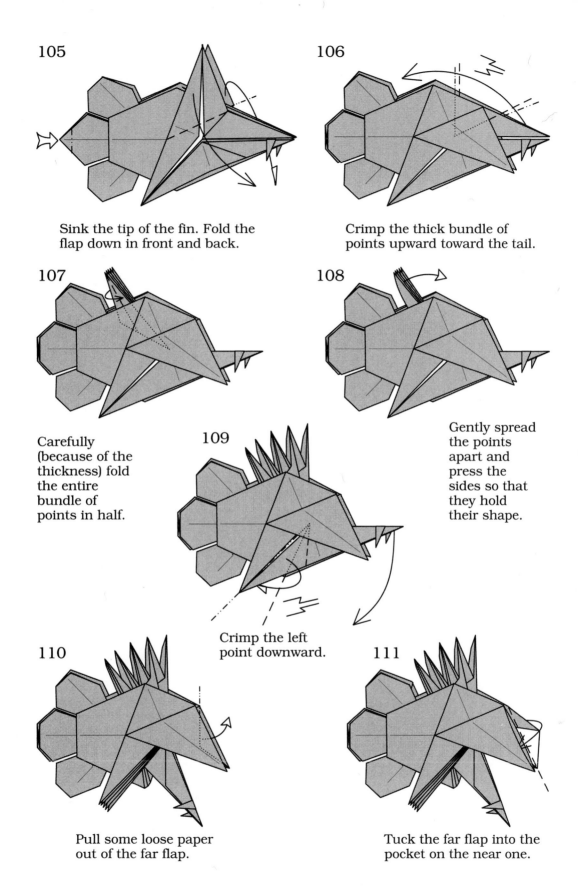

Sink the tip of the fin. Fold the
flap down in front and back.

106

Crimp the thick bundle of
points upward toward the tail.

107

Carefully
(because of the
thickness) fold
the entire
bundle of
points in half.

108

Gently spread
the points
apart and
press the
sides so that
they hold
their shape.

109

Crimp the left
point downward.

110

Pull some loose paper
out of the far flap.

111

Tuck the far flap into the
pocket on the near one.

Lionfish 183

112

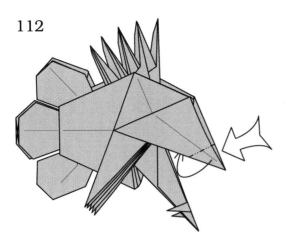

Reverse-fold the tip of the nose inside, which locks the two halves of the head together.

113

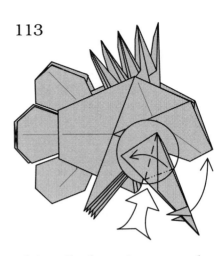

Crimp the lower jaw upward.

114

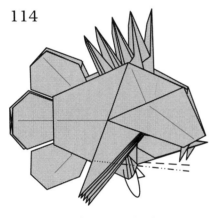

Mountain-fold the thick corners at the belly to the inside of the model (this locks the jaw crimp into place).

115

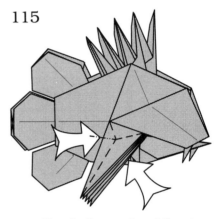

Pinch the pectoral fins in half, forming a rabbit ear through all layers.

116

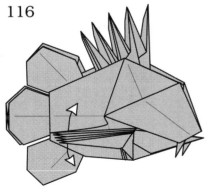

Spread the layers of the pectoral fins apart and pinch them at their base so they stand out away from the body.

117

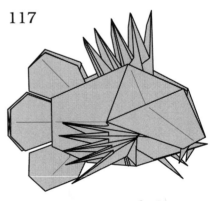

Lionfish

Echinoderms

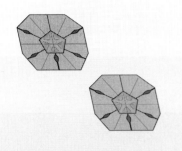

Echinoderms are built on a five-fold symmetry. There are six major groups—seastars, sea lilies, sea cucumbers, brittlestars, sand dollars, and sea urchins. All of these groups have representatives in every climate worldwide.

These spiny-skinned sea animals have an internal bony skeleton. The adult echinoderm has radial symmetry with a mouth in the center. They have many tiny tube feet which they use for moving, breathing, feeding, and feeling.

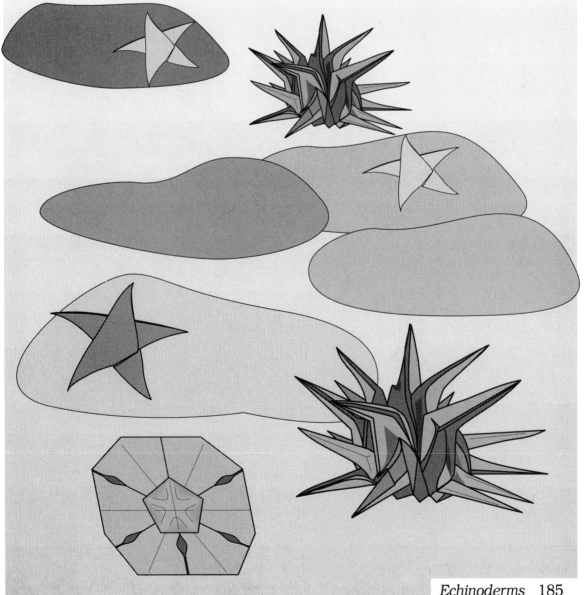

Starfish

These echinoderms usually have five arms. A newly hatched starfish swims around, settling after awhile to the bottom of the sea. It crawls around the sea floor using its tube feet. The mouth is on the underside of its body and the starfish turns its stomach inside out through the mouth to eat its prey. It feeds on oysters, clams, sponges, and other small animals. When cut, the starfish (*Asterias forbesi*) can grow new arms.

1
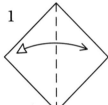

Fold and unfold.

2
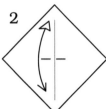

Make a small crease.

3
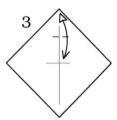

Fold the top corner to the center and unfold. Make a small crease.

4
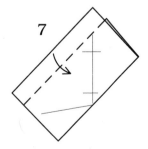

Fold up so that some point on line A–B meets the intersection in the circle.

5
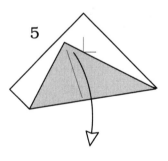

Unfold.

6
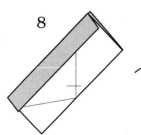

Fold behind using the intersection as a guide.

7
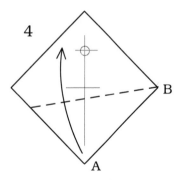

8
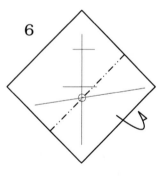

Fold along the existing creases.

9
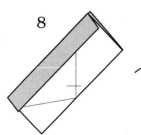

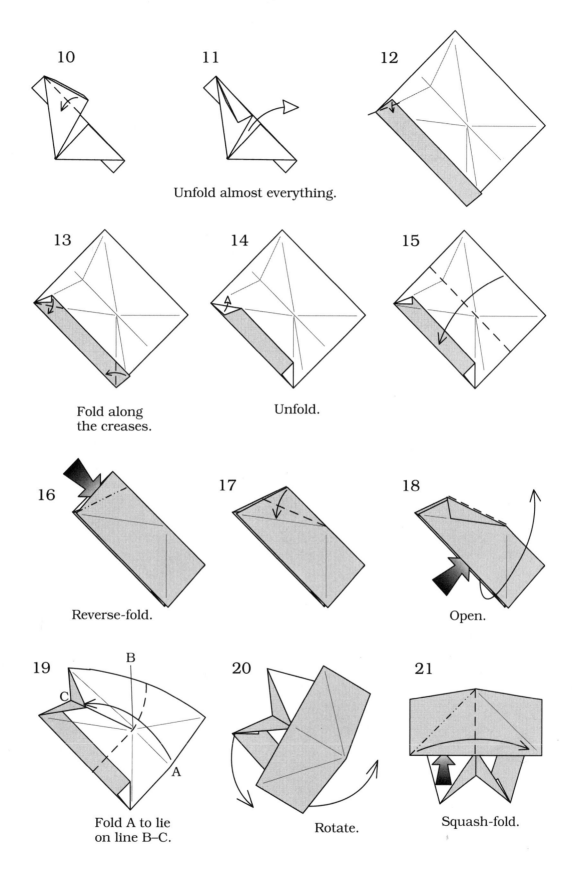

10

11

Unfold almost everything.

12

13

Fold along
the creases.

14

Unfold.

15

16

Reverse-fold.

17

18

Open.

19

B

C

A

Fold A to lie
on line B–C.

20

Rotate.

21

Squash-fold.

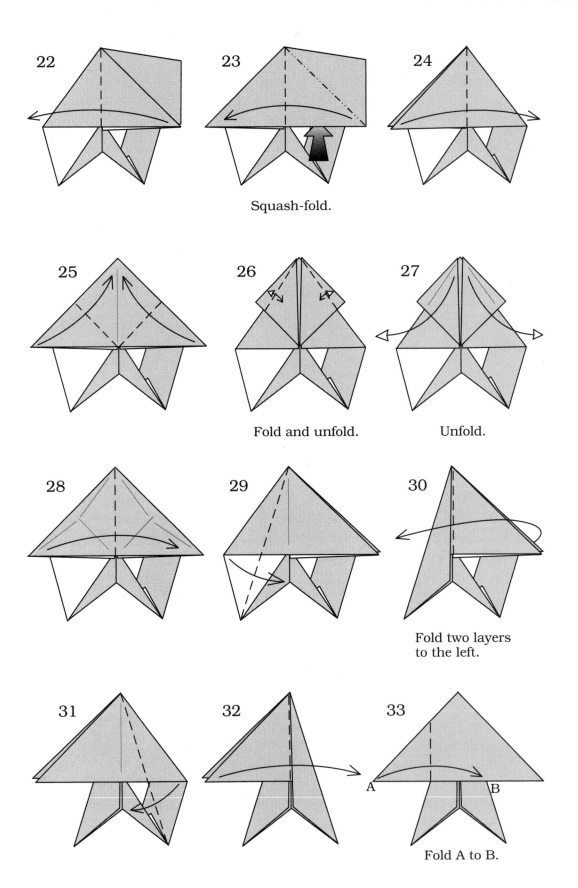

22

23

Squash-fold.

24

25

26

Fold and unfold.

27

Unfold.

28

29

30

Fold two layers
to the left.

31

32

33

A   B

Fold A to B.

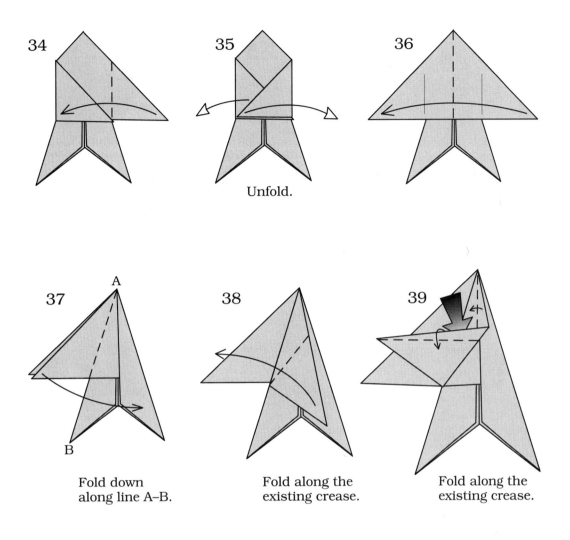

34

35

Unfold.

36

37

A

B

Fold down
along line A–B.

38

Fold along the
existing crease.

39

Fold along the
existing crease.

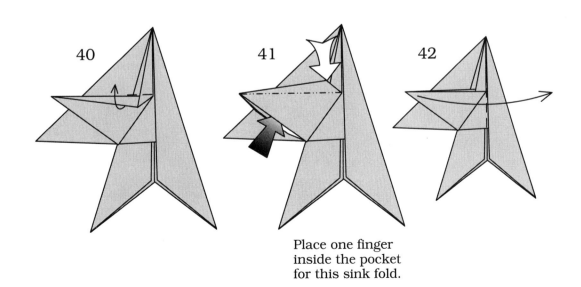

40

41

Place one finger
inside the pocket
for this sink fold.

42

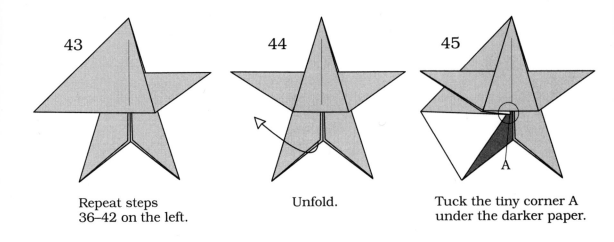

43

Repeat steps
36–42 on the left.

44

Unfold.

45

Tuck the tiny corner A
under the darker paper.

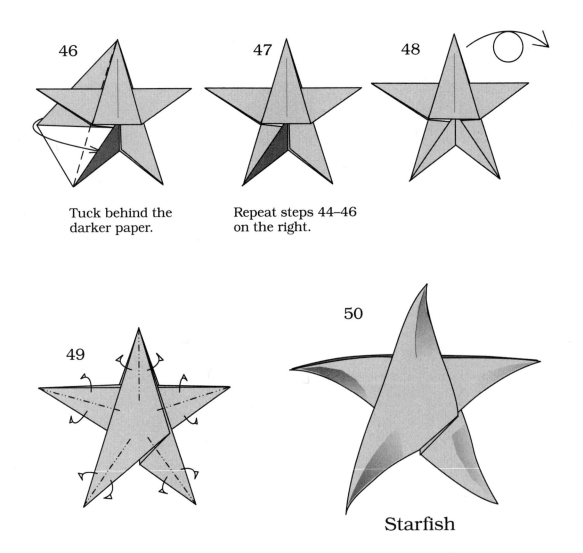

46

Tuck behind the
darker paper.

47

Repeat steps 44–46
on the right.

48

49

50

Starfish

Sand Dollar

Sand dollars are of the same class as sea urchins, but have shed their spines and adopted a flattened shape suitable for burrowing into sand. They typically stand up vertically in the sand and filter water for plankton. The Keyhole Urchin (*Millita quinquiespertorata*) lives in shallow water below low-tide lines from Cape Cod to the Caribbean and along coastal Mexico and Brazil. Its five slots begin as notches when the animal is young, but close off as it matures.

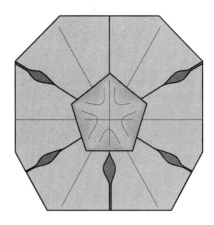

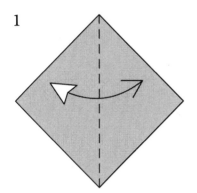

1

Crease the vertical diagonal.

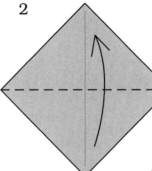

2

Fold the bottom corner up to the top.

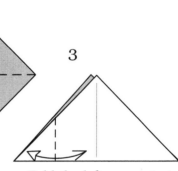

3

Fold the left corner in to the middle and unfold.

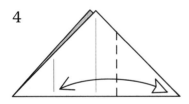

4

Fold the right corner over to the crease you just made and unfold.

5

Fold the left corner up so that the crease made in step 3 touches the crease made in step 4.

6

Fold the right corner up to cover the left one.

7

Unfold to step 3.

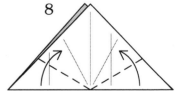

8

Fold the two bottom corners up so that their edges lie along the creases made in steps 5 and 6.

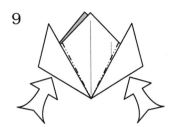

9

Reverse-fold the edges
into the model.

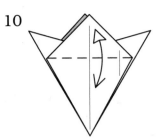

10

Crease through
one layer only.

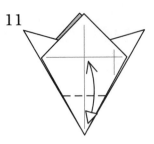
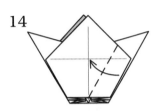

11

Fold and unfold.

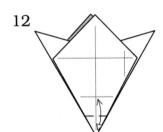

12

Fold and unfold.

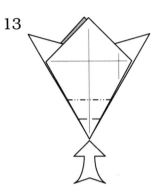

13

Double-sink the bottom
point, using the existing
creases as a guide.

14

Fold one flap up so
that its edge
touches the
intersection shown.

15

Repeat on the left, and
on both the right and
left in back.

16

Fold the two
remaining flaps
over the front flaps.

17

Fold one of the points at
the top downward and
open the model out flat.

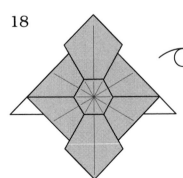

18

It looks like this.
Turn the paper over.

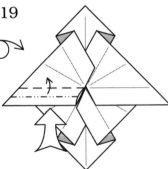

19

Symmetrically spread-
squash the flap shown.

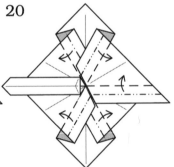

20

Repeat on the other
five similar flaps.

21

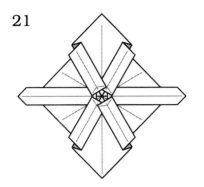

Like this. Turn
the paper over.

22

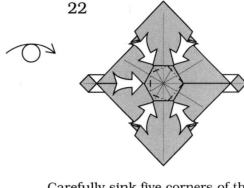

Carefully sink five corners of the
central hexagon. Note that each sink
is asymmetric, so that the result is a
pentagon. Also note that the point of
the pentagon goes toward the side,
rather than the top.

23

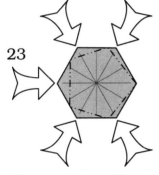

Close-up view of the sinks.

24

Rotate the model 1/4
turn counterclockwise.

25

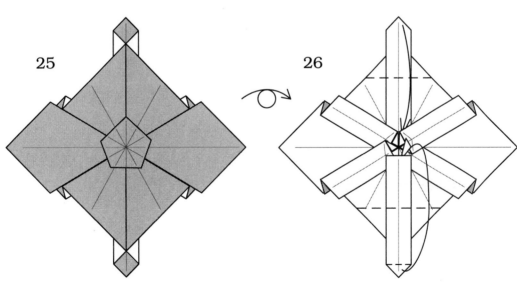

Like this. The long axis of the
model is vertical and the point of
the pentagon should point
upward. Turn the paper over
from side to side.

26

Fold the top point down and tuck its tip
under the two overlapping
spread-squashed flaps. Fold slightly more
of the bottom point up and fold its tip
over and tuck it into the pocket formed
by the bottom spread-squashed flap.

27

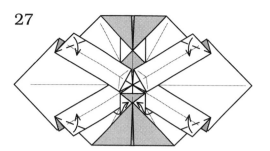

Fold the two upper corners down and the two lower corners up; tuck the sides of the lower central flap under the flaps to either side.

28

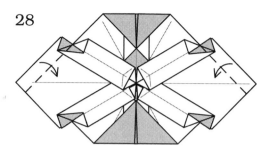

Fold the upper side edges down.

29

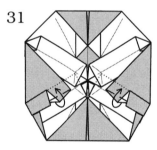

Fold the sides in.

30

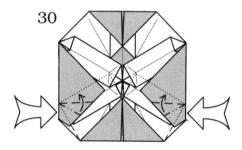

Swivel-fold the sides upward so that the mountain fold is aligned with the edge indicated by the x-ray line.

31

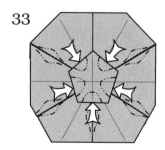

Tuck the colored flaps underneath the edges indicated by the x-ray line.

32

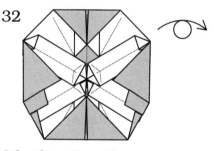

Like this. Turn the paper over from side to side.

33

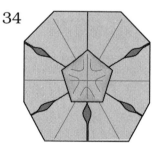

Shape the sides of the central pentagon with mountain folds. Mountain-fold the edges radiating out from the center to create the appearance of holes.

34

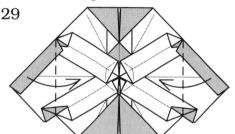

Sand Dollar

Atlantic Purple Sea Urchin

The Atlantic Purple Sea Urchin (*Arbacia punctulata*) lives on rocky coasts and shell bottoms from the low-tide line to waters 200 meters deep, and is responsible for much erosion of softer rocks and the production of sand. It has five very strong teeth in its mouth, which is located on the underside of the body. These teeth are used to rasp algae off rock surfaces and, if the rock is soft, some of it comes away as well. There are many species worldwide that range in color from delicate pink to powder blue; all are edible and are considered delicacies in Japan and France.

1

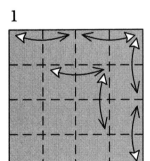

Crease the paper into fourths vertically and horizontally.

2

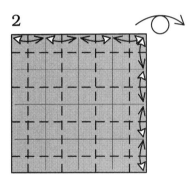

Crease it into eighths vertically and horizontally. Turn the paper over.

3

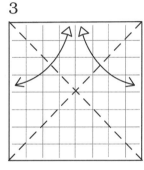

Crease the diagonals.

4

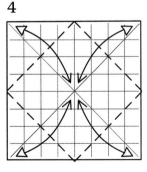

Bring the corners to the center, crease, and unfold.

5

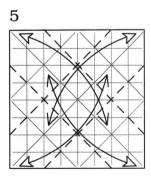

Add more diagonal creases.

6

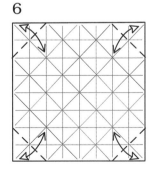

And more.

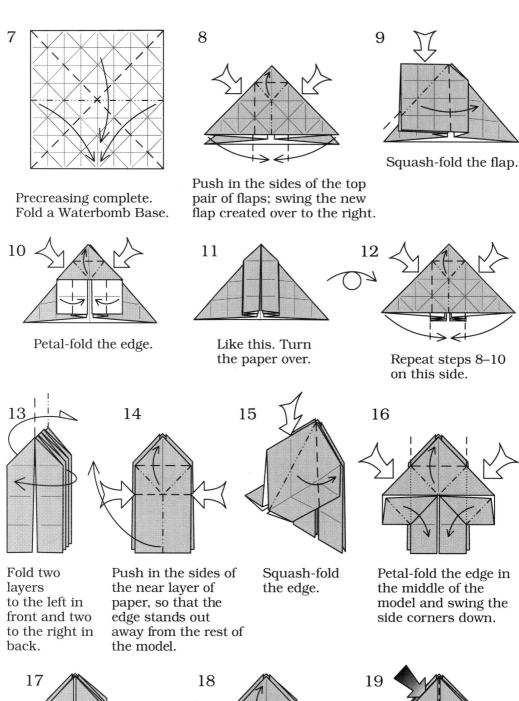

7

Precreasing complete.
Fold a Waterbomb Base.

8

Push in the sides of the top
pair of flaps; swing the new
flap created over to the right.

9

Squash-fold the flap.

10

Petal-fold the edge.

11

Like this. Turn
the paper over.

12

Repeat steps 8–10
on this side.

13

Fold two
layers
to the left in
front and two
to the right in
back.

14

Push in the sides of
the near layer of
paper, so that the
edge stands out
away from the rest of
the model.

15

Squash-fold
the edge.

16

Petal-fold the edge in
the middle of the
model and swing the
side corners down.

17

Like this.
Turn the
paper over.

18

Repeat steps 14–16
on this side.

19

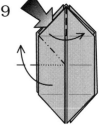

Fold one layer over to
the right and swing the
bottom left flap upward.

20

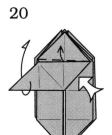

Closed-sink the corner upward.

21

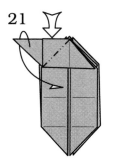

Reverse-fold the edge shown downward.

22

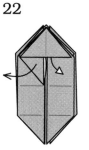

Rotate the flap clockwise and pull the loose paper out of the pocket.

23

Fold one corner to the left.

24

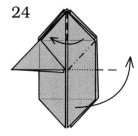

Repeat steps 19–23 on the right and on the other side.

25

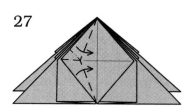

Squash-fold the point downward.

26

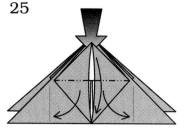

Fold down one more point.

27

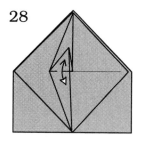

Fold a rabbit ear.

28

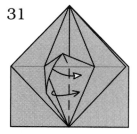

Fold the tip of the rabbit ear back and forth several times.

29

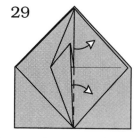

Pull a single layer of paper out from inside the rabbit ear. This is difficult because there are no loose edges to grab, but if you can get it started at the bottom corner, you can work your way up.

30

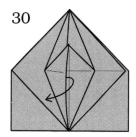

Open out the pocket slightly.

31

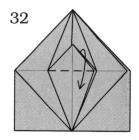

Pull the folded edge out from inside the pocket, turning a layer inside-out as you go.

32

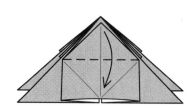

Fold the point down.

33

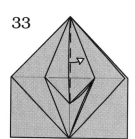

Repeat steps 30–31 on the top.

34

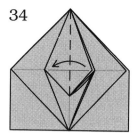

Fold one layer back to the left.

35

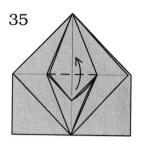

Fold the point upward.

36

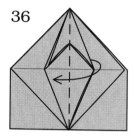

Fold all of the layers to the left.

37

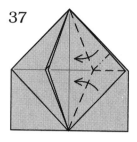

Repeat steps 27–36 on the right.

38

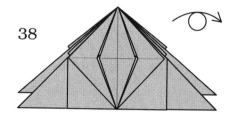

Like this. Turn the model over.

39

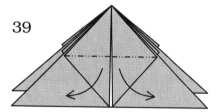

Repeat steps 25–37 on this side.

40

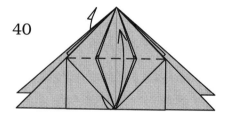

Fold one point up in front and one up in back.

41

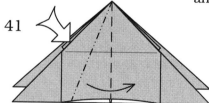

Squash-fold the indicated edge, but flatten only its upper half.

42

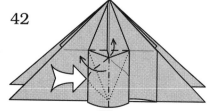

Pinch the sides of the lower part of the squash and swing the resulting flap to the left.

43

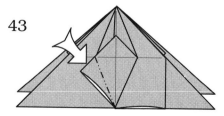

Reverse-fold the edge.

44

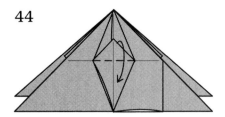

Fold the point down.

45

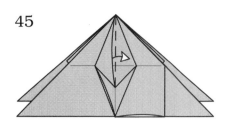

Pull the folded edge out of the pocket as in steps 30–31.

46

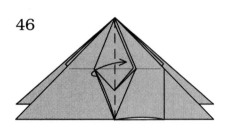

Fold all layers to the right.

47

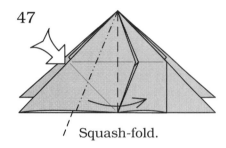

Squash-fold.

48

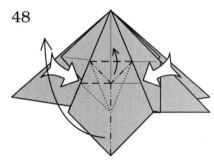

Pinch the lower edges of the squash fold together and swing the flap up to the left.

49

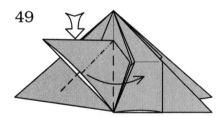

Squash-fold the new flap.

50

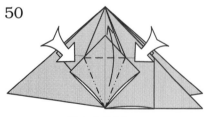

Petal-fold.

51

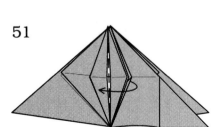

Fold all layers to the left.

52

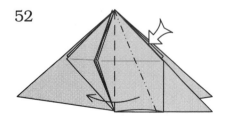

Repeat steps 41–51 on the right.

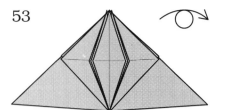

53

Turn the paper over.

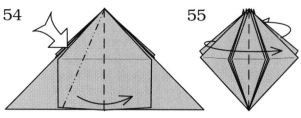

54

Repeat steps 41–52.

55

Rotate layers in front and back.

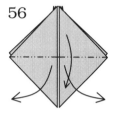

56

Squash-fold the point downward.

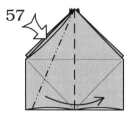

57

Repeat steps 41–45.

58

Fold the layers back to the left.

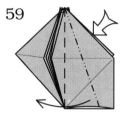

59

Repeat 41–46 on the right.

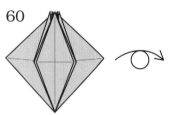

60

Turn the model over.

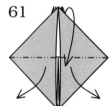

61

Repeat steps 55–60.

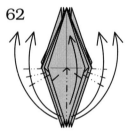

62

Reverse-fold all 12 points at the bottom upward. The model is very thick, and you should not try to flatten it out. Rather, fan the layers in all directions so that the model becomes conical and three-dimensional.

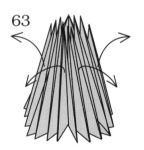

63

Rabbit-ear each of the 25 points outward and adjust them to point in all directions.

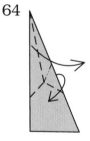

64

Detail of a single point. Fold a rabbit ear.

65

Like this.

66

Atlantic Purple Sea Urchin

Crustaceans

The crustaceans belong to the much larger group of arthropods. The phylum *Arthropoda* in turn, is the largest single grouping of animals in the world as it contains all the insects. The most well-known crustaceans, the crabs, shrimps, and lobsters, belong to the group known as decapods or ten-legged crustaceans (*deca* means ten and *pod* means leg or foot). They are found in all the waters of the world, fresh as well as salt, and from the poles to the equator.

Almost all crustaceans live underwater. Most of them have two pairs of antennas and some have eyes on movable stalks. Crustaceans have at least five pairs of legs. Their boneless bodies are protected by an outer shell.

Bay Barnacle

The Bay Barnacle (*Balanus improvisus*) is commonly found attached in great masses to rocks, pilings, oysters, and other hard-shelled animals. Unlike most barnacles, it tolerates fresh water at least occasionally, and is commonly found in bays and brackish estuaries. Barnacles are filter feeders, using their feathery legs to comb the water for plankton and other small organisms.

1

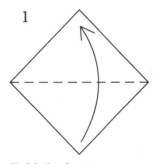

Fold the bottom corner up to the top.

2

Fold the bottom edge up almost to the top corner (the exact amount isn't critical).

3

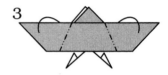

Fold the two corners down so that they cross each other.

4

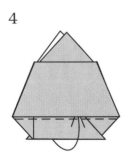

Fold all the layers together as one and tuck inside the model.

5

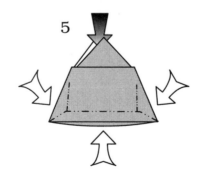

Push in the sides and bottom to make the model three-dimensional.

6

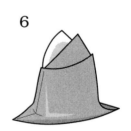

Bay Barnacle

Horseshoe Crab

The Horseshoe Crab (*Limulus polyphemus*) is the only American example of its subclass, the *Xiphosura*. The larvae are called "trilobite larvae" because of their resemblance to trilobite fossils, and it is believed that the trilobites were the ancestors of the *Xiphosura*. Horseshoe crabs have relatively simple eyes, which has resulted in their being extensively used in neurophysiological research.

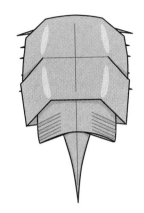
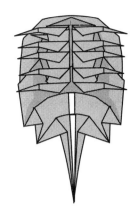

1

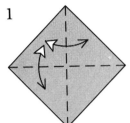

Crease the vertical and horizontal diagonals. Turn the paper over.

2

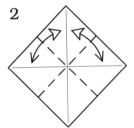

Fold the paper in half and unfold.

3

Fold a Preliminary Fold.

4

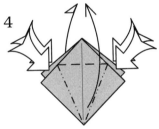

Petal-fold to make a Bird Base.

5

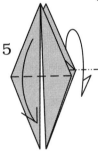

Fold the front and back flaps down.

6

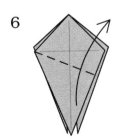

Fold the front flap up and to the right at right angles to the right edge.

7

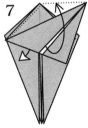

Pull the raw edge upward and release the loose paper under the flap.

8

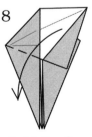

Fold the flap back down.

9

Fold the flap up to the left.

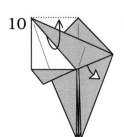

10

Pull out the
trapped layer.

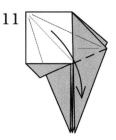

11

And fold the
flap back
down.

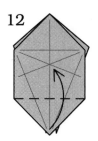

12

Fold the bottom
point up to the
intersection of
the two creases.

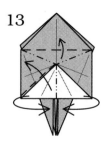

13

Bring the lower
corners together,
folding on
existing creases.

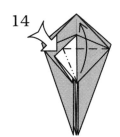

14

Squash-fold.

15

Pull out the
trapped layer
of paper.

16

Fold half of a
Preliminary
Fold with the
single layer.

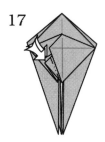

17

Reverse-fold
both edges.

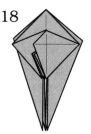

18

Turn the
model over.

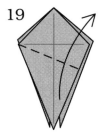

19

Repeat steps 6–17
on this side.

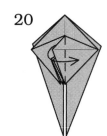

20

Fold the bundle
of layers over to
the right.

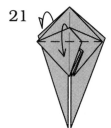

21

Fold the layer
down in front
and behind.

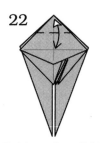

22

Fold and unfold.

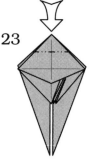

23

Sink the point
downward.

24

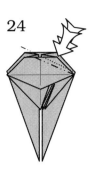

Sink two corners. They must be done simultaneously.

25

Fold one layer to the left in front and one to the right in back.

26

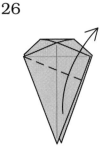

Repeat steps 6–11 on this flap.

27

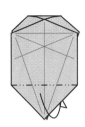

Mountain-fold the point underneath.

28

Bring the lower corners together as in step 13.

29

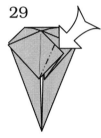

Reverse-fold the edge.

30

Valley-fold the two lower corners up to the sides.

31

Reverse-fold the corners.

32

Fold a Preliminary Fold through all of the thick layers.

33

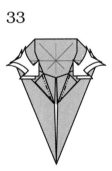

Reverse-fold four edges.

34

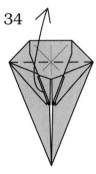

Lift the top pair of points upward as far as possible, letting the other four pairs fan out.

35

Like this.

36

Press in between the points and flatten them all downward, spacing them evenly. The dotted line indicates where the top pair folds down.

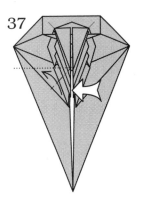

37

Like this. Reverse-fold the lowest corner out to the side.

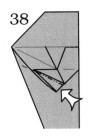
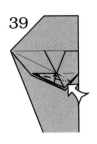

38

Only the lowest point is shown in steps 38–40. Reverse-fold the lower edge.

39

Reverse-fold a single edge.

40

Sink the corner and edges.

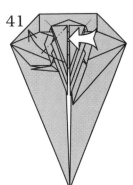

41

Reverse-fold the remaining four points on this side out to the side (only the top one is shown here).

42

Reverse-fold both edges of each point to narrow it. Repeat on the other four points.

43

Tuck the upper half of each leg inside the lower half.

44

Crimp each leg downward.

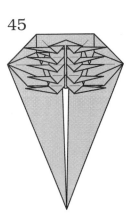

45

Repeat steps 37–42 on the right side.

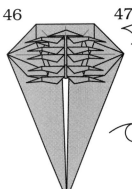

46

Like this. Turn the paper over.

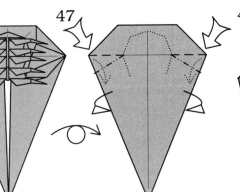

47

Round the body and crimp the corners as shown. Although it is difficult, the model will hold together better if you make each crimp symmetrical, thus making a closed sink of each corner.

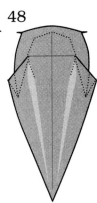

48

Like this.

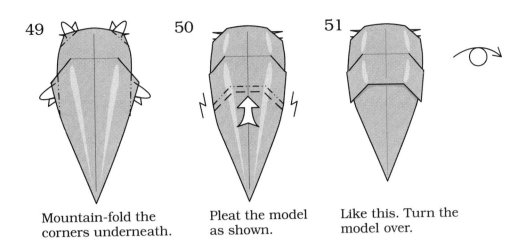

49 Mountain-fold the corners underneath.

50 Pleat the model as shown.

51 Like this. Turn the model over.

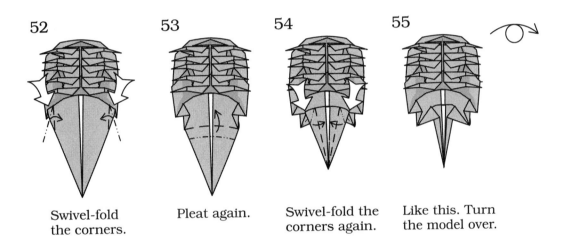

52 Swivel-fold the corners.

53 Pleat again.

54 Swivel-fold the corners again.

55 Like this. Turn the model over.

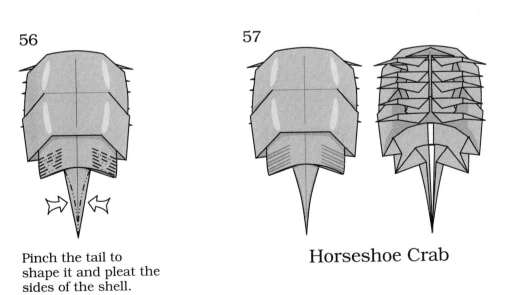

56 Pinch the tail to shape it and pleat the sides of the shell.

57

Horseshoe Crab

Hermit Crab

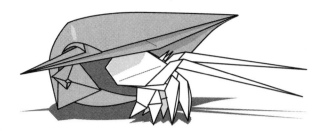

Hermit Crabs are represented by two families, *Coenbitoidea* and *Panguroidea*. Representatives of both families are notable in that they live inside the deserted shell of another animal, typically a whelk or snail. The rear of the hermit crab is soft and its hind legs are atrophied, except for a single pair used to hold the crab inside the shell. The crab keeps the shell until it outgrows it and must find another. Hermit crabs come in a rainbow of colors and make very good pets as they are clean and require little attention.

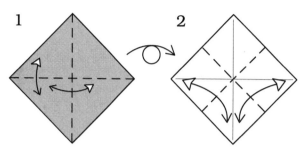

1

Crease the diagonals. Turn the model over.

2

Crease in half and unfold.

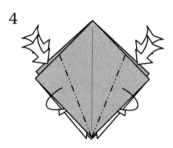

3

Fold a Preliminary Fold.

4

Enlarged view. Reverse-fold four corners to make a Bird Base.

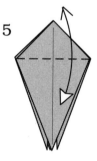

5

Enlarged view. Fold and unfold.

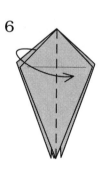

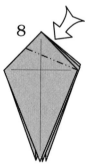

6

Fold one layer over from left to right.

7

Crease.

8

Open the top point out and sink it on the existing creases.

9

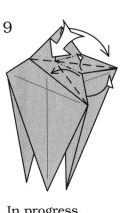

In progress.

10

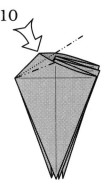

Sink the
remaining
corner.

11

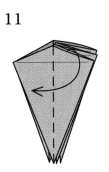

Fold one layer
over to the left.

12

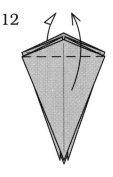

Fold one point
up in front and
in back.

13

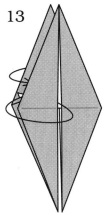

Color-change
both of the
flaps on the left.

14

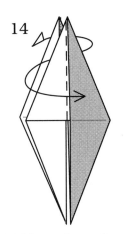

Fold one layer from
left to right in front
and one from right
to left in back.

15

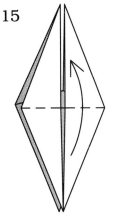

Lift up one
point.

16

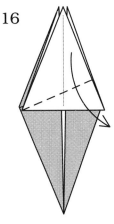

Fold the point
down along a line
perpendicular to
the right edge.

17

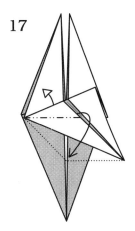

Pull out the
loose paper.

18

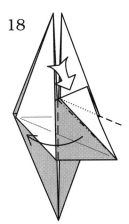

Squash-fold.

19

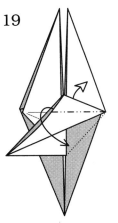

Pull out the
loose paper.

20

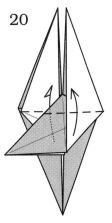

Outside-reverse-fold
the flap upward.

Hermit Crab 209

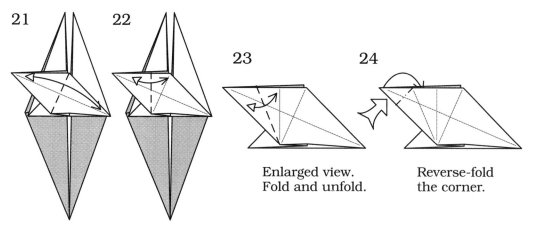

21 Fold and unfold.

22 Fold and unfold.

23 Enlarged view. Fold and unfold.

24 Reverse-fold the corner.

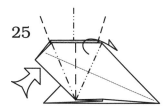

25 Crimp symmetrically.

26 Reverse-fold three hidden corners.

27 Reverse-fold the three corners again.

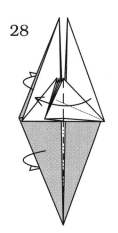

28 Fold one white layer over to the left in front and one colored layer over to the right behind.

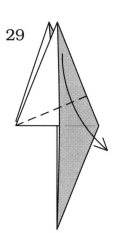

29 Fold one point down along a line perpendicular to the right edge.

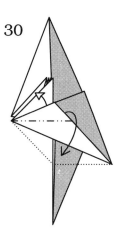

30 Pull out the loose paper.

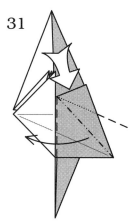

31 Squash-fold.

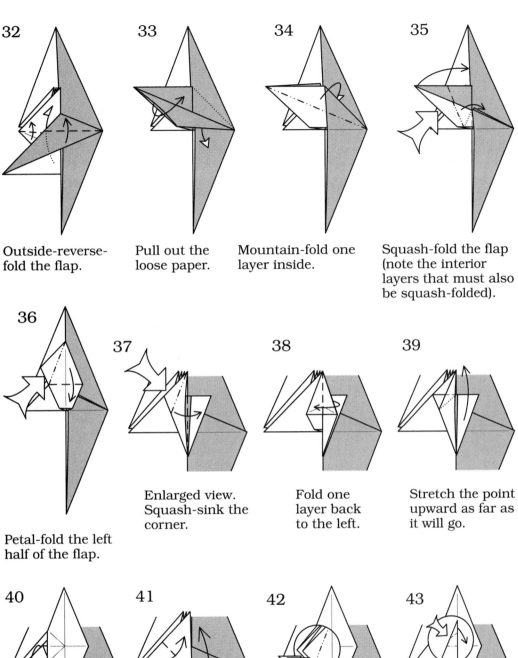

32 Outside-reverse-fold the flap.

33 Pull out the loose paper.

34 Mountain-fold one layer inside.

35 Squash-fold the flap (note the interior layers that must also be squash-folded).

36 Petal-fold the left half of the flap.

37 Enlarged view. Squash-sink the corner.

38 Fold one layer back to the left.

39 Stretch the point upward as far as it will go.

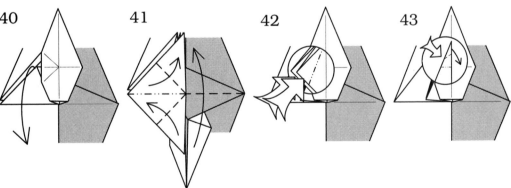

40 Fold down one layer from the left; the long flap comes too.

41 Form half of a Preliminary Fold from the left side and fold the point upward.

42 Reverse-fold the two corners.

43 Crimp the tiny hidden point with two reverse folds.

44

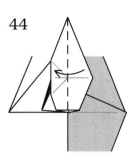

Fold one layer from right to left.

45

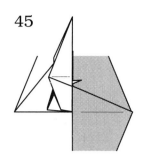

Repeat steps 29–45 on the other side.

46

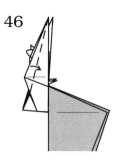

Narrow each of the two long points with valley folds.

47

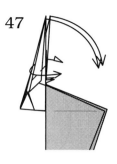

Outside-reverse-fold.

48

Sink the edges to narrow the points.

49

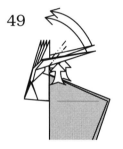

Inside-reverse-fold.

50

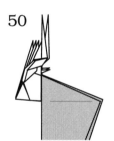

Like this.

51

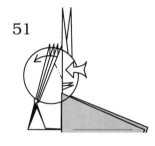

Enlarged view. Reverse-fold the next point. Repeat behind.

52

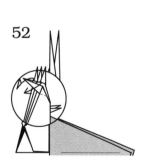

Outside-reverse-fold the point. Repeat behind.

53

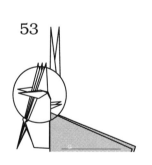

Like this.

54

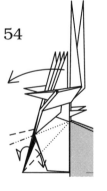

Crimp the group of four points downward.

55

Reverse-fold the middle corner.

56

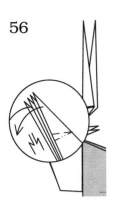

Crimp the outer pair of points downward.

57

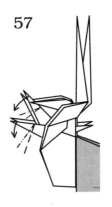

Crimp the tips of all four points downward.

58

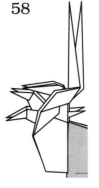

Like this.

59

Fold one layer from the right to the left, and rotate the body of the crab away from you.

60

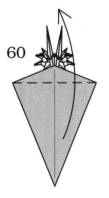

Fold the point upward.

61

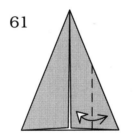

Crease lightly.

62

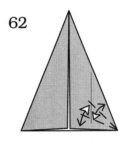

Fold and unfold.

63

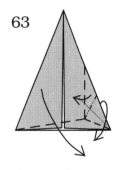

Fold a rabbit ear.

64

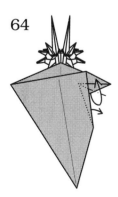

Swivel-fold.

65

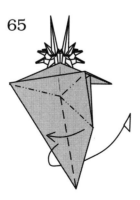

Fold a rabbit ear. The model becomes three-dimensional.

66

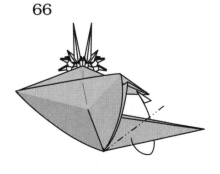

Mountain-fold the long point upward .

Hermit Crab 213

67

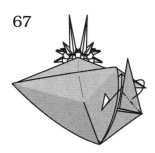

Mountain-fold the point behind again.

68

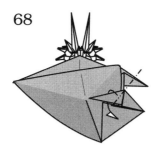

Continue mountain-folding the point until you run out of point.

69

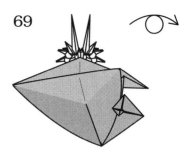

Like this. Turn the model over.

70

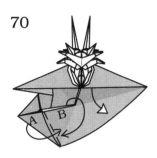

Bring points A and B together and pull out the loose paper on the right.

71

Push the excess paper upward and shape the shell by mountain-folding the rim; the body of the crab should be inside the shell.

72

Pinch the spine on the left side of the shell and shape the left side.

73

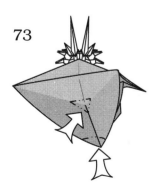

Sink the two corners shown; this helps the shell to keep its shape.

74

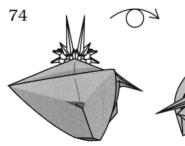

Like this. Turn the model over.

75

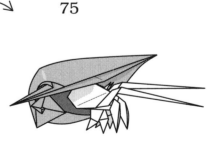

Hermit Crab

Blue Crab

The Blue Crab (*Callinectes sapidus*) is a commercially important species that supports a fishing industry in Chesapeake Bay and all along the Atlantic and Gulf coasts. This species has been overexploited through the years, and its numbers have been greatly reduced, but the population has now stabilized due to many fishing restrictions on size, sex, and season for harvest. Some fish farms are even experimenting to see if there is a practical method of culturing them. Blue crabs can get to be 5 or 6 inches across and have a hard shell that is blue above and white below. Immediately after molting, however, the shell is soft and papery, and they are sold (and devoured) as "soft-shell crab."

1

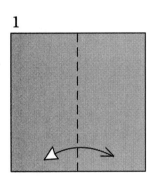

Fold the paper in half and unfold.

2

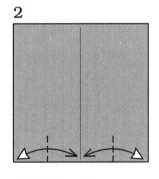

Fold the edges to the center, crease, and unfold.

3

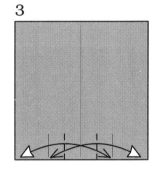

Fold and unfold.

4

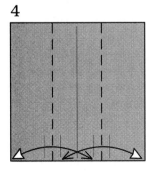

Fold and unfold.

5

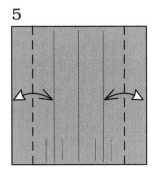

Fold and unfold.

6

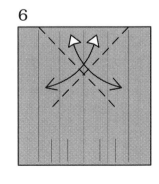

Fold and unfold.

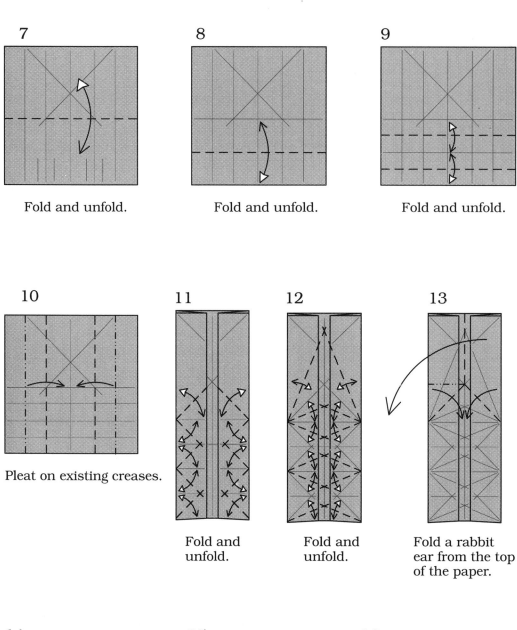

7

Fold and unfold.

8

Fold and unfold.

9

Fold and unfold.

10

Pleat on existing creases.

11

Fold and unfold.

12

Fold and unfold.

13

Fold a rabbit ear from the top of the paper.

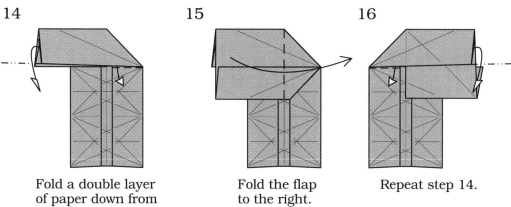

14

Fold a double layer of paper down from inside the rabbit ear.

15

Fold the flap to the right.

16

Repeat step 14.

17

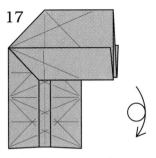

Like this. Turn the paper over from top to bottom.

18

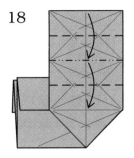

Pleat on existing creases.

19

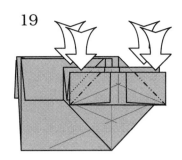

Reverse-fold four corners.

20

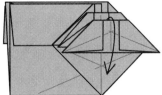

Fold one flap down.

21

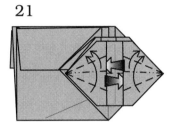

Fold it back up, incorporating the reverse folds shown.

22

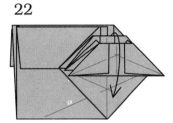

Fold two flaps down.

23

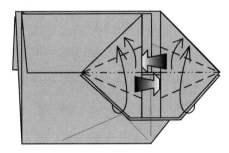

Fold them back up, incorporating the reverse folds shown.

24

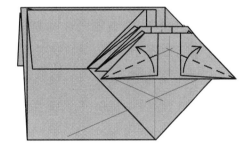

Valley-fold the flaps upward.

25

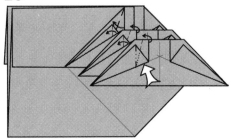

Reverse-fold all the layers on the left side of the pleats.

26

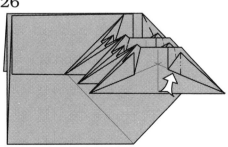

Reverse-fold the layers on the right.

27

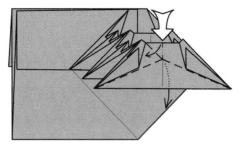

Push the middle of the top pleat down, making the small vertical pleat in the middle. The paper will not lie flat.

28

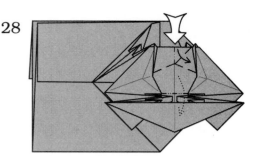

Repeat on the other pleat.

29

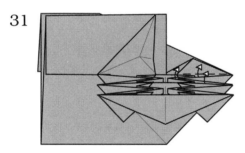

Reverse-fold the right edge and reassemble the creases that came unfolded in the previous step.

30

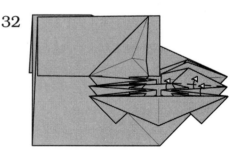

Pull out a single layer of paper from the double thickness rabbit ear to make it symmetric about a horizontal axis.

31

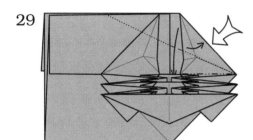

Again, pull out a single layer from the double thickness.

32

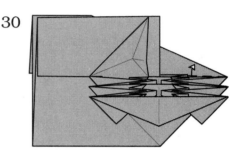

Again.

33

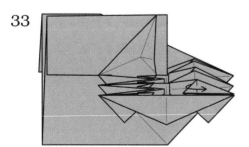

Fold the small flap over to the right.

34

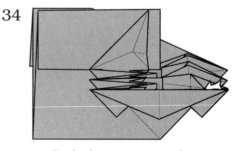

Sink the point into the interior of the model.

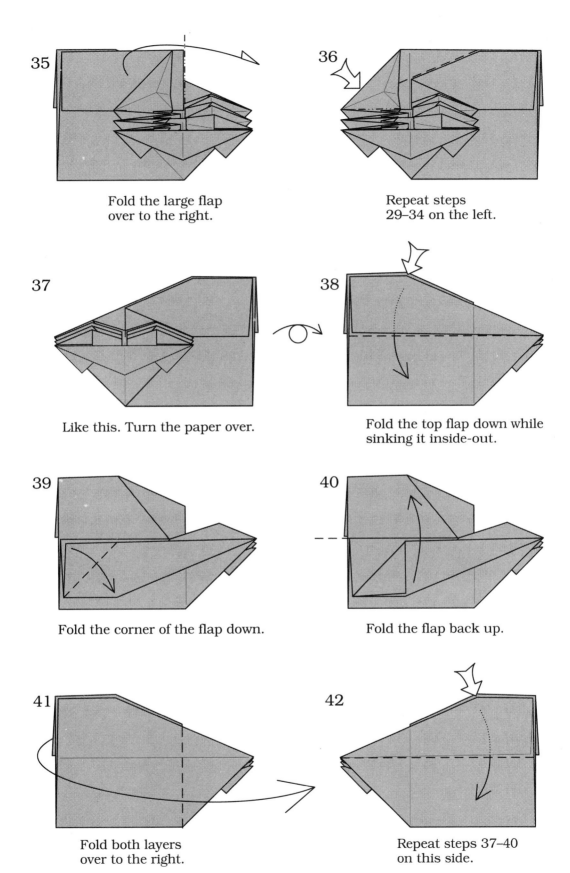

35 Fold the large flap over to the right.

36 Repeat steps 29–34 on the left.

37 Like this. Turn the paper over.

38 Fold the top flap down while sinking it inside-out.

39 Fold the corner of the flap down.

40 Fold the flap back up.

41 Fold both layers over to the right.

42 Repeat steps 37–40 on this side.

43

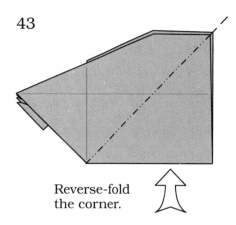

Reverse-fold the corner.

44

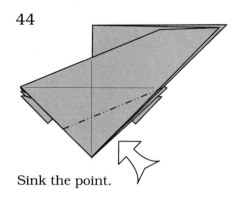

Sink the point.

45

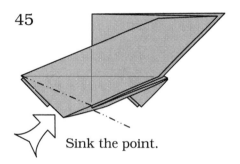

Sink the point.

46

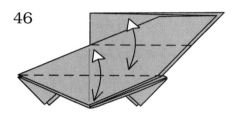

Fold and unfold.

47

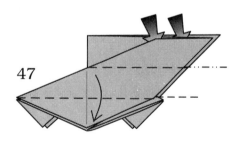

Pleat all layers individually, so that the two flaps remain separated.

48

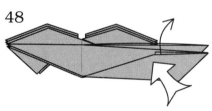

Grasp the original corner of the square that is inside the near flap and pull it entirely out of the flap.

49

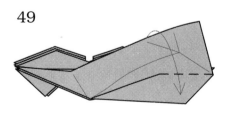

Fold down. The paper will not lie flat.

50

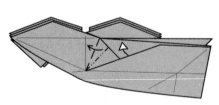

Crimp the paper toward the middle of the model and pull out the paper where shown.

51

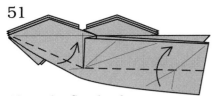

Close the flap back up.

52

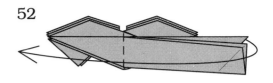

Fold both flaps
over to the left.

53

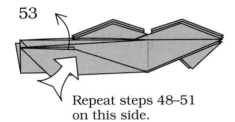

Repeat steps 48–51
on this side.

54

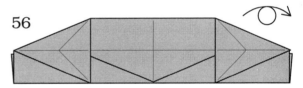

Fold one flap over to the right.

55

Lift one layer up and
sink the corners.

56

Like this. Turn the paper
over from side to side.

57

Fold and unfold.

58

Fold and unfold.

59

Reverse-fold both corners.

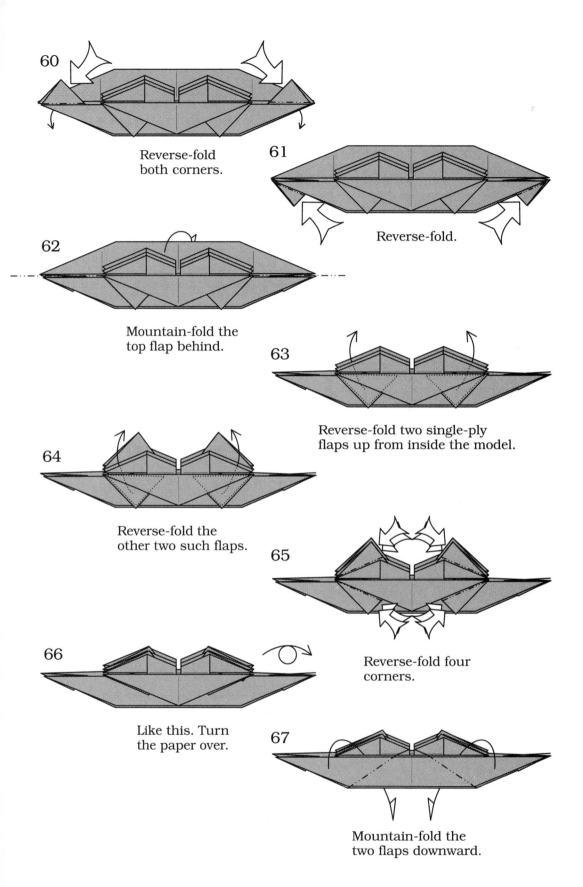

60 Reverse-fold both corners.

61 Reverse-fold.

62 Mountain-fold the top flap behind.

63 Reverse-fold two single-ply flaps up from inside the model.

64 Reverse-fold the other two such flaps.

65 Reverse-fold four corners.

66 Like this. Turn the paper over.

67 Mountain-fold the two flaps downward.

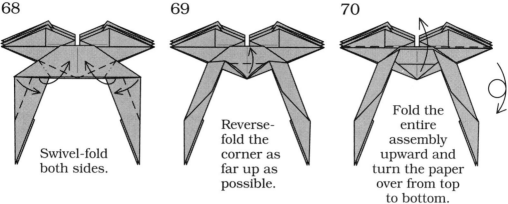

68

Swivel-fold both sides.

69

Reverse-fold the corner as far up as possible.

70

Fold the entire assembly upward and turn the paper over from top to bottom.

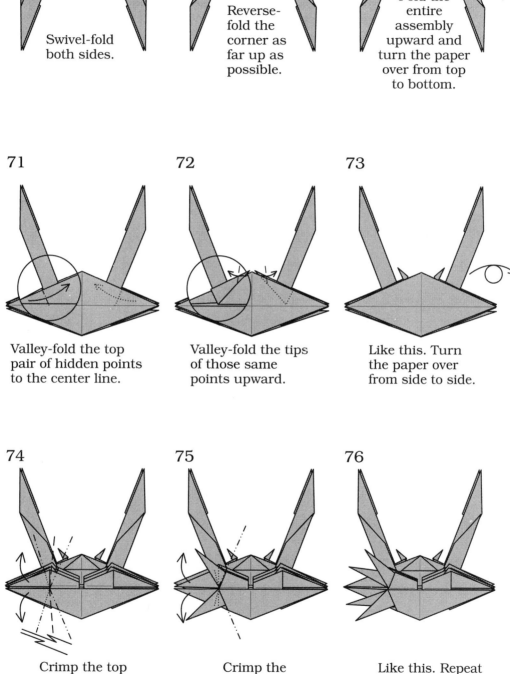

71

Valley-fold the top pair of hidden points to the center line.

72

Valley-fold the tips of those same points upward.

73

Like this. Turn the paper over from side to side.

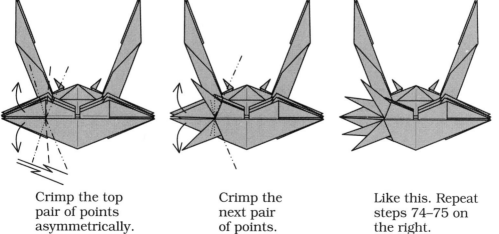

74

Crimp the top pair of points asymmetrically.

75

Crimp the next pair of points.

76

Like this. Repeat steps 74–75 on the right.

77

Mountain-fold the layers at the bottom.

78

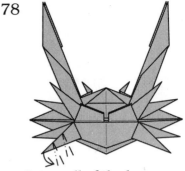

Crimp all of the legs (only one is shown here).

79

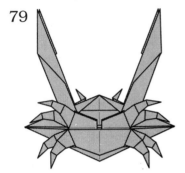

Like this. Turn the model over.

80

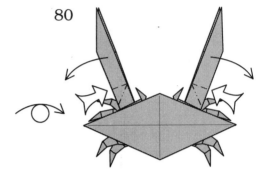

Crimp the two long flaps outward.

81

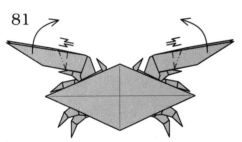

Crimp again.

82

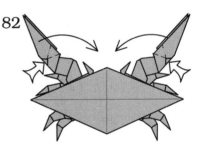

Squash-fold the claws toward each other.

83

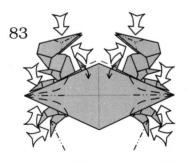

Pinch the tips of the claws and the spines on the sides of the shell. Shape the body to be three-dimensional, and squash-fold the bottommost pair of legs.

84

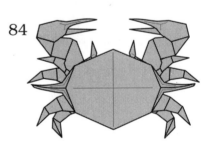

Blue Crab

Fiddler Crab

Fiddler crabs are members of the genus *Uca* and are named for the single enlarged pincer possessed by the male of the species. They use their large claw primarily for courtship displays and battles with other males. If the claw breaks off, as occasionally happens, it will regenerate as a small claw while the other claw enlarges to take its place. Most fiddler crabs are found in the mangrove swamps of the tropics, where they eat the detritus left by the receding tide. They are among the most numerous inhabitants of the mangroves and as a result, are the prey of almost every larger creature.

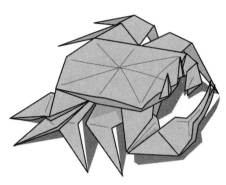

1

Crease the diagonals.

2

Fold two rabbit ears, with the points going in opposite directions.

3

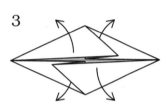

Unfold.

4

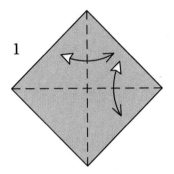

Crease as shown, making the creases sharp only where the dashed lines are.

5

Mountain-fold the top half behind.

6

Fold the corner upward so that its edge hits the intersection shown; repeat behind.

7

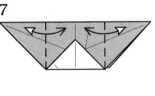

Fold and unfold.

8

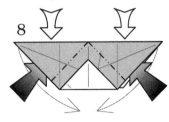

Reverse-fold two corners.

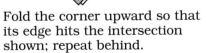

9

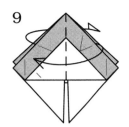

Fold one layer to the
left in front and one to
the right in back.

10

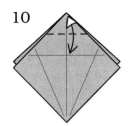

Fold and unfold.

11

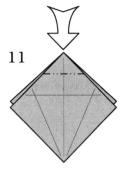

Sink.

12

Repeat step 9, folding
down the top edge in
front and back.

13

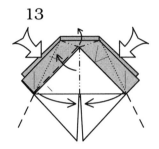

Squash-fold the sides and
swing the white flap over
to the left.

14

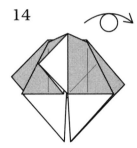

Like this. Turn
the paper over.

15

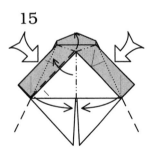

Repeat step 10
on this side.

16

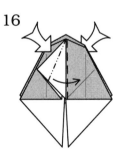

Squash-fold.
Repeat behind.

17

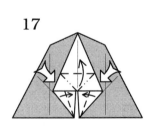

Enlarged view.
Petal-fold.

18

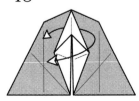

Unwrap one layer.

19

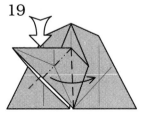

Squash-fold.

20

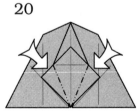

Reverse-fold
the edges.

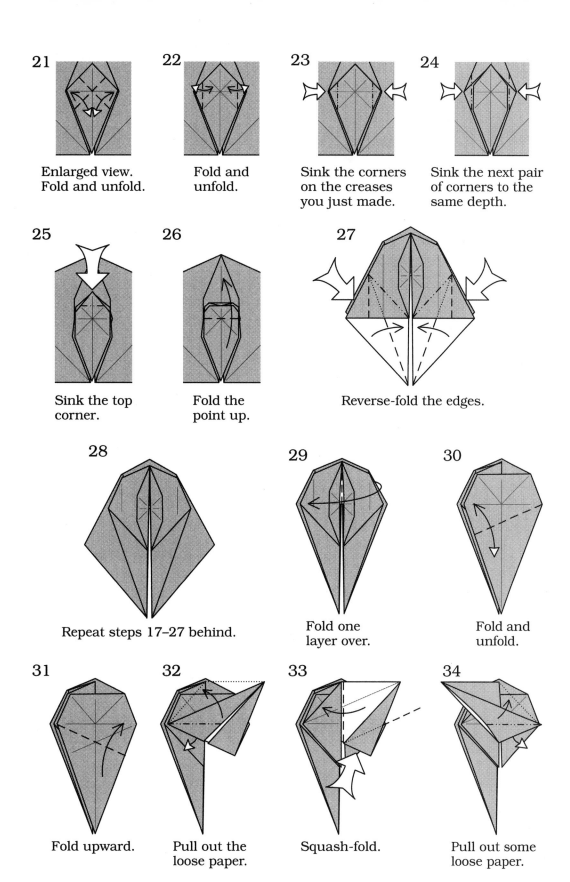

21 Enlarged view. Fold and unfold.

22 Fold and unfold.

23 Sink the corners on the creases you just made.

24 Sink the next pair of corners to the same depth.

25 Sink the top corner.

26 Fold the point up.

27 Reverse-fold the edges.

28 Repeat steps 17–27 behind.

29 Fold one layer over.

30 Fold and unfold.

31 Fold upward.

32 Pull out the loose paper.

33 Squash-fold.

34 Pull out some loose paper.

Fiddler Crab 227

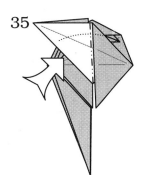

35

Reverse-fold
the point over
to the right.

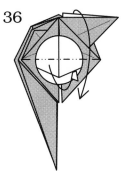

36

Fold the top point
down; at the same
time swing the
hidden point up
inside the model.

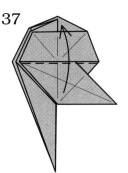

37

Fold the point
back up.

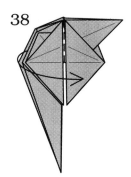

38

Fold one layer
over to the right.

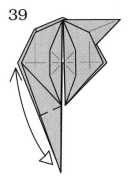

39

Fold and unfold.

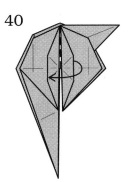

40

Fold one layer
over to the left.

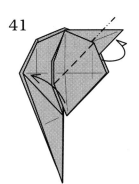

41

Fold one layer
up to the left;
repeat behind.

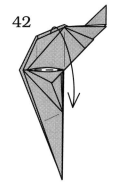

42

Fold the top down
and flatten it.

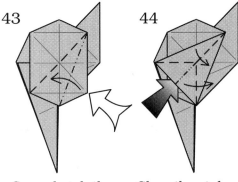

43

Spread-sink the
indicated point.

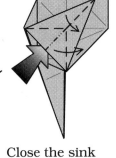

44

Close the sink
up, incorporating
the reverse fold
at the bottom.

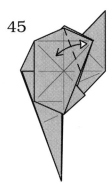

45

Fold and
unfold.

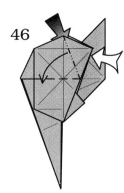

46

Open out the upper
edges of the point to
form a three-sided
pyramid.

47

Push in the right side of the pyramid while reverse-folding its upper edge to the right.

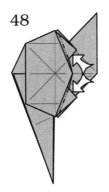

48

Reverse-fold both edges.

49

Like this. Turn the paper over.

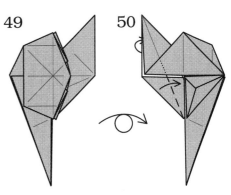

50

Valley-fold one layer.

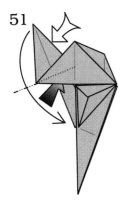

51

Reverse-fold the top corner down.

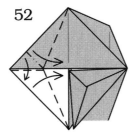

52

Fold a rabbit ear.

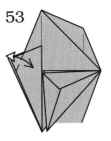

53

Fold and unfold.

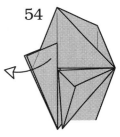

54

Unfold the rabbit ear.

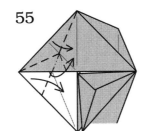

55

Fold a different kind of rabbit ear.

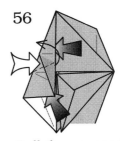

56

Pull the upper edge to the left and sink the lower edge.

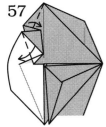

57

Tuck the two-toned corner into the pocket and flatten.

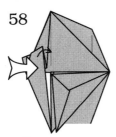

58

In progress.

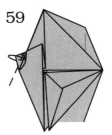

59

Tuck the corner into the pocket.

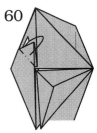

60

Tuck the corner into the pocket.

Fiddler Crab 229

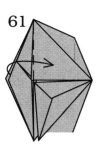

61 Fold one corner to the right.

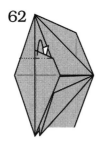

62 Mountain-fold the corner.

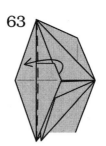

63 Fold the layer back to the left.

64 Swivel the right point upward.

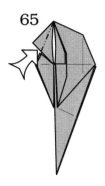

65 Reverse-fold the edge.

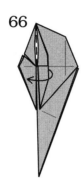

66 Fold all of the narrow layers over to the left.

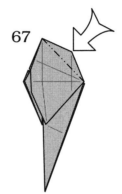

67 Sink the corner.

68 Fold upward.

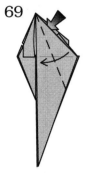

69 Open flat the sunk corner.

70 Close it back up.

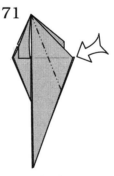

71 Sink the corner.

72 Squash-fold the corner asymmetrically, with three layers going to the right and one to the left.

73

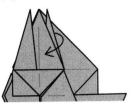

Lift the right point
up to release it.

74

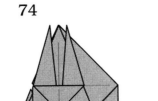

Like this.

75

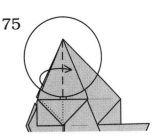

Behind the two points, fold
one layer over to the right,
releasing two more points.

76

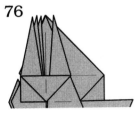

Like this.

77

Fold the long
point upward.

78

Fold one layer
upward.

79

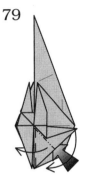

Swivel the
right point
downward.

80

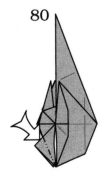

Reverse-fold
the edge.

81

Bring the
hidden point
to the front.

82

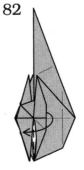

Fold all narrow
layers over to
the left.

83

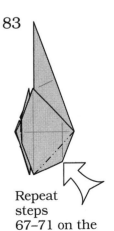

Repeat
steps
67–71 on the
bottom.

84

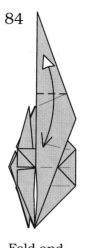

Fold and
unfold.

85

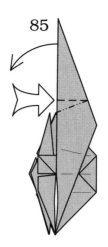

Crimp the point
over to the left.

86

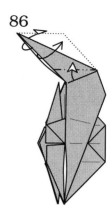

Pull out some loose
paper; repeat behind.

87

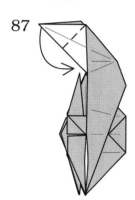

Reverse-fold
the corner.

88

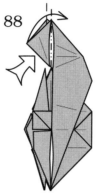

Reverse-fold
the corner.

89

Narrow the long
point with a
rabbit ear on
both sides.

90

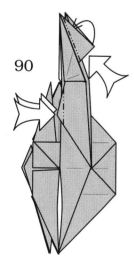

Sink the two lower corners
that protrude beyond the
left edge. Reverse-fold the
edge at the top.

91

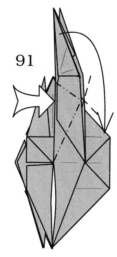

Simultaneously make
two reverse folds. Then
rotate the model 1/4
turn counterclockwise.

92

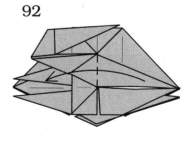

Fold one point over
from right to left.

93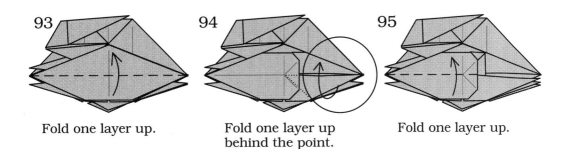

Fold one layer up.

94

Fold one layer up
behind the point.

95

Fold one layer up.

96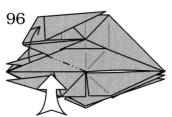

Reverse-fold the point
upward to match the
larger one.

97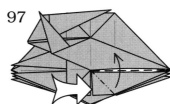

Squash-fold the corner
symmetrically.

98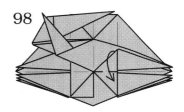

Fold one layer
downward.

99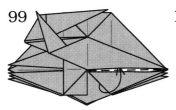

Tuck the layer under-
neath the raw edge.

100

Swing two points
over to the right.

101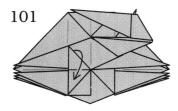

Repeat steps 98–99
on this flap.

102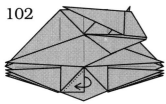

Tuck the corner into
the pocket behind it.

103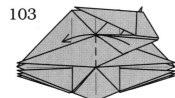

Fold the large point
over to the left.

104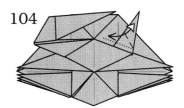

Fold the right edge of the
point down to the dotted
line and unfold.

105

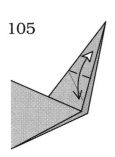

Fold and unfold.

106

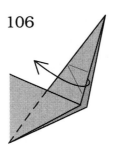

Open the flap.

107

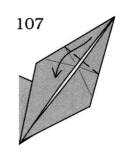

Fold the tip down.

108

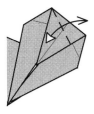

Fold and unfold.

109

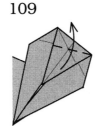

Fold the point upward
so that its left edge is
aligned with the layer
behind it.

110

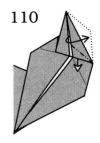

Pull out the
loose paper.

111

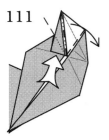

Squash-fold.

112

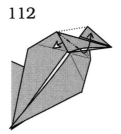

Pull out the
loose paper.

113

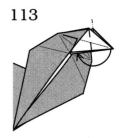

Reverse-fold.

114

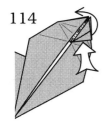

Reverse-fold.

115

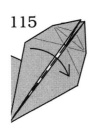

Close the
flap up.

116

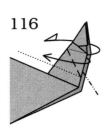

Outside-reverse-fold
on the creases you
made in step 104.

117

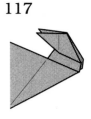

Like this.

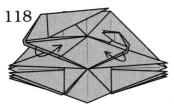

118

Tuck the "elbows" of the claws into the pockets beneath them (similar to steps 98–99).

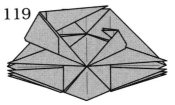

119

Like this. Turn the model over.

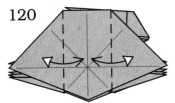

120

Fold and unfold.

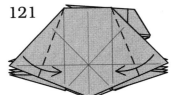

121

Fold the upper edges in to the creases you just made.

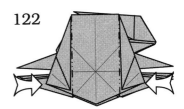

122

Carefully closed-sink the corners into the body.

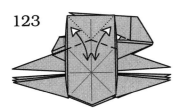

123

Fold and unfold.

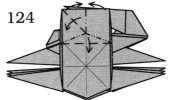

124

Crimp the body and swing the two points toward each other.

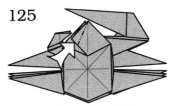

125

Reverse-fold the edge.

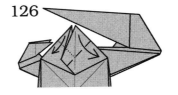

126

Spread the two points at the top out to the sides.

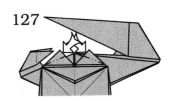

127

Reverse-fold the edges.

Fiddler Crab 235

128

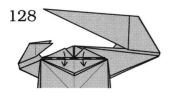

Fold the two thick edges downward.

129

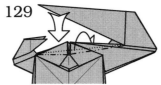

Reverse-fold the left side and mountain-fold the right side at the top of the body.

130

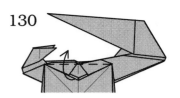

Fold all the layers upward.

131

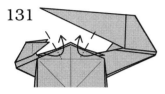

Twist the two trapped points forward so that they point up and out.

132

Like this.

133

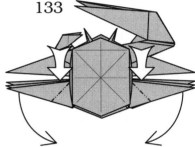

Reverse-fold the thick pair of points downward.

134

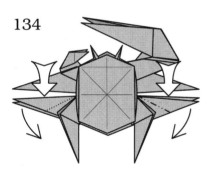

Reverse-fold the next pair of points downward (note that the left one is inside another point).

135

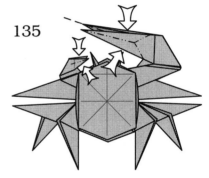

Pinch both pincers of each claw to shape them.

136

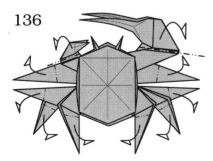

Mountain-fold all of the legs and claws downward and puff up the body to shape it.

137

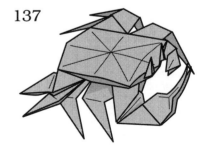

Fiddler Crab

American Lobster

This dark green crustacean has large claws used for crushing and cutting its prey of mollusks and small fish. The lobster (*Homarus americanus*) grows to about two feet long and walks along the ocean floor. It is protected by a hard outer exoskeleton. To grow, it sheds its exoskeleton. While the new one is forming, the lobster hides in holes in the ocean floor.

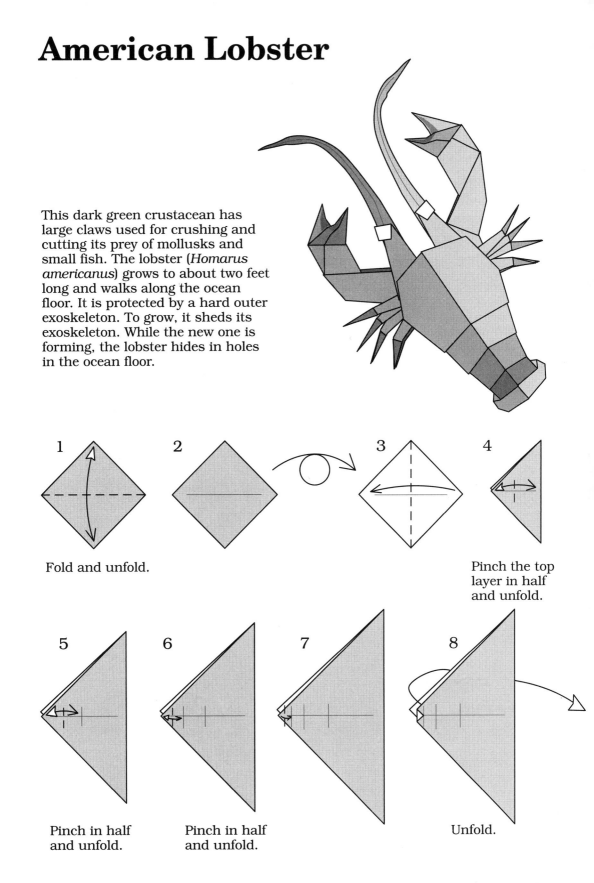

1

Fold and unfold.

2

3

4

Pinch the top layer in half and unfold.

5

Pinch in half and unfold.

6

Pinch in half and unfold.

7

8

Unfold.

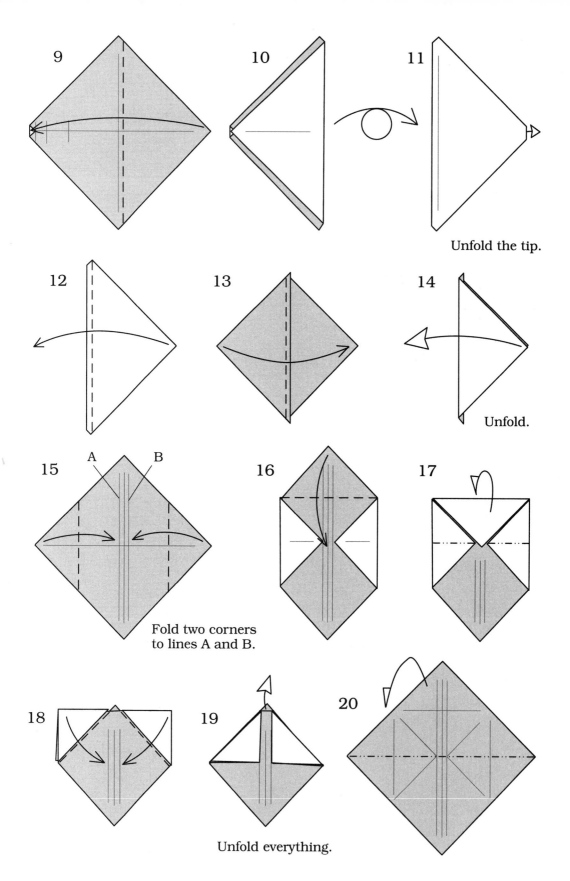

9

10

11

Unfold the tip.

12

13

14

Unfold.

15

A   B

Fold two corners
to lines A and B.

16

17

18

19

20

Unfold everything.

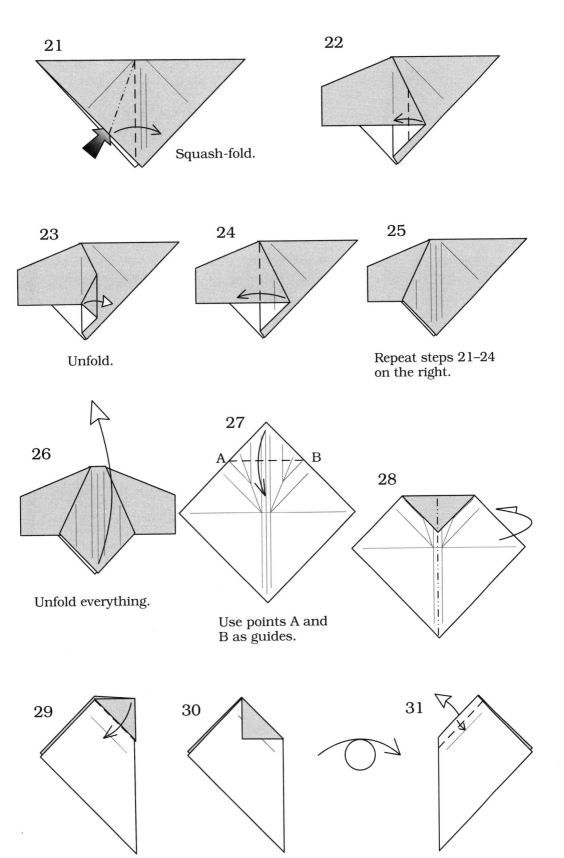

21 Squash-fold.

22

23 Unfold.

24

25 Repeat steps 21–24 on the right.

26 Unfold everything.

27 Use points A and B as guides.

A   B

28

29

30

31

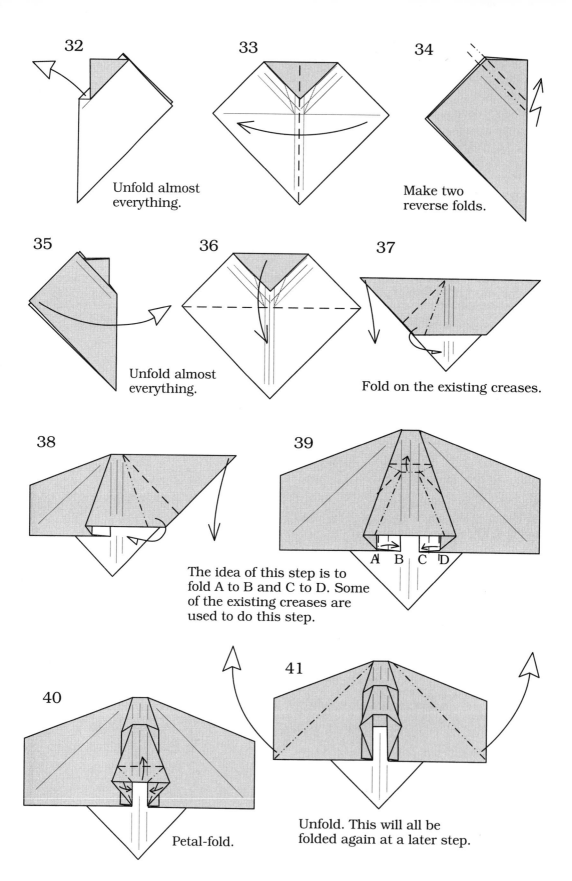

32 Unfold almost everything.

33

34 Make two reverse folds.

35 Unfold almost everything.

36

37 Fold on the existing creases.

38 The idea of this step is to fold A to B and C to D. Some of the existing creases are used to do this step.

39 A B C D

40 Petal-fold.

41 Unfold. This will all be folded again at a later step.

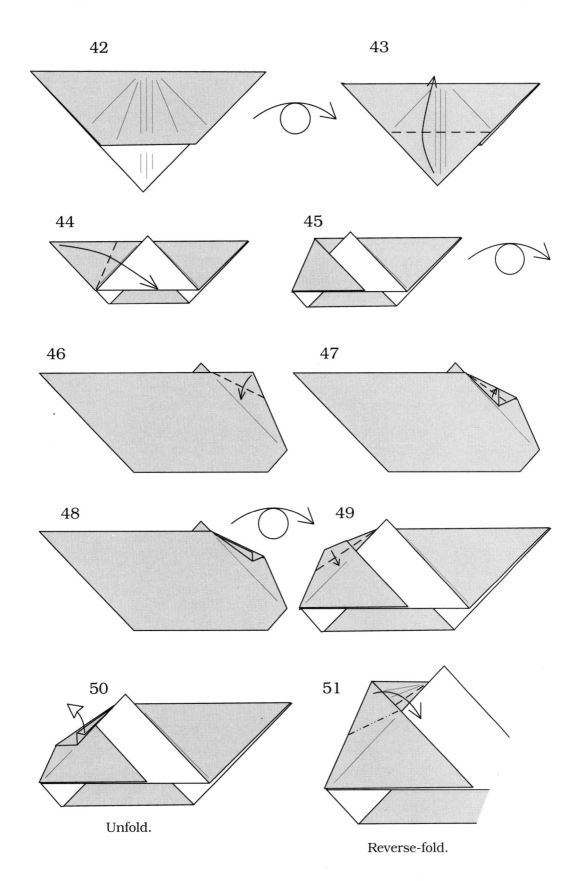

50

Unfold.

51

Reverse-fold.

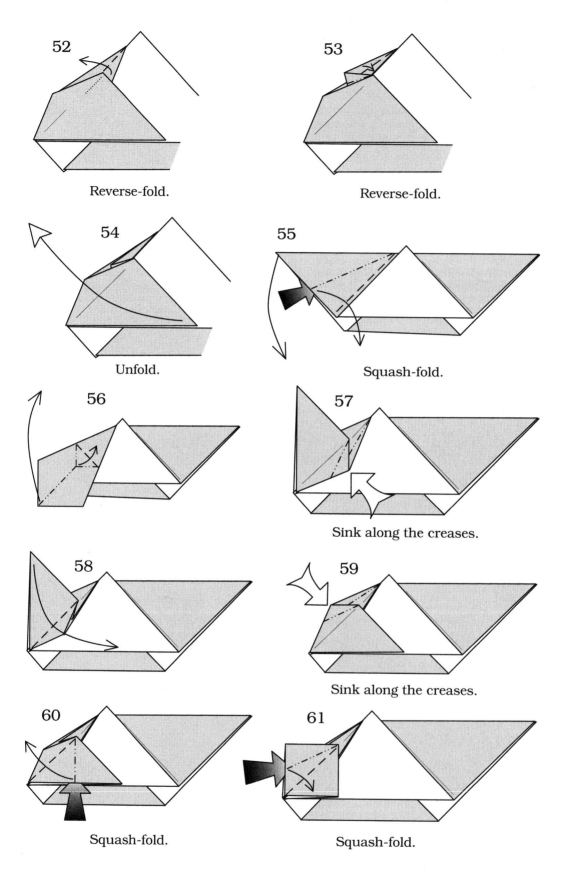

52 Reverse-fold.

53 Reverse-fold.

54 Unfold.

55 Squash-fold.

56

57 Sink along the creases.

58

59 Sink along the creases.

60 Squash-fold.

61 Squash-fold.

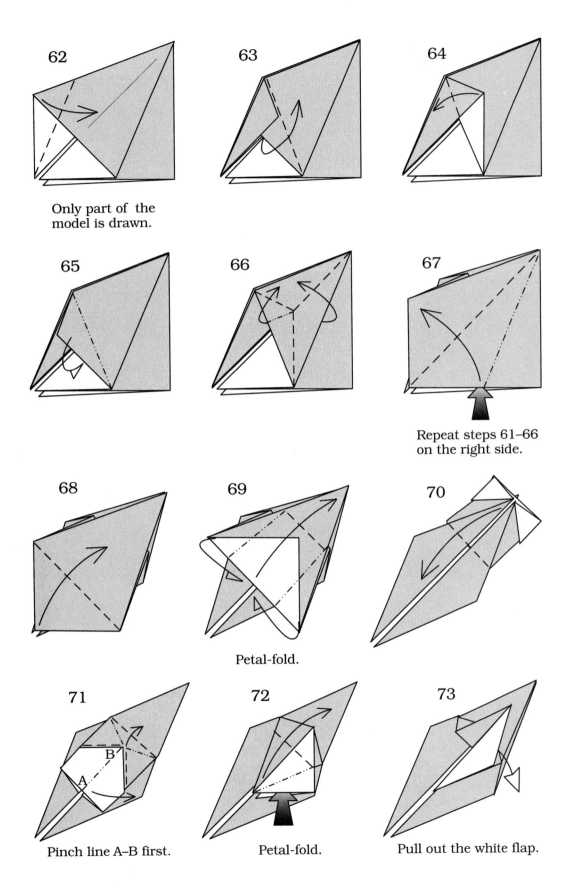

62

Only part of the model is drawn.

63

64

65

66

67

Repeat steps 61–66 on the right side.

68

69

Petal-fold.

70

71

Pinch line A–B first.

72

Petal-fold.

73

Pull out the white flap.

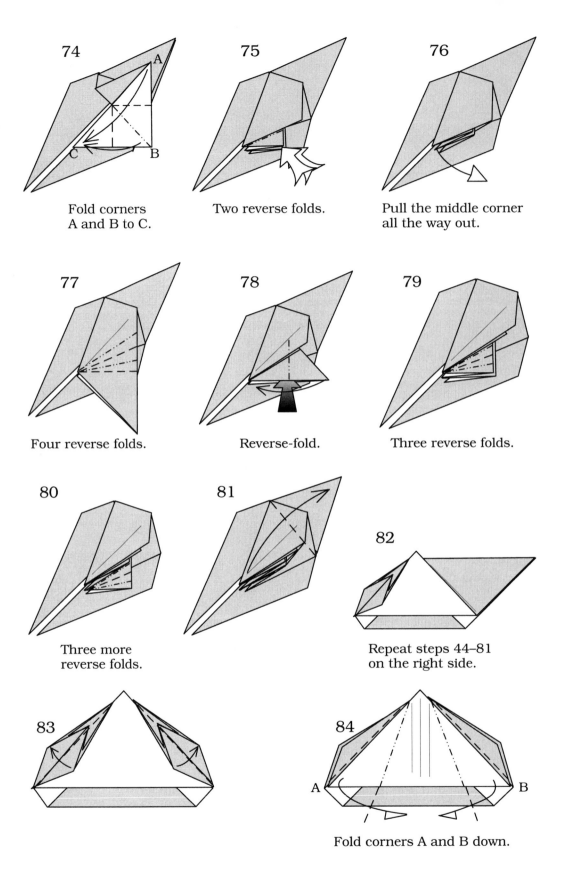

74

Fold corners
A and B to C.

75

Two reverse folds.

76

Pull the middle corner
all the way out.

77

Four reverse folds.

78

Reverse-fold.

79

Three reverse folds.

80

Three more
reverse folds.

81

82

Repeat steps 44–81
on the right side.

83

84

Fold corners A and B down.

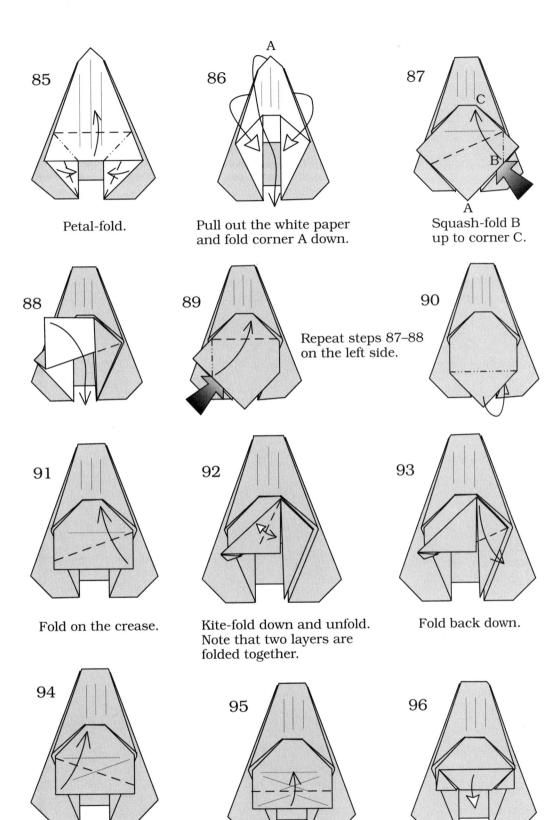

85 Petal-fold.

86 Pull out the white paper and fold corner A down.

87 Squash-fold B up to corner C.

88

89 Repeat steps 87–88 on the left side.

90

91 Fold on the crease.

92 Kite-fold down and unfold. Note that two layers are folded together.

93 Fold back down.

94 Repeat steps 91–93 on the left side.

95

96 Unfold.

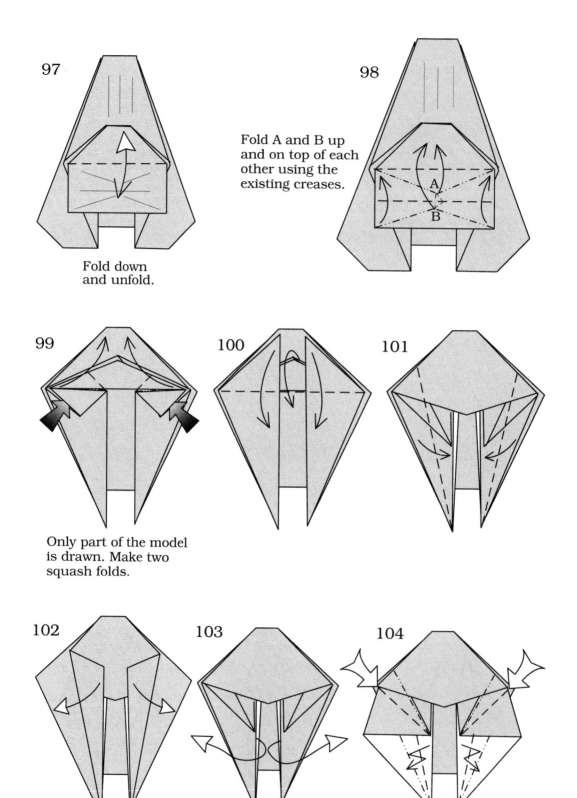

97

Fold down
and unfold.

98

Fold A and B up
and on top of each
other using the
existing creases.

A
B

99

Only part of the model
is drawn. Make two
squash folds.

100

101

102

Unfold.

103

Pull out some paper.

104

Make two reverse
folds on each side.

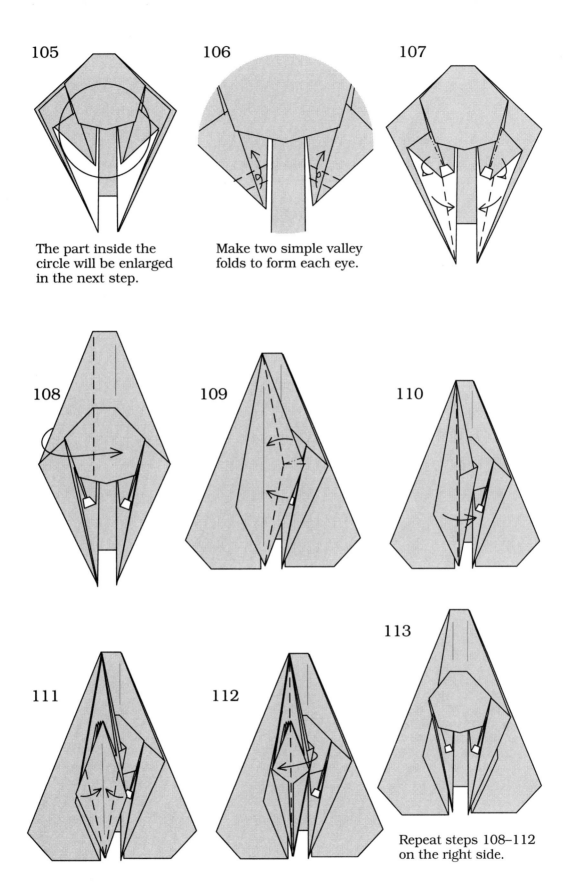

105

The part inside the circle will be enlarged in the next step.

106

Make two simple valley folds to form each eye.

107

108

109

110

111

112

113

Repeat steps 108–112 on the right side.

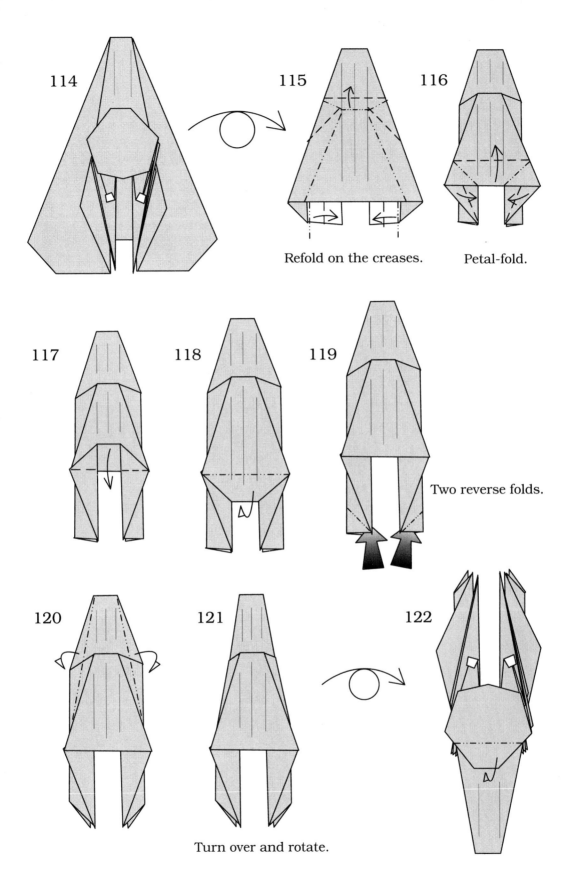

114

115

Refold on the creases.

116

Petal-fold.

117

118

119

Two reverse folds.

120

121

Turn over and rotate.

122

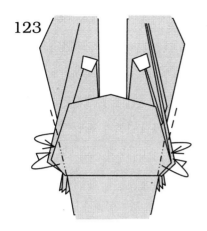

123

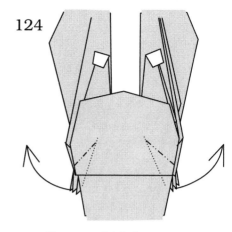

124

Reverse-fold three corners together on each side.

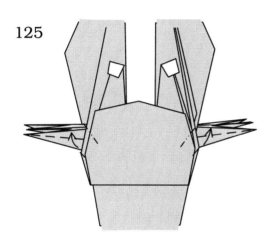

125

Repeat behind.

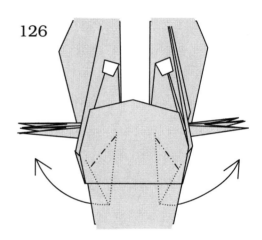

126

Two reverse folds.

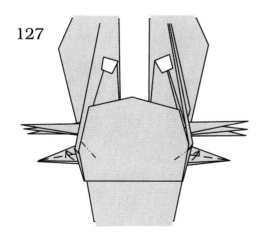

127

Repeat behind.

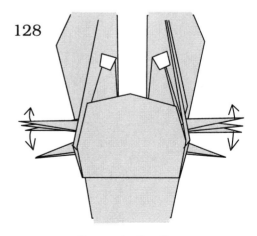

128

Separate the three legs on each side.

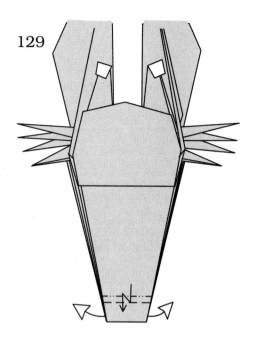

129

To form the tail, separate as much paper as possible at the bottom. The mountain and valley folds are only for the top layer.

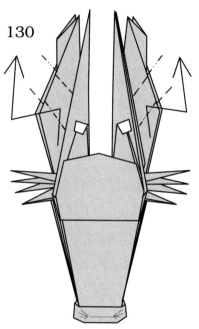

130

Make two reverse folds on each side to begin the formation of the claws.

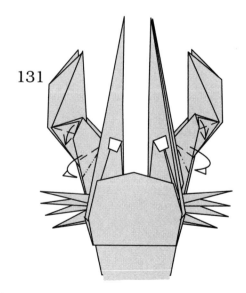

131

Repeat behind.

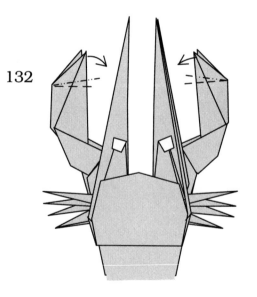

132

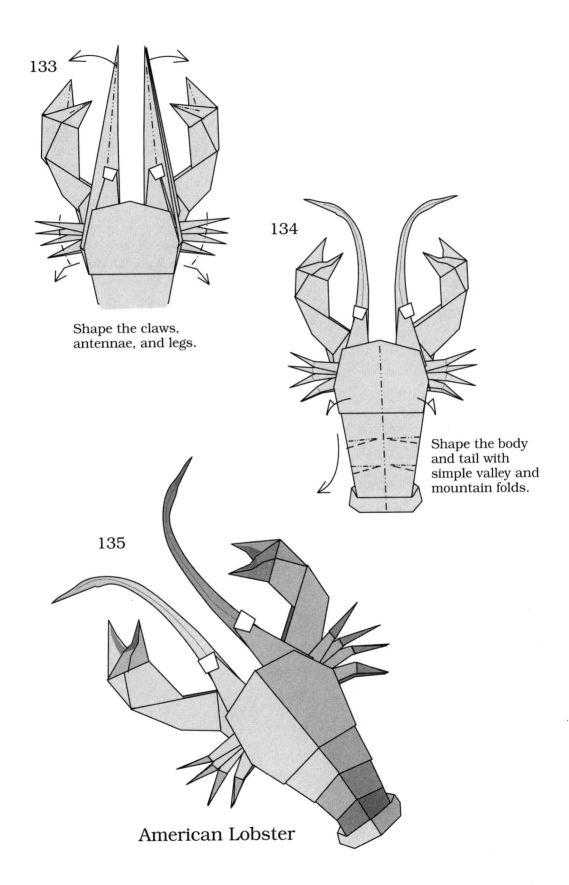

133

Shape the claws,
antennae, and legs.

134

Shape the body
and tail with
simple valley and
mountain folds.

135

American Lobster

Basic Folds

Rabbit Ear.

To fold a rabbit ear, one corner is folded in half and laid down to a side.

See the Fish Base (page 255) for a detailed folding method.

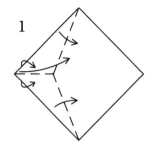

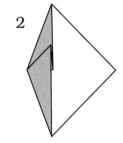

Fold a rabbit ear.

Double Rabbit Ear.

If you were to bend a straw you would be folding the double rabbit ear.

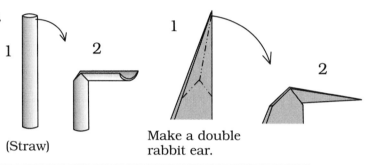

(Straw)

Make a double rabbit ear.

Squash Fold.

In a squash fold, some paper is opened and then made flat. The shaded arrow shows where to place your finger.

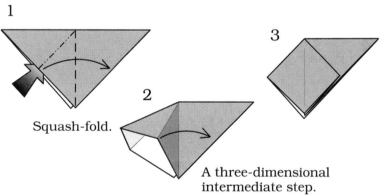

Squash-fold.

A three-dimensional intermediate step.

Petal Fold.

In a petal fold, one point is folded up while two opposite sides meet each other.

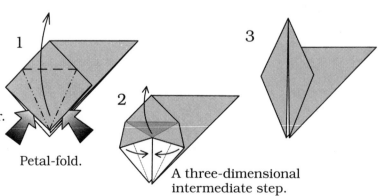

Petal-fold.

A three-dimensional intermediate step.

Inside Reverse Fold.

In an inside reverse fold, some paper is folded between layers. Here are two examples.

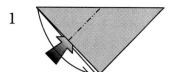

Reverse-fold.

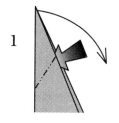

Reverse-fold.

Outside Reverse Fold.

Much of the paper must be unfolded to make an outside reverse fold.

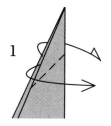

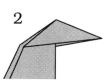

Outside-reverse-fold.

Crimp Fold.

A crimp fold is a combination of two reverse folds.

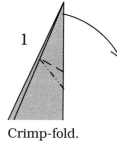

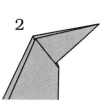

Crimp-fold.

Sink Fold.

In a sink fold, some of the paper without edges is folded inside. To do this fold, much of the model must be unfolded.

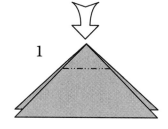

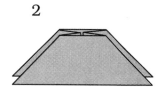

Sink.

Spread Squash Fold.

A cross between a squash fold and sink fold, some paper in the center is spread apart and then made flat.

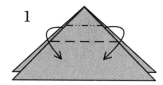

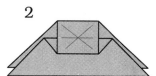

Spread-squash-fold.

Preliminary Fold.

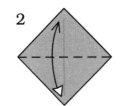

1 Fold and unfold.

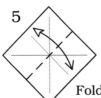

2 Fold and unfold.

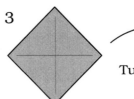

3 Turn over.

4 Fold and unfold.

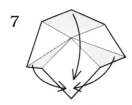

5 Fold and unfold.

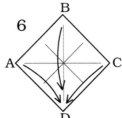

6 Collapse the model using the creases. Bring A, B, and C to D.

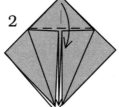

7 This is a three-dimensional intermediate step.

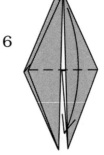

8 Preliminary Fold

Bird Base.

1 Begin with the Preliminary Fold. Kite-fold.

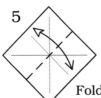

2

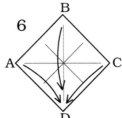

3 Unfold.

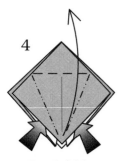

4 Petal-fold.

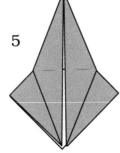

5 Repeat steps 1–4 behind.

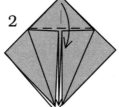

6 Repeat behind.

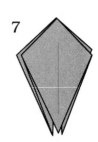

7 Bird Base

Fish Base.

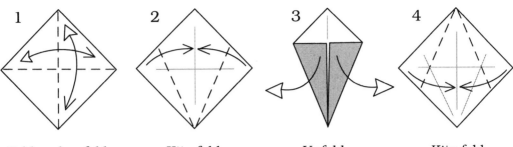

1 Fold and unfold.

2 Kite-fold.

3 Unfold.

4 Kite-fold.

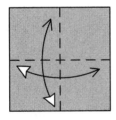

5 Squash-fold.

6 Squash-fold.

7 Fold behind.

8 Fish Base

Waterbomb Base.

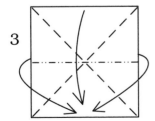

1 Fold and unfold.

2 Fold and unfold.

3 Collapse along the creases.

4 A three-dimensional intermediate step.

5 Waterbomb Base

Credits

The following models were designed by John Montroll:

Tadpole	Triggerfish
Tadpole with Hind Legs	Angelfish
Froglet	Goldfish
Frog	Cichlid
Sperm Whale	Sailfish
Humpback Whale	Barracuda
Dolphin	Blue Shark
Seahorse	Deep Sea Angler Fish
Carp	Starfish
Ocean Sunfish	American Lobster

The following models were designed by Robert J. Lang:

Walrus	Blackdevil Angler
Killer Whale	Lionfish
Giant Clam	Sand Dollar
Hawk-Wing Conch	Atlantic Purple Sea Urchin
Spider Conch	Bay Barnacle
Murex	Horseshoe Crab
Chambered Nautilus Shell	Hermit Crab
Cuttlefish	Blue Crab
Brill	Fiddler Crab

Additional software used in the production of this book was written by Robert J. Lang.

The authors would like to acknowledge the contributions of several individuals who helped to bring about this book. Ron Levy and Terry Hall proofread the diagrams, catching many mistakes and making numerous helpful suggestions towards improving their clarity. Matt Harnick provided much of the zoological information about the different sea life. Barbara Hofer proofread the manuscript. Beth Panitz and Marjorie Wood helped with some of the text. Andy Montroll designed the cover and took the photographs. Yushima No Kobayashi Co., LTD. supplied washi paper which was used for some of the models on the cover.